ESSAYS
IN HONOR OF
CONYERS READ

CONYERS READ

ESSAYS
IN HONOR OF
CONYERS READ

EDITED BY NORTON DOWNS

TRINITY COLLEGE · HARTFORD · CONNECTICUT

THE UNIVERSITY OF CHICAGO PRESS

THE UNIVERSITY OF CHICAGO PRESS, CHICAGO 37
Cambridge University Press, London, N.W. 1, England

FOREWORD

A SINGLE volume would be far from adequate if papers were included from the host of students who owe their interest in history to the inspiring teaching and example of Conyers Read. The present volume perforce contains only a few of the many studies that might be included here if space permitted; but these few are a token of the deep respect and affection of the many who can look back to their contact with a great scholar, teacher, and friend as one of the main influences that shaped their lives. The wide range of these papers is an indication of the breadth of Professor Read's own interest and of his influence upon others.

It is doubly fitting that the present volume was conceived during Professor Read's term as president of the American Historical Association, for, in addition to his writings and his teaching, American historians are all deeply in his debt for his term as executive secretary of the association during the troubled years from 1933 to 1941, when his services were of especial value on account of his previous business experience.

Dr. Read, after his graduation from Harvard in 1903, remained there to obtain his Ph.D. degree in 1908, after which he moved to Oxford, where he received the degree of B.Litt. in 1909. In the latter year he accepted an invitation to Princeton to take part in President Wilson's new preceptorial system. In 1910 he was called to the University of Chicago, becoming professor of history there in 1919. Since 1934 he has been professor of English history in the University of Pennsylvania.

In 1925 Dr. Read published his great life of Sir Francis Walsingham in three volumes, *Mr. Secretary Walsingham and the Policy of Queen Elizabeth.* As the title indicates, this is far more than a mere biography: it is one of the most valuable studies ever made of Elizabethan England. This was followed in 1936 by *The Tudors,* a piece of brilliant condensation. Of Professor Read's

Bibliography of British History covering the Tudor period, it is sufficient to say that it has become the model for all subsequent bibliographical publications on English history.

It is a pleasure and an honor to have a part, even a minor part, in this tribute to one of America's foremost historical scholars.

C. H. McILWAIN

HARVARD UNIVERSITY

PREFACE

TEMPERAMENT and conviction have never permitted Mr. Read to take his stand with those who hold that the pursuit of knowledge exonerates the scholar from the responsibilities of the citizen. As a student in England, if not before, he came across the tradition which links learning with action and requires that education be repaid by service to the community. Twenty years ago his arduous labors in the cause of more intelligent teaching of history in the schools testified to his public spirit. More recently, in his concern for the international position of the country, he devoted time and effort to the organization of a Council on Foreign Relations in Philadelphia. And, finally, his presidential address to the American Historical Association in 1949 dealt characteristically with the "Social Responsibility of the Historian."

It is no cause for wonder, then, that Mr. Read should have taken an active and vigorous part in the great war debate which rocked the country between 1939 and 1941 or that, as the national emergency became acute, he should have abandoned his academic work entirely in order to devote four years of his life to government service. From the very onset of the international crisis, his feelings were unmixed and his convictions unclouded. Like almost all Americans, he detested Hitler and naziism and, indeed, any and all forms of authoritarianism or totalitarianism, with their challenge to the ideals and tenets of democracy. But, unlike most of his compatriots, he had the moral courage to think the issue through. He saw that it was not a question of liking or disliking war, not a question of interfering in the affairs of others or of trying to right the wrongs of Europe, least of all a question of embarking upon a new crusade to make the world safe for democracy. On the contrary, he held with President Roosevelt, Secretary Hull, and a relatively small number of other influential Americans that naziism and fascism were a threat to democracy everywhere, that the aggressive dictatorships of Europe, once they had wiped out France and Britain, were bound to turn their attention to the Western Hemisphere. It was all very well, he felt, to talk about minding one's own business and about making the United States a haven of democracy in a war-torn world. But there was no way of insulating this or any other country against the impact of war or of immunizing it against hostile designs. The issue was not one of our choosing, and we therefore ran a grave risk, by ignoring or underestimating it, of finding ourselves face to face with disaster.

The argument between the so-called "isolationists" and "interventionists" could retain something of the theoretical or academic flavor so long as the European war continued in the "phony" stage, that is, so long as France and Britain stood unassailed and, in appearance at least, had an even or better chance of ultimate victory in a long contest of economic power. But the unexpected and almost incredibly successful Nazi assault upon the Low Countries and France in May, 1940, brought pure speculation to an abrupt close. With France on the verge of collapse and Britain momentarily defenseless, something akin to panic swept over the United States. Most Americans, though still wedded to the determination to stay out of war if humanly possible, suddenly realized the implications of the German victories and saw that raw self-interest, if nothing more, demanded aid to the Allies in the hope of staving off defeat.

These were the ideas underlying the famous appeal of William Allen White for the formation of a Committee To Defend America by Aiding the Allies, a committee which could mobilize and channel public opinion and, when necessary, bring pressure on Congress or lend support to the President in behalf of a policy of national defense conceived in more positive and extensive terms than those traditional on this side of the Atlantic. White suggested the organization of local chapters, by which the work of the Committee could be carried into numerous communities. His appeal supplied all the spark that was needed to set Mr. Read in motion. He wired at once, congratulating White on his courageous stand and offering his services. The immediate response was a request that he organize a chapter of the committee at the University of Pennsylvania.

Mr. Read lost no time in making a start. But, like others of his compatriots everywhere and notably in the universities, he found that the tide of aloofness, indifference, and fear was still running strong. Abandoning the college campus, he therefore turned to the larger arena of the city of Philadelphia itself. It was a formidable undertaking, for the city, strong in Quaker pacifist influences, had long been a field for active propaganda by the Nazi Bund. Nonetheless, there was at least a handful of energetic, clearheaded citizens who were willing to rally behind Mr. Read. A chapter of the White committee was promptly established and embarked upon an aggressive campaign of public education. In the course of the ensuing year, part of the press was enlisted in the cause, radio programs were devised and floated, and thousands of leaflets were distributed. In the end, the local chapter had the satisfaction of knowing that it had contributed substantially to the conversion of popular sentiment and that it had served effectively in promoting such important measures as the destroyers-for-bases deal, the Universal Service Act, and the Lend-Lease legislation.

Within the Committee To Defend America by Aiding the Allies there had been, almost from the beginning, an advanced group which favored support of Britain, even at the risk of American involvement in the war. White himself drew the line at active participation and, when the pressure from the "all-outers" became too great, resigned from the chairmanship. Thereupon, the activist group launched an organization of its own, the Fight for Freedom, which, before long, completely overshadowed the older and more modest movement. Mr. Read was a charter member of the new committee. He had taken a lively part in the discussions in New York which led to its formation, and he was one of the first publicly to indorse its program. For him there was never the slightest doubt that the national interest required the maintenance of the British position, no matter what the cost. He explained all this with the utmost frankness to his Philadelphia associates and offered to resign if they felt unable to go with him all the way. No better testimony to his influence and leadership could be found than in the action of the local chapter, which declined his resignation and, instead, voted to transfer its allegiance to the new Fight for Freedom organization.

By the summer of 1941 the situation not only in Europe but also in Asia had pretty nearly reached the breaking point, and therefore the work of education and agitation had become ever more imposing. Mr. Read devotedly spent on it all the time he could possibly spare from his teaching. Much of the locally used material he and Mrs. Read prepared personally. Among other things, he himself replied in detail to a series of newspaper articles written by a prominent journalist who was highly critical of Britain's efforts and prospects and violently opposed to any risk of involvement. Without surcease Mr. Read continued, despite obloquy and an ever increasing number of threats, to hammer home the arguments on which he rested his own convictions. To men like him, throughout the country, belongs in large measure the credit for having brought the American people to a realization of their vital stake in the conflict abroad.

At this point an opportunity for a direct and more concrete contribution was presented to Mr. Read. At the request of President Roosevelt, Colonel (later General) William J. Donovan was setting up a new government agency, to be known as the Office of the Co-ordinator of Information. The basic idea behind this venture was the need for collecting, sifting, and analyzing the mass of information flowing into Washington from abroad. The United States government had never previously had anything approaching a unified intelligence service. From our diplomatic representatives reports of all kinds were being sent to the State Department, while the War and Navy Departments were being served by their military and naval attachés, and the Treasury, Commerce, and other departments also maintained special agents abroad. For the sound formulation of national policy and strategy it had become urgently necessary that all data bearing on the national security should be co-ordinated, tested, and checked against information known from published sources and familiar to experts. To General Donovan it had seemed that the first step in solving the problem should be to draw on the universities and to enlist the aid of those who not only had wide and deep knowledge of foreign countries and conditions but also had training and experience in the critical treatment of evidence. At General Donovan's request, President James P. Baxter, 3rd, of Williams College, undertook to assemble a group of specialists, around whom as a nucleus an adequate research and analysis staff could be built up.

President Baxter and those with whom he consulted were convinced that the task in hand would require an organization to cover the entire world and that, for a well-rounded picture of the problems of any specific region, the resources of all the social sciences—economics, history, political science, geography, anthropology, etc.—would have to be drawn upon. For the crucial area of Great Britain and the British Commonwealth there was agreement from the outset that the obvious person to direct the work was Conyers Read, not only because of his long and intensive studies of English history, but because of his profound study of Britain's position in the war and its bearing on American interests. In mid-summer of 1941 Mr. Read was therefore invited to join the small group of organizers. Like all new departures, the project was bound to be experimental, but it was a real challenge to American scholarship and fitted perfectly with Mr. Read's ideas of public service. Without hesitation he accepted. Among the half-dozen members of the initial group that went to Washington on a hot August night, he was one. In these days, when the organization which later became the Office of Strategic Services has become famous, he can look back with satisfaction to the time when it began its operations in a suite of offices, all of which had desks, a few of which had chairs, and none of which had a telephone.

For a period of somewhat less than a year the agency of the Co-ordinator of Information was directly under the supervision of the President and consisted very largely of the Research and Analysis Branch, on the one hand, and a Foreign Information Branch, concerned with radio broadcasting to foreign countries, on the other. In June, 1942, it was renamed the Office of Strategic Services and became part of the organization of the Joint Chiefs of Staff. Thereafter, it took over a number of other activities, such as secret intelligence and secret operations, of world-wide scope. But throughout its history, until October, 1945, when it was disbanded, the Research and Analysis Branch continued to be one of the largest and most important sections of the agency. It eventually comprised in the neighborhood of four hundred trained scholars, and maintained field staffs abroad in critical localities all the way from London to Chungking. During the final months of the war, Mr. Read himself was to become the historian of the OSS, and it is to be hoped that the work of his historical staff, never intended for publication, has been properly preserved for posterity.

It would be utterly hopeless, in the present connection, to attempt a sketch of even the one division of the agency with which Mr. Read was himself connected. His assignment, from the beginning, was to build up a competent staff of experts and to study every aspect of British and Commonwealth affairs which might be of significance for the successful prosecution of the war. He threw himself into this task with his usual interest, energy, and conviction. In a remarkably short time he had enlisted a group of key experts, around whom over the years a considerable staff grew up. As a measure of Mr. Read's success as a discriminating recruiter, it is necessary only to list a few of the men and women who served under his direction: Dean Ralph J. Bunche, of Howard University, who later transferred to the State Department and subsequently to the United Nations, recently to become famous as the acting mediator between the new state of Israel and its Arab neighbors; Professor W. Norman Brown, expert on the affairs of India; Professor Ephraim A. Speiser, expert on the Near East, later chief of the Near Eastern Section of the OSS; Professor Holden Furber, widely traveled throughout the British Empire and an authority on imperial problems; James Green, also deeply versed in imperial relations, later a member of the State Department; and Elizabeth Armstrong, specialist on Canadian problems and at the present time a member of the Canadian desk in the State Department.

But Mr. Read was not satisfied with merely having enlisted his staff. He knew that for effective work there must be solidarity of interest and readiness to co-operate—in short, good *esprit de corps*. Of all the sections of the Research and Analysis Branch, it may be safely said that none had this spirit in greater measure than the

British Empire Section. After Mrs. Read came to Washington to join her husband, she, too, took an active interest in promoting close contacts and a sense of common effort. At pleasant social gatherings the members of the group came together at the Read home, where there was ample opportunity to further friendships and to discuss mutual problems.

It was not to be expected that Mr. Read would take a narrowly professional view of his responsibilities. From the very beginning the entire organization benefited from his experience and his advice. In this connection it ought to be remembered that the road for any new government agency is likely to be a rough one. It stands to reason that other agencies were not eager to put all their information at the disposal of a newcomer, the more so as the latter was so largely composed of suspicious-looking scholars. Furthermore, the directive under which the new group operated was characteristically vague. There was no precedent for co-ordinated intelligence work. Everything had to be blocked out by trial and error, with many false starts and even more disappointments. At an early date it had become clear that, in order to be effective, the work of the staff would have to be carefully planned, so that no unnecessary studies would be embarked upon and so that assignments should be clearly outlined, with proper provision for co-operation between the various sections of the organization. For that purpose a Projects Committee was set up, and, as a member of this body, Mr. Read, by untiring, hardheaded criticism, was able to do much in the way of blocking out the right tasks in the right way. Until the organization became too large, very few of the finished products in turn escaped his keen scrutiny.

In much the same spirit Mr. Read refused to regard the assignment of his section as a bookish one, to be pursued in cloistered solitude. He spent much time and effort in establishing contacts with other agencies and in drawing upon them for useful information. More important still, he made a special point of developing close relations with the numerous and varied British and Empire delegations in Washington. Through personal friendship he kept himself exceptionally well posted on what was going on and on what the crucial problems in the British war effort were.

As American representatives returned from abroad, he was sure to pump them for all they were worth. British visitors were always welcome at his home, where, indeed, Mrs. Read frequently arranged stag dinners, to give senior members of the branch an opportunity to discuss matters at length. In September, 1942, Mr. Read flew to England for a four weeks' stay. The present writer, who was his companion on that occasion, still has a vivid recollection of his unflagging industry on that trip. In London he was in and out of every office that might be helpful to him. He spent several days at Oxford, so familiar to him, where he showed less interest in old haunts than in the British research center that was carrying on work similar to his own. To top it all off, he made trips to various industrial centers to acquaint himself at first hand with methods and problems. Before leaving, he laid the foundations for a London representation of his own section, encouraging his men, then and later, to get around the country as much as possible and to participate in meetings that would bring them in touch with the rank and file of the population.

Enough has been said at least to indicate the nature of Mr. Read's task and the methods by which he undertook to meet it. His own section looked upon him with reverence and affection, while throughout the organization generally he was known and admired for his loyalty and devotion, as well as for his clearsighted, realistic approach to the common problem. By the end of the war, the OSS was not only a large, but an extremely influential, power in government. It had made countless valuable studies and was relied on for the solution of many baffling questions. It is surely no exaggeration to say that it had proved itself even to the most skeptical and that it had demonstrated to the hilt that scholars, if properly organized and directed, can make an impressive contribution even to the waging of a great war. This was not the achievement of one man or of a few men but rather the result of the combined thought and effort of many. Among them, Mr. Read has long since been assured an important and honorable place.

WILLIAM L. LANGER

HARVARD UNIVERSITY

TABLE OF CONTENTS

BIBLIOGRAPHY OF CONYERS READ

1909

Editor, *The Bardon Papers: Documents Relating to the Imprisonment and Trial of Mary, Queen of Scots.* Camden Society, 3d Series, Vol. XVII.

1911

"Factions in the English Privy Council under Elizabeth," *American Historical Association Report,* I, 109–19.

1912

REVIEWS

BATES, E. S. *Touring in 1600: A Study in the Development of Travel as a Means of Education* (Boston, 1911), *American Historical Review,* XVII, 656.

OGG, DAVID. *Cardinal de Retz, 1613–1679* (London, 1912), *American Historical Review,* XVII, 872.

1913

"Walsingham and Burghley in Queen Elizabeth's Privy Council," *English Historical Review,* XXVIII, 34–58.

1914

"English Foreign Trade under Elizabeth," *English Historical Review,* XXIX, 515–24.

1915

"The Fame of Sir Edward Stafford," *American Historical Review,* XX, 292–313.

1917

REVIEW

GLADISH, DOROTHY M. *The Tudor Privy Council* (Retford, 1915), *American Historical Review,* XXII, 435.

1920

"Political Progress of the English Workingman," *Journal of Political Economy,* XXVIII, 505–17, 601–18.

1921

REVIEWS

HOGAN, JAMES. *Ireland in the European System,* Vol. I (London, 1920), *American Historical Review,* XXVI, 769.

MAINWARING, G. E. (ed.). *The Life and Works of Sir Henry Mainwaring,* Vol. I (London, 1920), *American Historical Review,* XXVI, 828.

HAMMOND, J. L. and BARBARA. *The Village Labourer 1760–1832; The Town Labourer 1760–1832; The Skilled Labourer 1760–1832* (1919). FURNISS, EDGAR S. *The Position of the Labourer in a System of Nationalism* (1920), *Quarterly Journal of Economics,* XXXV, 341–53.

1923

REVIEW

MAINWARING, G. E., and PERRIN, W. G. (eds.). *The Life and Works of Sir Henry Mainwaring,* Vol. II (London, 1922), *American Historical Review,* XXVIII, 354.

1924

REVIEWS

THOMSON, GLADYS SCOTT. *Lord Lieutenants in the Sixteenth Century: A Study in Tudor Local Administration* (London, 1923), *American Historical Review,* XXIX, 323.

EVANS, FLORENCE GREIER. *The Principal Secretary of State: A Survey of the Office from 1558–1680* (Manchester, 1923), *American Historical Review, XXIX,* 543.

1925

Mr. Secretary Walsingham and the Policy of Queen Elizabeth. 3 vols. Oxford.

1926

"Good Queen Bess," *American Historical Review,* XXXI, 647–61.

"The Proposal To Assassinate Mary Queen of Scots at Fotheringay," *English Historical Review,* XL, 234–35.

Introduction to "Despatches of Castelnau de la Mauvissiere (on Frobisher, Gilbert, de la Roche, Drake, 1577–1581)," *American Historical Review,* XXXI, 285–96.

1927

REVIEWS

MULLER, JAMES ARTHUR. *Stephen Gardiner and the Tudor Reaction* (New York, 1926), *American Historical Review,* XXXII, 102.

WAKE, JOAN (ed.). *A Copy of Papers Relating to Musters, Beacons, Subsidies, etc. in the County of Northampton, 1586–1623* (Kettering, 1926), *American Historical Review,* XXXII 314.

1928

REVIEW

WILLIAMSON, JAMES A. *Sir John Hawkins, the Times and the Man* (Oxford, 1927), *American Historical Review,* XXXIII, 863.

1930

"The Fame of Sir Edward Stafford," *American Historical Review,* XXXV, 560–66.

REVIEW

POLLARD, A. F. *Wolsey* (New York, 1929), *American Historical Review,* XXXV, 337.

1931

REVIEWS

MAHON, MAJOR GENERAL R. H. *The Tragedy of Kirk o'Field* (Cambridge, 1930), *American Historical Review,* XXXVI, 428.

BELLOC, HILAIRE. *Wolsey* (Philadelphia, 1930), *American Historical Review,* XXXVI, 633.

1932

REVIEW

BRUGMANS, H. (ed.). *Correspondentie van Robert Dudley, Graaf van Leycester, en andere Ducumenten betreffende zijn Gouvernement-Generaal in de Nederlanden 1585–1588* (3 vols.; Utrecht, 1931), *American Historical Review,* XXXVII, 312.

1933

Editor, *Bibliography of British History, 1485–1603, Tudor Period.* Oxford.
"Queen Elizabeth's Seizure of the Duke of Alva's Pay-Ships," *Journal of Modern History,* V, 443–64.

REVIEW

CONWAY, AGNES. *Henry VII's Relations with Scotland and Ireland, 1485–1498* (Cambridge, 1932), *American Historical Review,* XXXVIII, 97.

1934

REVIEWS

WILSON, MONA. *Sir Philip Sidney* (New York, 1932), *American Historical Review,* XXXIX, 112.

MATHEW, DAVID. *The Celtic Peoples and Renaissance Europe:A Study of the Celtic and Spanish Influences on Elizabethan History* (New York, 1933), *American Historical Review,* XXXIX, 506.

NEALE, J. E. *Queen Elizabeth* (New York, 1934), *American Historical Review,* XXXIX, 718.

1935

"Sir Francis Walsingham." In GARVIN, KATHERINE (ed.), *The Great Tudors.* London.

REVIEWS

RUSTON, ARTHUR, and WITNEY, DENIS. *Hooton Pagnell: The Agricultural Evolution of a Yorkshire Village* (New York, 1934), *Journal of Modern History,* VII, 471.

MULLER, JAMES ARTHUR. (ed.). *The Letters of Stephen Gardiner* (New York, 1933), *American Historical Review,* XL, 322.

PICKTHORN, KENNETH. *Early Tudor Government* (2 vols.; Cambridge, 1934), *American Historical Review,* XL, 495.

1936

The Tudors. New York.

"A Letter from Robert, Earl of Leicester to a Lady," *Huntington Library Bulletin,* IX, 15–26.

REVIEWS

SARGENT, RALPH M. *At the Court of Queen Elizabeth: The Life and Lyrics of Sir Edward Dyer* (New York, 1935), *American Historical Review,* XLI, 326.

CHAMBERS, R. W. *Thomas More* (New York, 1935), *American Historical Review,* XLI, 529.

1937

"School History and the College Entrance Examinations," *Education, LVIII,* 51–55.

REVIEWS

CARDINAL, EDWARD V. *Cardinal Lorenzo Campeggio, Legate to the Courts of Henry VIII and Charles V* (Boston, 1935), *American Historical Review,* XLII, 111.

WHITE, BEATRICE. *Mary Tudor* (New York, 1935), *American Historical Review,* XLII, 301.

HINTON, EDWARD M. *Ireland through Tudor Eyes* (Philadelphia, 1935), *American Historical Review,* XLII, 588.

WERNHAM, RICHARD BRUCE. *Calendar of State Papers, Foreign Series of the Reign of Elizabeth, Preserved in the Public Record Office,* Vol. XXII (London, 1936), *American Historical Review,* XLII, 745.

1938

Editor, *The Constitution Reconsidered.* New York: American Historical Association.

"Mercantilism: The Old English Pattern of a Controlled Economy." In *The Constitution Reconsidered,* pp. 63–77. New York: American Historical Association.

REVIEWS

STEINBECKER, CARL B. *Poor-Relief in the Sixteenth Century* (Washington, 1937), *American Historical Review,* XLIII, 673.

WEDGWOOD, COL. THE RT. HON. JOSIAH C., and HOLT, ANNE D. *History of Parliament: Biographies of the Members of the Commons House 1439–1509* (London, 1936), *Journal of Modern History,* X, 411.

CODE, JOSEPH BERNARD. *Queen Elizabeth and the English Catholic Historians* (Louvain, 1935), *American Historical Review,* XLIII, 113.

MACKENZIE, AGNES MURE. *The Rise of the Stuarts* (New York, 1935); *The Scotland of Queen Mary and the Religious Wars* (New York, 1936), *American Historical Review,* XLIII, 346.

CAMPBELL, LILY B. *Tudor Conceptions of History and Tragedy in "A Mirror for Magistrates"* (Berkeley, 1936), *American Historical Review,* XLIII, 445.

SCOTT, WILLIAM ROBERT. *Adam Smith as Student and Professor* (Glasgow, 1937), *Pennsylvania Magazine of History and Biography*, LXII, 107.

1939

REVIEWS

GARRETT, CHRISTINA HALLOWELL. *The Marian Exiles: A Study in the Origins of Elizabethan Puritanism* (Cambridge, 1938), *American Historical Review*, XLIV, 350.

CHEW, SAMUEL C. *The Crescent and the Rose: Islam and England during the Renaissance* (New York, 1937), *American Historical Review*, XLIV, 601.

1940

"The English Elements in Benjamin Franklin," *Pennsylvania Magazine of History and Biography*, LXIV, 314–30.

REVIEWS

Calendar of the Patent Rolls Preserved in the Public Record Office: Philip and Mary (3 vols.; London, 1936–38), *American Historical Review*, XLV, 119.

History of Parliament, Register of the Ministers and of the Members of Both Houses, 1439–1509 (London, 1938), *Journal of Modern History*, XII, 234.

1941

REVIEWS

Calendar of the Patent Rolls Preserved in the Public Record Office: Philip and Mary, Vol. IV; *Elizabeth*, Vol. I (London, 1939), *American Historical Review*, XLVI, 627.

PRESCOTT, H. F. M. *A Spanish Tudor: The Life of "Bloody Mary"* (New York, 1940), *American Historical Review*, XLVI, 89.

MAYNARD, THEODORE. *Queen Elizabeth* (Milwaukee, 1940), *Journal of Modern History*, XIII, 240.

BECKER, CARL L. *Modern Democracy* (New Haven, 1941), *Pennsylvania Magazine of History and Biography*, LXV, 381.

1943

REVIEWS

MOZLEY, J. F. *John Foxe and His Book* (New York, 1940), *American Historical Review*, XLVIII, 91.

BELLOC, HILAIRE. *Elizabeth, Creature of Circumstance* (New York, 1942), *American Historical Review*, XLVIII, 641.

CAMPBELL, MILDRED. *The English Yeoman under Elizabeth and the Early Stuarts* (New Haven, 1942), *American Historical Review*, XLVIII, 777.

1945

REVIEW

PEEL, ALBERT (ed.). *The Notebook of John Penry, 1593* (London, 1944), *American Historical Review*, L, 790.

1946

REVIEWS

JUDSON, ALEXANDER C. *The Life of Edmund Spenser* (Baltimore, 1945), *American Historical Review*, LI, 538.

AYDELOTTE, FRANK. *The American Rhodes Scholarships: A Review of the First Forty Years* (Princeton, 1946), *Pennsylvania Magazine of History and Biography*, LXX, 430.

1947

REVIEW

CAMPBELL, LILY B. *Shakespeare's "Histories": Mirrors of Elizabethan Policy* (San Marino, Calif., 1947), *American Historical Review*, LII, 725.

1948

REVIEW

HOBBES, THOMAS. *Leviathan*, ed. OAKSHOTT; LOCKE, JOHN. *The Second Treatise of Civil Government and a Letter concerning Toleration*, ed. GOUCH; MILL, J. S. *Liberty and Considerations of Representative Government*, ed. McCALLUM (Oxford, 1947), *William and Mary Quarterly*, 3d ser., V, 409.

1949

"Recent United States and British Government Publications on the London Naval Conference of 1930," *American Historical Review*, LIV, 307–14.

"More Light on the London Naval Treaty of 1930," *American Philosophical Society Proceedings*, XCIII, No. 4, 290–308.

1950

"Social Responsibilities of the Historian," *American Historical Review*, LV, 275–85.

1951

Editor, with READ, EVELYN PLUMMER. CLAPHAM, JOHN. *Elizabeth of England*. Philadelphia.

REVIEWS

ROWSE, A. L. *The England of Elizabeth: The Structure of Society* (New York, 1950), *William and Mary Quarterly*, 3d ser., VIII, 458.

WILLCOX, WILLIAM B. *Star of Empire: A Study of Britain as a World Power, 1485–1945* (New York, 1951), *William and Mary Quarterly*, 3d ser., VIII, 124.

SOME RELATIONSHIPS BETWEEN BRITISH INDUCTIVE LOGIC AND FRENCH IMPRESSIONIST PAINTING

By GEORGE HAINES IV

Connecticut College, New London

INTRODUCTION

I PROPOSE in this paper to point out certain analogies between a mode of thinking and a mode of feeling. That such analogies exist in almost any historical period is increasingly recognized; that they contribute to a better understanding of both modes of expression by revealing some of the otherwise less obvious implications is also clear. Nor would we ever have doubted their usefulness, had we not come to make radical distinctions between expressions formalized in words and those formalized in other media. No one doubts that there are differences implicit in these media, that each has its own autonomy. But the differences are not absolute; both the artist's forms and the thinker's concepts are means of responding to and influencing society. As Pablo Picasso wrote in a moment of exasperation:

What do you think an artist is? An imbecile who has only his eyes if he's a painter, or ears if he's a musician, or a lyre at every level of his heart if he's a poet, or even, if he's a boxer, just his muscles? On the contrary, he's at the same time a political being, constantly alive to heart-rending, fiery or happy events, to which he responds in every way. . . . No, painting is not done to decorate apartments. It is an instrument of war for attack and defense against the enemy.[1]

And if we have learned nothing else of recent years, surely we know now that this is equally true of the man of ideas.

Artists and thinkers, like all of us, come into contact with and are influenced by the events, the ideas, the pressures of their day. The principal concepts or forms they develop—what in Mill we call his "utilitarianism" or his "empiricism" and what in Pissarro

1

we call his "impressionism"—are created in response to such pressures and reveal their general attitude toward the world. Usually, once the thinker has established the fundamental conceptual pattern of his thought or an artist has established the fundamental formal pattern of his expression, later pressures will appear only in variations within these. And if a thinker or artist makes a considerable alteration in his fundamental pattern, as Renoir and Cézanne did in the eighties, we are justified in looking for the new pressures responsible.

But the result of the various pressures will not be necessarily found in some obvious concern with specific subject matter. Particularly is this true of the impressionists, who rejected the interest of their predecessors in painting historical or anecdotal subjects. However revolutionary these artists may be, they will not paint pictures of the storming of barricades. And this remains generally true of creative painters from that day to this. Their mode of persuasion, the means by which they "battle against the enemy," is by prevailing upon us to see what they see the way they see it. This is peculiarly the painter's way.

We shall be seeking here to define the fundamental formal characteristics of French impressionist painting and the fundamental conceptual characteristics of British empiricist thought as developed in psychology and logic during the middle years of the nineteenth century. After showing how these characteristics reveal analogous modes of thinking and feeling, I shall also indicate how these characteristics differentiate them from other schools in their respective "fields" in comparable ways.

Before entering upon the discussion, some misconception may be avoided by stating explicitly that no relations between specific individuals are insisted upon. It will be convenient to make considerable use of the names of John Stuart Mill and Camille Pissarro, for example; but, unless otherwise clearly implied, it is in each instance as representative of a school of thought or a group of painters. Also, though I shall indicate some acquaintance by one group with the work of the other, it is important to understand that no direct influence of one of these groups upon the other is either predicated or required for my purpose. Having indicated that they lived in similar "climates of opinion" and were subject to similar pressures of various kinds, the burden of proof will rest entirely upon the strength of the analogies. If we are dealing with multiple variables, as I believe, impressionism in painting was the consequence of a multitude of factors, one of the least of which, perhaps, was the thinking of Englishmen. But since the multitude of factors which resulted in impressionism in painting were not very different from the multitude of factors which resulted in British empiricist concepts in psychology and logic in the middle decades of the nineteenth century, that these modes of thinking and feeling should exhibit similar basic characteristics can hardly be astonishing.

Granting this, it might also be expected that many other topics or "fields" would in the same years reveal similar characteristics, and the question be asked: For what reason choose these? The simplest answer might be the interest of the writer. But something more can be said for the choice.

The importance of the cultural role played by the sciences in the nineteenth and twentieth centuries is generally acknowledged. But if the applications of science justify it in terms of utility, only the logic of science can justify such claims as scientists may make to be discoverers of reliable knowledge. In such a connection one need hardly urge the importance of British empiricism, the associationist psychology, and inductive logic, especially as the latter was developed by Mill. If these have been long superseded, their influence remains very great, and the logic of science remains indebted to Mill. Something not dissimilar may be said of French impressionism in painting. The developments in twentieth-century painting constitute distinctive manifestations of our culture. But what is often called "modern art" begins with French impressionism; as Fernand Leger has said, "It was the Impressionists who 'broke the line.' "[2] Hence, to establish relations between that logic and that painting would give promise of being an important step toward laying a basis for the delineation and understanding of the culture of our own time.

THE FORMATIVE PRESSURES

It is a historian's commonplace that the decades of the third quarter of the nineteenth century were "a period of realism."

Though the term is so vague as to cover almost anything and everything, that is its function. More discriminating for the intellectual and artistic movements of the time is "the return to English empiricism" noted by the French authors of the volume entitled *Du libéralisme à l'impérialisme (1860–1878).*[3] The very note of transition in the title is warranted: by 1880 British empiricism, like the Utilitarian individualism associated with it, was declining in influence.

From the time of Francis Bacon, British empiricism had been closely associated with scientific investigation; its renewed influence in these decades was closely allied with the special triumphs of the sciences in the same years. After the disappointments and defeats of the revolutions of 1848, men sought a more secure basis for their hopes of a better world than the idealist philosophies seemed to offer and turned to the methods of thinking which they believed were responsible for the achievements of the sciences. A respect for, even a "humility before," the facts, whether those facts were the facts of political and financial power or the empirically given facts of nature, was an attitude encouraged both by British empiricism and by the sciences.

The common characteristic of the scientific concepts developed during the Newtonian era of science has been defined by E. A. Burtt:

> The whole magnificent movement of modern science is essentially of a piece; the later biological and sociological branches took over their basic postulates from the earlier victorious mechanics, especially the all important postulate that valid explanations must always be in terms of small, elementary units in regularly changing relations. To this has been added, in all but the rarest cases, the postulate that ultimate causality is to be found in the motion of the physical atoms.[4]

In other words, the whole tendency of scientific thought was analytical; in every subject the effort was to discover the "small, elementary units" in terms of which valid explanation was possible. The atoms of chemistry, the molecules of physics, the cells of biology, the small variations of evolutionary biology, the elementary sensations of the associationist psychology, the elementary facts of inductive logic—these were the necessary terms in which explanation was to be sought. The compounds, organisms, bodies, or generals formed out of these were the products of association. So the student of society reduced the compounds of his subject matter—society and social institutions—to their "elements," the individuals of which they are composed,[5] insisting that the compounds or collectivities should be voluntary, contractual associations. It was a rationalistic empiricism which decreed that, whether in the market place or in the legislative assembly, the individual should enter and take part by choice, since social relationships, group ties, responsibility, if dependent upon the individual, would follow the pain-pleasure calculus and so be in harmony with the laws of nature. This was the basis of the radical liberalism of the middle decades of the century.

As such, liberalism was primarily analytical and disintegrative. The difficulty we shall find that the movements we are concerned with had in accounting for the discrete objects of the natural world, for "bodies" or "generals," either in perception or in conception, reflected the lack of any constructive, organizing, unifying principle in their philosophy.

This was evidenced in their distrust of all institutions other than voluntary, contractual associations. Leslie Stephen wrote that for John Stuart Mill: "Old institutions awake no thrill; they are simply embodiments of prejudice."[6] And, since "bad institutions" were supported by false philosophy, one purpose of his *Logic* was "to provide a logical armory for all assailants of established dogmatism." It was enormously successful and provided "the philosophical creed of an important section of the rising generation, partly biassed, it may be true, by the application to 'bad institutions.'"[6] The liberalism of this tradition was, as it had been earlier, directed against the institutions of feudalism and the dynastic monarchies.[7]

Concerning Mill, William James wrote: "Mr. Mill's habitual method of philosophizing was to affirm boldly some general doctrine derived from his father, and then make so many concessions of detail to its enemies as practically to abandon it altogether."[8] As James hinted, this was at least partly due to Mill's essential fair-mindedness. But it was partly due, also, to the difference between his experience, private and public, and that of his father —or Jeremy Bentham. For, even while the program of the radical philosophers was being realized—the abolition of slavery and serfdom, the breaking-down of the guilds and old chartered companies, the disestablishment of religion, the secularization of education, the relaxation of police regulations of domicile—even as the individual was becoming the free atomic integer of a mass society, not merely a fear of, but the problems of, a mass society were appearing. The Saint-Simonians and Comte, Owen, Carlyle, Maurice, Kingsley, and Ruskin were, in their diverse ways, seeking means of achieving the values of a responsible social order. Influenced by these and by Tocqueville's analysis of democracy as developed in the United States, Mill must have recognized the application to his inherited creed of Comte's criticism of the radicalism of the *philosophes:*

> It essentially consists in attributing an organic character to the negative principles which served to destroy the Feudal and Theological System; in other words, it takes mere modification of the Old System as the foundation of the system which is to be established.[9]

The consequences of utilitarian individualism, with its emphasis upon laissez faire, Malthus' doctrine of population, Ricardo's iron law of wages, its secularism, and its pain-pleasure calculus, were the slums of the factory and commercial towns, the grinding poverty of the "operatives," the whole dismal factory system, on one side, and, on the other, the replacement of the old nobility and gentry by aggressive entrepreneurs and their dependents, professionals, and *rentiers*.

Yet Mill was unable to accept any of the proposed solutions for the organization of the new society; he would only alter the emphasis in the inherited creed. In ethics he would alter Bentham's crude analysis by admitting qualitative as well as quantitative differences in pleasures; he would introduce the concept of "mental chemistry" into his father's system of psychology; and in political economy, while maintaining the position of laissez faire, individualist competition, he would not only stress co-operatives but urge that the state confiscate from landholders the "unearned increment," restrain "imprudent marriages," regulate labor where individual competition failed, and use its power to equalize wealth. In brief, Mill marked the turning point at which the old individualist liberalism gave place to the new socialist liberalism.

Mill could hardly go further while the fight for the old program was not ended. Even in Britain its work was far from complete, while in France yet more remained to be done. Acquainted from boyhood with French liberals, Mill was particularly interested in French affairs. Against the aspersions of British conservatives, he defended the Revolution of Forty-eight.[10] The French reciprocated this interest, if only because the British had already achieved many of the prerequisites of a liberal society, as well as an undisputed industrial leadership. Science rather than philosophy or religion, an internationalism based upon nationalism, free trade, parliamentary government and an extended franchise, secular education, free speech and free press, and the right freely to associate—these were the pressing issues of the day for all liberals.

Evidence that such pressures were contributing to a similar "climate of opinion" in Britain and France can be found in the particular subjects of our interest. As the war against Russia and the Cobden treaty suggest, the political and economic relations of the two countries were relatively good; but these were paralleled by even closer intellectual relations. British empiricism, to which he was, in turn, indebted, prepared the way for a sympathetic response to the ideas of Auguste Comte in England. The leading British empiricists early recognized the relevance to their own endeavors of his efforts to extend scientific method to social problems. They not only translated his work but made it the subject of lengthy exposition and criticism.[11]

But if British empiricism prepared the way for the positive philosophy in Britain, not only that philosophy but Condillac and the ideologists had prepared the way for the work of Mill, Bain, Lewes, and Spencer in France. Rejecting the eclectic philosophy of Cousin, Jouffroy, and others, Hyppolite Taine called for a return to "the old and good path, so long abandoned, of induction and experience."[12] Devoting himself appropriately to a monumental *Histoire de la littérature anglaise* (1864), he concluded that work with a detailed exposition of Mill's *Logic*. The same year M. Mervoyer introduced the French to the work of Bain and Spencer in his *Étude sur l'association des idées*. A. Binet would later date the founding of experimental psychology in France from the publication of Taine's *De l'intelligence* (1870). In that work Taine not only accepted the basic concepts of British associationism but quoted, verbatim, page after page from the works of Mill, Bain, and Spencer, as well as from the laboratory monographs of the German sensationists and the French school of abnormal psychology. T.-A. Ribot provided an even fuller and more systematic account of British association psychology the same year in *La Psychologie anglaise contemporaine*. Nine years later he followed this with *La Psychologie allemande contemporaine,* in which he noted the difference between the German and British schools—the German experimental rather than speculative in method—and the similarity of their basic concepts, the British having more systematically elaborated their views.

The association psychology, especially as conceived by James Mill, provided the foundation of John Stuart Mill's *System of Logic, Ratiocinative and Inductive* (1843). This work probably did as much to spread the principles of associationism as any of the more specifically psychological works of the school, with the possible exception of Spencer's. Many other logics appeared during the century, but none commanded the almost universal acceptance of Mill's. If in the seventies Spencer was sometimes regarded as "a new Aristotle," no less was thought of Mill in logic. In the eighties, J. B. Stallo observed:

> There are few German physicists and mathematicians who have not been diligent students of Mill's *Logic,* particularly since the appearance of Schiel's translation [1849; 2d ed., 1863; 3d ed., 1876] and the extravagant praises of Liebig. . . . The interest with which each new edition of Mill's *Logic* has been received by scientific men everywhere is mainly due, doubtless, to its frequent references to scientific methods and results. The fact is that Mill has, for a series of years, been the official logician and metaphysician of the Continental naturalists and mathematicians, and the regard in which he is held by contemporary men of science is not unlike that which Aristotle enjoyed among the early Medieval scholastics.[13]

Writing about the same time, F. H. Bradley in his own *Logic* complained that in England Mill's had become practically a text.[14] There it had gone through no less than ten editions.

As for Mill's general influence in France, little more impressive evidence can be offered than the dates of the French translations of his works and their reprinting:

1854—*Principes d'économie politique*
1861—*La Liberté;* and *Principes d'économie politique* (2d ed.)
1862—*Le Gouvernement représentatif*
1864—*La Liberté* (2d ed.)
1865—*Le Gouvernement représentatif* (2d ed.)
1866–67—*Système de logique déductive et inductive*
1868—*Auguste Comte et le positivisme*
1869—*La Philosophie de Hamilton* and *L'Assujettissement des femmes*
1873—*Principes d'économie politique* (3d ed.)
1874—*Mes mémoires; histoire de ma vie et de mes idées*
1875—*Essais sur la religion* and *La Révolution de 1848 et ses détracteurs*
1877—*La Liberté* (3d ed.)
1880—*Système de logique* (2d ed.)

At the same time the works of other British empiricists were far from neglected. Bacon's works received a revised translation at the hands of M. F. Riaux in 1843, went into a second edition in 1851 and a third in 1859. Hume's essay on psychology was first translated and published with other philosophical essays in 1878. Alexander Bain's *L'Esprit et le corps considérés au point de vue de leurs rélations,* first published in 1873, and his *La Science de l'éducation,* first published in 1879, were both in their fifth editions in 1885; while his *Le Sens et l'intelligence* appeared in 1874 and his *Logique déductive et inductive* in 1875, and both went into second editions in the eighties. Spencer's *First Principles* appeared in French translation in 1871, his *Principles of Psychology* in 1874, and so on. Certainly, the French were well provided with the sources of British empirical thinking, and, during the regime of Louis Napoleon, those of liberal tendencies must have found stimulus in Mill's work in particular.

But at the same time that French political liberals were engaged in a conflict with the Second Empire, the realistic artists were engaged in conflict with their own "bad institutions." As Bentham had long before observed, the aristocracy held "as much and as long as possible to the principle of taste, taking furthermore great pains to constitute itself its supreme arbiter."[15] A dictation of taste was exercised by the art academies, especially opposing any kind of realism, and landscape painting itself was regarded as an inferior form of art. Even the sentimental landscapists of the French Barbizon school were denounced as "democrats...who don't change their linen" by Count Nieuwerkerke, the imperial director of fine arts.[16] The effects of such dictation upon the history of impressionism offers material for interesting speculation.

Of the leading impressionist painters with whom we shall be concerned, those who carried the form to its logical extreme and were the group around whom disciples gathered during the seventies—Claude Monet, Camille Pissarro, Alfred Sisley, and Auguste Renoir—it is worth noting that the first three lived and painted for some months in England. Sisley was himself an Englishman, born of English parents in France and, except for a short time in 1870 or 1871, resident in France. Monet and Pissarro were together in England during the year 1870. In addition to having studied the English painters, Pissarro, at least, had read in Mill. In 1884 he wrote his son Lucien, then living in London:

> Why doesn't Alfred read the two little books on socialism which I lent him? They are easy reading and should give him a general idea of the movement which points to the new road our society must take. . . . Let him read John Stuart Mill, the last works especially; look what Mill acknowledged before he died![17]

Such intimate familiarity with Mill was unusual; in England at the same date few even of the more intelligent writers appeared to be aware "of the conflict within Mill or of his trend toward socialism."[18]

This is merely incidental, however. If we are to suppose a relationship between British empiricist thinking and any kind of painting, we might expect that form of painting to originate in England. Nor are we wholly disappointed. Impressionism was in its origin largely English.

Among the painters whom Monet and Pissarro studied in England were Turner and Constable. Pissarro wrote:

> We were struck chiefly by the landscape painters, who shared more in our aim with regard to "plein air," light and fugitive effects. . . . Turner and Constable, while they taught us something, showed us in their works that they had no understanding of the *analysis of shadow* which in Turner's painting is simply used as an effect, a mere absence of light. As far as tone division is concerned, Turner proved the value of this as a method among methods, although he did not apply it correctly and naturally.[19]

After quoting this, Rewald adds that the two Frenchmen, "through direct observation, had already in 1870 come closer to nature than Turner." But, whatever that may mean and however much or little the English painters actually influenced the Frenchmen, the formal tendencies of impressionism appeared earlier in Britain, where the empiricist tradition orginated and was more consistently maintained.

It is well known how Delacroix was influenced by Constable's use of color contrasts, and the French impressionists were early influenced by Delacroix. But Constable had gone much farther toward the extreme of impressionism than any of the pictures which were on exhibit in 1870 could have indicated.[20] The full extent of Constable's development of the impressionist manner was concealed by the painter; only when he had made second copies of his pictures, the latter completed to suit the taste of the Royal Academy and its patrons, were they exhibited. In brief, British painting began to develop in the direction later taken by French impressionism. But, meeting with discouragement, the English painters left completion of that development to the French and returned to it only when the French movement had triumphed.[21]

In France the academy's Institute of Fine Arts, established and supported by the dynastic monarchs as a means of controlling taste, was the center upon which the artists' opposition to conservatism in art focused. This institution controlled not only the public educational facilities for artists but also the principal sales opportunities, the salons, expositions, awards of prizes and honors, and especially the government's purchases for museums in Paris and throughout the country. The academy's strict regulations of the seventeenth and eighteenth centuries had been slightly modified, particularly the right of students to work under individual masters had been granted; but its defense of the tradition of neoclassicism was staunchly and, on the whole, successfully maintained. And when the artists' dissatisfaction and opposition forced the emperor to make some changes in the institute's procedure in the sixties, the changes made, like the "liberalizing" of the political institutions of the empire at the same time, were "opportunistic" rather than substantial.[22]

Hence it was that, in a country which spent a large amount of public money upon art, it was yet necessary for artists who rejected the academic tradition, whatever their merit, to seek outlets for the sale of their work among the private dealers, with an accompanying dependence upon market conditions and the bargaining of speculative monopolists. Painters with private incomes, no matter how modest, such as Degas, Manet, and Cézanne, felt vexation of the spirit in being denied a place in the official exhibitions; but others, like Monet before his second marriage, Sisley after 1871, and Pissarro throughout his life, endured the misery of poverty. This combination of public largess with private misery even for worthy nonconformists was responsible for the attacks upon the academy.

Those who distrust coincidences may regard it as accidental that French impressionism awaited for its full development the triumph of the Third Republic. But as a historian of the academies writes:

> Liberalism and realism go hand in hand, and as the nineteenth century was the Golden Age of the one, it also saw the acme of the other. . . . This irresistible development forced academies everywhere to give in. Though they tried to uphold their ideals, they had grudgingly to accept one innovation after another. But . . . they never did it in time.[23]

That impressionism in art was realistic in the same sense that British empiricism was will be suggested by the analogies to follow. That impressionism as an art form, like empiricism as a mode of thinking, represented bourgeois liberal views will be indicated later.

CHARACTERISTICS AND ANALOGIES

I. FRENCH IMPRESSIONIST PAINTING

Landscapes, frequently landscapes with figures but as frequently simply landscapes, furnished the staple subject matter of the impressionists. They were, however, unconcerned with landscape as the embodiment of the spiritual or as the environment of human life—a fact which may account for the declining interest of their early champion, Zola, in their art.[24] They were interested in landscape as a revelation of particular effects which only the artist as painter could seize and reveal.

The contribution of the impressionists to our vision was their discovery of the enchantment of color and color alone. That our vision of the world is the effect of the play of light upon the retina of our eye, a play of atmospheric effects, was their endless theme. In pursuit of this vision in all its evanescence, the importance of *what* was seen diminished. A turn in the road, a street scene, a vision of boats on water, or men and women in a garden, all alike furnished the painters with a thematic play of light and color, "the motif."

But the effect of sunlight was discovered to be a blurring of contours and a dissolution of individual objects into simply complex color concentrations. As a result, even the human figures, like the natural objects, became dabs of a variety of colors; their women were simply the brightest colored of the flowers of the field.

It is a kind of realism when men and women are reduced by the artist to the status of the natural. But it was an impressionist realism which reduced the human and all other objects to the terms of the painter's medium, color. This suggests that the importance of their ostensible subject matter was itself technical. Their real subject was simply the world of appearance.

Since we are accustomed to seeing color as local color, to reduce the world to sensations of atmospheric color required a special education of the power of vision. What was called for was an acute and tireless analysis of the effects of light. This was the reason the impressionists took their easels into the field and, unlike their predecessors, remained there to complete their paintings, becoming "field workers" in the arts.[25] As long as the artist remained in the studio or developed his field sketches into finished pictures in the studio, his painting was an artificial creation, a construction, governed either by an ideal, by preconceived form, or by his imagination. But if the sensations of color given by light to the eyes were to form the material of art, observation and accurate recording were essential.

To reproduce their sensations of light effects, the impressionists applied color to canvas in small, perceptible strokes and, to eliminate the dull muddiness of mixed colors, used only the primary and immediately derivative colors. These were placed upon an otherwise blank canvas without the preparatory brown base, which, following the old tradition, Courbet and Degas used. The multitude of small strokes made possible an intermingling of a variety of colors within a limited area, thus imitating the composite effects of light and reflected lights which they discovered in their analysis of the shadowed and luminous. In the effort to present only their sensations of color, they renounced drawing, and lines defining boundaries disappeared as contours were subordinated to the color relations of the discrete forms with the whole visual scene.[26]

Impressionist painting thus represented a reduction of the visual world to a kind of unity in terms of the medium of the art, and the discrete objects of our everyday experience survived only as defined by associations of color. This is perhaps most apparent in the landscapes with figures, where the latter become mottled with the greens and blues of their surroundings. But it is also evident in the impressionists' portraits. The profound insight into character of the great portrait painters was not theirs. Often the more revealing lines of a face are scarcely hinted at in their pictures; what appears is more a tableau of color, a vivid, lively play of light on human features, than the lineaments of character.

The decomposition of bodies into disconnected dabs of color was what most confused the critics of their day. For, beyond the association of color sensations, the harmony of the film of color, objects and formal structure were alike notable chiefly by their absence from these pictures. The familiar world of objects, like the familiar world of neoclassic composition, had been replaced by a confused and confusing vision of atoms of paint.

II. BRITISH ASSOCIATION PSYCHOLOGY

As the impressionists took the visual appearance of the natural world as their subject matter, reporting it by means of small strokes of pure color, separate, merged, or interwoven, the British psychologists took consciousness as their subject matter and analyzed it in terms of elementary sensations received from the external world. With such concepts as the "unconscious," "subconscious," and "instincts" they had no concern and until late in the period thought only in terms of the consciousness of the normal, white, European adult. Postulating of mind little more than Locke's blank tablet, only an "expectancy" in Mill's phrase, they maintained that consciousness was formed wholly by the experience of sensations; the mind's activity was confined to registering and recalling or reproducing these sensations and their associations with one another. Mill set down four laws of association: (1) similar phenomena tend to be thought of together; (2) phenomena experienced or conceived in "close contiguity to one another tend to be thought of together. The contiguity is of two kinds; simultaneity and immediate succession.... Of facts which have been experienced or thought of in immediate succession, the antecedent, or the thought of it, recalls the thought of the consequent, but not conversely" (3) associations become "irresistible" by repetition; (4) when an association has attained this "character of inseparability," the phenomena "come to seem inseparable in existence."[27]

The painters analyzed the world of vision, reducing it to terms of sensations of color; the psychologists reduced consciousness to their term "sensations." But the psychologists' results were not very different from what the painters arrived at: analyzed into elementary sensory impressions, the discrete unities or bodies of our common experience seem inadequately accounted for. Particularly was this true in James Mill's psychology. John Stuart Mill introduced the notion of "mental chemistry." He thought that sometimes a melting or coalescing of the elements occurred when they entered into a combination. The section is worth quoting from Mill; it is so apposite to the impressionist technique:

> When many impressions or ideas are operating in the mind together, there sometimes takes place a process of a similar kind to chemical combination. When impressions have been so often experienced in conjunction, that each of them calls up readily and instantaneously the ideas of the whole group, those ideas sometimes melt and coalesce into one another, and appear not several ideas but one; in the same manner as when the seven prismatic colors are presented to the eye in rapid succession, the sensation produced is that of white. But in this last case it is correct to say that the seven colors when they rapidly follow one another *generate* white, but not that they actually *are* white.[28]

We are not so much concerned here with his illustration from color—Mill was treating of light rather than of pigment—but the notions of coalescing, generating, as well as association, are not without parallel implications for the technique of the painters.

We should note also that, even in "coalescence," white was regarded as a kind of general, "generated" by the elementary parts and not "actually" a whole or unity. For these psychologists, objects were clusters of associated impressions.

They distinguished, however, between an "active mode" of perceiving and a "passive mode." Of the latter, Bain wrote:

> In purely passive feeling, as in those of our sensations that do not call forth our muscular energies, we are not perceiving matter, we are in a state of subject consciousness. . . . All our senses may yield similar experiences, if we resign ourselves to their purely sensible or passive side. . . . It is just possible, although difficult, to make light a subject experience; mere formless radiance would be an approach to it; the recognition of form or boundary introduces an object property, embodied in ocular movements.[29]

That is a close approach to a description of impressionism, the extreme envisioned by Bain being almost realized by some of Monet's pictures painted in the nineties. The second, or "active mode," which included "ocular movements," was the means by which the psychologists accounted for visual effects other than color, for "visible movement, visible form, apparent size, distance, volume, and situation." However, though the psychologists called upon a greater range of sensations than did the painters, this "active mode" differed from the "passive" only in the addition of more sensations; objects remained, in their pages, complex concentrations of various sensations.

As the French painters developed the impressionist aesthetic to its extreme, so Taine carried the logic of the association psychology to its extreme conclusion and revealed that, in fact, it dealt only with the "state of subject consciousness." If localization of our sensations in external objects is an error and what exists in the external world is only the "possibility of sensations," then normal perception (as distinguished from abnormal) can be defined in his words as "an accurate hallucination" (as abnormal perception is inaccurate). In the words of an unsympathetic critic: "Just as he evaporates the outer world into a void, so Taine reduces the inner world to a nonentity; the ego becomes a conglomeration of images. Reality is thus all surface, beneath which there is nothing at all."[30] Lionello Venturi writes that the "Impressionists were well aware that what they painted was not reality, but the *appearance of reality.*"[31] And many a critic of impressionism would add "beneath which there is nothing at all." For the reality of the impressionist paintings is all surface, a brilliant, shimmering screen.

III. BRITISH INDUCTIVE LOGIC

In contrast to the traditional syllogistic logic, with its emphasis upon consistency of thought deduced from a major premise, the inductive logic emphasized discovery and proof. Built upon the association psychology, the peculiarity of this logic was its insistence upon the empirical foundation of knowledge. Proofs from intuition, from definition, from any sort of a priori basis, were discarded by Mill. All axioms, even those of mathematics, were regarded as generalizations from experience. This meant that the logic was less concerned with the activity of thought, of judgment, than with the determination of constancies in the facts given in experience.

This is immediately apparent from Mill's analysis of the syllogism. He begins by noting that the syllogism is a means of finding the implications of the major premise. Though admitting that all its implications are not at once obvious, nevertheless he insists that the implications are not genuine unknowns. But the whole purpose of inquiry is the discovery of unknowns. Proceeding with the analysis, he finds that the major premise itself is a generalization arrived at by inference from particulars.

Taking the syllogism, "All men are mortal, Socrates is a man, therefore Socrates is mortal," he argues that, from our knowledge of "the deaths of John and Thomas and every other person we ever heard of in whose case the experiment had been fairly tried," we have reasonably concluded that "all men are mortal." But this reveals that the major premise itself is a general resulting from an observation of particulars:

Now, all which man can observe are individual cases. From these all general truths must be drawn and into these they may again be resolved; for *a general truth is but an aggregate of particular truths;* a comprehensive expression, by which an indefinite number of individual facts are affirmed or denied at once. . . . From instances which we have observed, we feel warranted in concluding, that what we found true in those instances, holds in all similar ones, past, present, and future, however numerous they may be. We then, by that valuable contrivance of language which enables us to speak of many as if they were one, record all that we have observed, together with all that we infer from our observations, in one concise expression; and have thus only one proposition, instead of an endless number, to remember or to communicate.[32]

However, despite the usefulness of the general proposition, if the evidence "is sufficient to support the general proposition, it is sufficient also to support an inference from particulars to particulars without passing through the general."[33] Thus the basic method of science must be induction, by which generals or laws are arrived at. And though deduction is an indication of the perfection attained by a science, nevertheless it rests originally upon induction. The consequences of the deduction must, of course, in turn be tested by observation and experiment. Deduction is, however, but half, the latter half, of the process of scientific logic of which the preceding, and more important, half is induction.

Assuming the "uniformity of nature," a general yielded by simple enumeration, Mill asserts: "The Law of Causation, the recognition of which is the main pillar of inductive science, is but the familiar truth that invariability of succession is found by observation to obtain between every fact in nature and some other fact which has preceded it."[34] This is the logic of associationism. The associated sensations, the "contiguous phenomena," of the psychology become the "invariable succession of facts" of the logic. The problem of logic is accordingly to determine which of the associated phenomena are connected in invariable sequence; and this "process of ascertaining what consequents in nature are invariably connected with what antecedents . . . is in some sort a process of analysis." We must reduce the complex phenomena into their elements by a mental process of observation and then by experiment:

> The order of nature, as perceived at first glance, presents at every instant a chaos followed by another chaos. We must decompose each chaos into single facts. We must learn to see in the chaotic antecedent a multitude of distinct consequents. This, supposing it done, will not of itself tell us on which of the antecedents each consequent is invariably attendant. To determine that point, we must endeavor to effect a separation of the facts from one another, not in our minds only, but in nature.[35]

Having arrived at the ultimate particulars, we are then ready to apply the four methods, or the five canons, of induction.

Commenting upon Mill's suggestions for the symbolization of his methods, L. S. Stebbing wrote: "Here, as always, Mill assumes a one-one correspondence of the cause-factors and effect-factors. His symbols *suggest* a likeness between cause and effect, since to capital letters correspond the same small letters."[36] This procedure, however unfortunate logically, would appear to be partly a consequence of his psychology. For what in the *System of Logic* Mill designated "cause" and "effect" factors were surely those "contiguous phenomena" of the psychology which, having been "experienced or thought of in immediate succession, the antecedent, or the thought of it, recalls the thought of the consequent. . . . "[27] The "methods" are simply the means of assuring the selection of the invariables in any specific series.

If, in this account of Mill's logic, it may seem that I have ignored unduly the genuine sense of contiguity which holds cause and effect together or the various methods of agreement, difference, and concomitance which are designed to assure a genuine thread of causation, it may be worth while to reiterate that, in the thinking of this school, inference moves from particulars to particulars. H. Levy and others among Mill's followers insisted upon this: the great virtue of his *Logic* was that it taught men to reason from particulars to particulars.[37] It is not so much that these particulars never form a group and such groups, generals; they do. But the particulars are never wholly lost in the group. So in the impressionist paintings it would be nonsense to pretend that there is *no* composition apparent or that we cannot discern the discrete figures. Nevertheless, the particulars are not wholly lost; the figures remain a cluster of closely associated particulars. Granting all the necessary differences between a system of logic and a form of painting, if we can say that the general laws are arrived at and consist in an aggregate of particulars and that the composition of a painting is similarly arrived at by means of and consists in an aggregate of particulars, the analogy is not without a reasonably adequate foundation.

Whether Pissarro or any of his companions ever read the following passage in Mill may be doubted. That they would have found in it an expression of their own belief, as Pissarro expressed it: "work, observation and sensation are the real forces,"[38] can hardly be doubted. Mill was writing of the "mental analysis" which must precede the analysis to be "made in nature":

> And everyone knows that in the mode of performing it, one intellect differs immensely from another. It is the essence of the act of observing, for the observer is not he who merely sees the thing which is before his eyes, but he who sees what parts that thing is composed of. To do this well is a rare talent. One person, from inattention, or attending only the wrong place, overlooks half of what he sees; another sets down much more than he sees, confounding it with what he imagines, or with what he infers; another takes note of the *kind* of all the circumstances, but being inexpert in estimating their degree, leaves the quantity of each vague and uncertain; another sees indeed the whole, but makes such an awkward division of it into parts, throwing things into one mass which require to be separated, and separating others which might more conveniently be considered as one, that the result is much the same, sometimes even worse, than if no analysis had been attempted at all.[39]

The impressionists would have seen the relevance of this. They would have agreed with the individualism said to be implicit in the art of observing; they would have rejoiced in the recognition of the careful practice of analytical observation necessary to see "what parts that thing is composed of"; even the pitfalls enumerated would have been familiar to them.

The basis for our analogy should now be sufficiently evident. As in psychology, so in logic, so in painting, consciousness, natural laws, the visual scene, were regarded as truly arrived at only by an analysis of the given chaotic reality into its elements and a methodical association of the products of the analysis: of sensations in psychology, of elementary facts in logic, of strokes of color in painting. And as the empiricists recognized no mental powers or faculties or "native determinations," no a priori truths or formal concepts, so the impressionists recognized no a priori or necessary visual forms. The associationist analysis of consciousness predicated a passive mind, whose content was made up of sensations, which were, in turn, "facts" and "ideas," and whose only activity consisted in the recording, recollecting, and associating of these sensations. Mill's logic predicated induction, which consisted of analysis by observation of facts and association according to the canons; when this was done, the generalizations were revealed. Impressionism predicated observational analysis and a passive recording of the associations of the observed sensations. All depended upon "experience," which meant, for all, upon sensations and the observation of sensations. All represented a kind of copy theory: truth is arrived at by accurately reproducing sensations or impressions from external reality; all depended upon this "given," which was merely to be analyzed into its elements and their associations recorded.

COMPARABLE WAYS OF DIFFERING

To exhibit these relations in greater detail would require a tedious examination, which, in the end, could hardly be warranted. However, I shall examine one aspect of Mill's logic which was at variance with other logics of the period, since this will also clarify distinctions between the painters. A crucial point at issue in scientific logic was the matter of hypotheses. The traditional empiricist position was hostile to these "phantoms," as Bacon called them. But by Mill's time their importance in relation to scientific experiment had become so evident that they could not be ignored. Mill recognized this: "the function of hypotheses is one which must be reckoned absolutely indispensable in science," and "the hypothesis by suggesting observations and experiments puts us on the road to independent evidence."[40]

But William Whewell had forced the issue. A Tory and High Churchman, influenced by Kant, he was the author of *The Logic of the Inductive Sciences,* a work which both helped and stimulated Mill to write his own. Whewell distinguished between sensations and ideas "with reference to a fundamentally fixed line of demarkation between what is passively *given* to the mind and the *activity* put forth by the mind."[41] This led him to his conception of a hypothesis generated by the mind, an activity not arising from the factual evidence:

The ideal conception which the mind itself supplies is superinduced upon the facts as they are originally presented to observation. Before the inductive truth is detected, the facts are there, but they are many and unconnected. The conception which the discoverer applies to them gives them conception and unity.[42]

With this Mill could not agree; it hinted of innate, a priori forms and ideas, of that "intuition" which he repudiated. His problem was therefore to reconcile hypotheses with his psychology in which "sensations are somehow finally and completely given as ultimate facts, and . . . ideas are mere re-registrations of such facts."[43] In the effort to solve that problem, he returned to a strict empiricist position, retracting much of what he had already written concerning hypotheses. His conclusion was that the ideas which order the facts arise from the impress of the facts themselves:

> The conceptions [hypotheses] which we employ for the colligation and methodization of facts, do not develop themselves from within, *but are impressed upon the mind from without;* they are never obtained otherwise than by way of comparison and abstraction, and, in the most important and most numerous cases, are evolved by abstraction *from the very phenomena which it is their office to colligate.*[44]

For Whewell the mind imposed general ideas upon the chaos of the given facts; for Mill the ideas originated from without, from the very chaos of facts which the ideas order.

One of the painters associated with the impressionists, though never an impressionist himself, was Edgar Degas. The difference between his conception of the art of painting and that of his impressionist friends is summarized by Rewald:

> "You need natural life," he explained to his colleagues, "I, artificial life." But the difference between him and the impressionists was not entirely defined by this statement. "I always tried," Degas later explained to the English painter Sickert, "to urge my colleagues to seek for new combinations along the path of draftsmanship, which I consider a more fruitful field than that of color. But they wouldn't listen to me, and have gone the other way." Degas apparently considered their approach to nature too passive and disapproved of their complete fidelity to a chosen motif. Their principle of not omitting or changing anything, their sole preoccupation with their immediate sensations made them, in his eyes, slaves of the chance circumstances of nature and light. "It is very well to copy what one sees," he said to a friend, "it's much better to draw what one has retained in one's memory. It is a transformation in which imagination collaborates with memory. One reproduces only that which is striking; that is to say, the necessary. Thus one's recollections and invention are liberated from the tyranny which nature exerts."[45]

Though concerned to record the life of his time, Degas stressed draftsmanship and distrusted painting directly from the model. What he sought to render was not the particulars but the typical, the "essential."[46] And is there not a fundamental similarity between his idea of the "transformation in which imagination collaborates with memory" and Whewell's "ideal conception which the mind" superinduces "upon the facts as they are originally presented to observation"? It is this product of the mind or imagination which, applied to the chaos of our sensations, imposes order and brings out the "essential" or the "necessary." Only by this something given by the mind from within, Degas asserted, are "one's recollections and invention liberated from the tyranny which nature exerts."

The impressionists submitted to, took a passive attitude toward, the "tyranny" of nature. The only vestige of some peculiar contribution of the mind in their aesthetic may be said to lie in their choice of the motif. Yet what was this motif if it was not just the peculiar concatenations or associations of the sensations, since the painters were so faithful to the latter as given and the more fugitive the effect, the more certainly this was true? As Mill might have said, the motif was given with the impressions, and a better illustration of his contention would be hard to find. For, in the selection of the motif, the conception to be employed "for the colligation and methodization of facts" was actually given with and by the sensations. If so little design is discoverable in their pictures, if they are so lacking in form as to be almost meaningless, is it not because the design is simply an association of particulars and that only too frequently no "general" is drawn from the "particulars," that the coexistences and contiguities remain mere aggregates?

The same kind of difference between these artists appeared in their contrasting attitudes toward the Japanese color prints, first known to Western artists during the late fifties and early sixties. Though the impressionists admired these works, they were uninfluenced by them. But many other artists found them instructive, and among these was Degas. Rewald notes: "Their graphic style, their subtle use of line, their decorative qualities, their daring foreshortenings and, above all, the way in which their principal subjects were often placed off-center, the whole composition and organisation of space seem to have impressed him [Degas] deeply."[47] Similarly Degas's disciples, especially Mary Cassatt, were deeply influenced, often to the point of painting little more than a pastiche.

Degas and his group were to a degree sympathetic with impressionism, as Whewell and similar logicians were sympathetic with the logic of induction; both, however, felt the lack of organizing principles, the one in the logic of impressionism, the other in the logic of empiricism. Because Degas and his associates felt the need of order, an aesthetic order, in a way the impressionists did not, they were particularly interested in any means of "colligating and methodizing" their observations of nature. The Japanese prints presented them with "new combinations along the path of draftsmanship," with a new a priori scheme, as it were, upon which to build or compose. The impressionists, trusting wholly to observation and sensation, believed in no such schemes and sought none.

During the late seventies, the "climate of opinion" was changing. One of those doing much to bring about this change in England was T. H. Green at Oxford. In his *Lectures on Logic,* delivered in 1874–75, he attempted a refutation of Mill. Mill's contention that mathematical concepts are derived from sensations of experience was always under attack by idealists.[48] This need not concern us except that Green, in challenging that part of Mill's argument, criticized his contention that real lines are sensations. According to Green:

> It is impossible to hold that real lines are sensations. . . . What I see is colour (or light), but line is not a colour nor a relation between colours. To make sense you have to say that it is a relation between coloured surfaces, but it is not as coloured that the surfaces are thus related, for the colours may be changed in any way you please, while that relation between the surfaces which constitutes the line remains the same. It is only by taking "sight" to express an act of intellectual combination exercised on materials which are given by sense, but which in virtue of this act become quite different from what they are merely as feelings, that we can be said to see bodies. The idea of the line is obtained by the detachment of a purely intellectual element, a mere relation, involved in this "sight" of bodies. This intellectual element, this mere relation, *is* the real line.[49]

No lines from sensation; the line is an intellectual element. Had the works of the impressionists been submitted as evidence, they would have confirmed it, as Degas might have agreed with the argument. The impressionists found no lines in their visual sensations and painted none. Degas, following the advice of Ingres and the practice of the neoclassic painters, regarded the line as the foundation of the art.

CONCLUSION

In the eighties the French impressionist school broke up, as many of the members themselves came to recognize the limitation of their procedure. When in 1880–81 Renoir began to doubt the validity of the impressionist aesthetic and turned to draftsmanship, studying the works of Raphael and Ingres, he wrote: "While painting directly from nature, the artist reaches the point where he looks only for the effects of light, where he no longer composes, and he quickly descends to monotony."[50] And surely that is one way of describing the result of an analytic reduction and passive recording, whether in terms of sensations of color or in terms of the sensations of the pain-pleasure calculus.

During the middle eighties even Pissarro was seeking means of achieving "synthesis," the key word of the next decades, as "sensations" and "observation" had been of the earlier. For a few years he became a disciple of Seurat and Signac, only to return to "the suppleness, liberty, spontaneity, and freshness postulated by our impressionist art."[51] Sisley changed his manner little; Monet carried impressionism to its ultimate refinement in his studies of haystacks and water lilies. But many of their important disciples, including Cézanne, were forsaking them.

That impressionism was a liberal bourgeois form of art is neither a new nor a startling idea. Meyer Shapiro has pointed out that the impressionists drew upon bourgeois entertainments for their subject matter:

These urban idylls not only present the objective forms of bourgeois recreation in the 1860's and 1870's; they also reflect in the very choice of subjects and in the new aesthetic devices the conception of art as solely a field of individual enjoyment, without reference to ideas and motives. . . . In enjoying realistic pictures of his surroundings as a spectacle of traffic and changing atmospheres, the cultivated rentier was experiencing in its phenomenal aspect that mobility of the environment, the market and of industry to which he owed his income and his freedom.[52]

If we can accept Beatrice Webb's account of her father's home as representative of the life of the entrepreneur in the seventies, it was not only the mobility of the environment in a material sense but the mobility of all human relationships that found expression in impressionism:

> The world of human intercourse in which I was brought up was in fact an endless series of human beings, unrelated one to the other, and only casually connected with the family group. . . . Our social relations had no roots in the neighborhood, in vocation, in creed, or for that matter in race; they likened a series of moving pictures—surface impressions without depth—restlessly stimulating in their glittering variety.[53]

Nor could this have been a rare experience in a period of mass migrations from country to city and from continent to continent.

During their own time the impressionists were associated by unfriendly critics with movements of the political left, as were realistic painters of all descriptions throughout the century. Under the Republic, whenever fear of *le spectre rouge* was being used by conservatives in their attacks on the Republic, as during the Boulanger episode, impressionism was denounced as socialist or communist art. And from the standpoint of the political conservative or monarchist, for whom a bourgeois republic was "left," this was accurate enough, though it was indiscriminate labeling as far as the political views of the individual painters were concerned.

Degas, whom we have distinguished from the impressionists, was, like Whewell again, a political conservative, actually a monarchist. The genial, but continually disappointed Manet, who became an impressionist in his last period, was a liberal Republican. Sisley and Renoir were indifferent to politics. Monet was a liberal with socialist inclinations. Pissarro, a gentle Jew who suffered as much from the private monopolist as from the academy, and was the most interested of the group in political theory, was a philosophical anarchist. Equally as informative as this, however, is a later incident, an incident which occurred after the deaths of Manet and Sisley. It will be recalled that Pissarro and Monet were the ones who remained most faithful to the impresssionist aesthetic. Now, when in the nineties Zola espoused Dreyfus' cause, though the novelist had only a short time before deeply offended the painters, nevertheless Monet and Pissarro "overcame their resentment and immediately supported him," while Degas "joined the militarists, turned anti-Semitic and henceforth avoided Pissarro, while Cézanne . . . also failed to rally behind Zola."[54]

Pissarro thought it ironical to be classed as a bourgeois—in overalls and without a penny in his pocket—and believed that impressionism reflected his own anarchist thought.[55] Nor was he wholly mistaken. Impressionism was anarchist in tendency in the same sense that, as Matthew Arnold indicated in his essay "Culture and Anarchy," anarchy was one logical extreme of empirical and utilitarian thinking. British empiricist thought was, as we have seen, analytical and destructive, whether of generals, bodies, or institutions. Utilitarian laissez faire doctrines postulated a minimum of institutional authority. Anarchism carried such anti-institutionalism to the extreme of positive social doctrine. The political theories of the left in the mid-century sought to free the individual in the interest of his fullest development and, like bourgeois liberalism, emphasized co-operation and denounced class-conservative institutions. The envisaged ends of these theories were not greatly different; it was upon methods of achieving those ends that they were most radically at odds. Finally, these doctrines were alike in promoting the development of the mass society.

Élie Halévy has pointed out that the individualism of the utilitarians, when combined with their pain-pleasure calculus, led to an equalitarianism in which men would be merely interchangeable integers and so to a uniform society in which all individualism, perhaps in any sense but certainly in the sense understood up to that time, would be lost, as Carlyle asserted and Mill came to fear.[56] But we have seen something similar in impressionism: the reduction of the visual world of colored objects to the sensations of color, leading to a world in which the discrete forms tended to lose all reality, being replaced by a mass of associated colors. And "the conception of art as solely a field of individual enjoyment, without reference to ideas and motives," is an anarchical position in its freedom from institutional loyalties and responsibilities. We can, I think, conclude that just as in the logic of empiricism and utilitarian liberalism the extreme of anarchism was implicit, so it was in impressionism as a form of painting. Within the general conceptual patterns we call "empiricism" or "utilitarianism" and within the general formal pattern we call "impressionism," many variations were developed by individual thinkers and painters so classified; the bourgeois liberalism of the middle decades was the more conservative political position, as anarchism was one of the radical political extremes, of these patterns of thought and feeling.

Who would dispute that, meanwhile, the mass society was appearing in the actuality of social life? With the passage of general incorporation acts and acts permitting workingmen's combinations, with the passage of the Education Act and the Third Reform Bill in Britain, with the establishment of the Third Republic and the passage of the laic laws in France, the problem was no longer to bring to an end old institutions. They were gone or going, as were most of the old distinctions by which individualism had previously been fostered. The new problems were the problems of a mass society. The new problem was to discover what constituted the true whole or unit of which the multitudinous new voluntary and contractual institutions were the particulars or to create a unified structural pattern, a composition, out of these competing units.

Nor was it only the impressionist movement that was giving place to a movement for "synthesis" of some sort in the eighties. The revolt against the empirical philosophy of the previous decades was gaining strength everywhere: "Even in England by 1878 the vein of empiricism appears exhausted."[57] The younger psychologists were ridiculing associationism and sensationism as "mosaic" or "atomistic" and were seeking a unity of psychological reality in "acts" or "motor impulses" or "instincts." Idealists in philosophy were emphasizing the whole or unity within which, or subordinate to which, all analysis occurs; the empiricists in logic were turning to statistics in an effort to establish structural or formal relations in the chaos of their empirical data.

Of the younger painters who were dissatisfied with impressionism—Seurat, Signac, Cross, Bonnard, Vuillard, Gauguin, and Van

Gogh—one who worked with Gaugin, Maurice Denis, has explained what it was these younger men found to admire in the later work of Cézanne that seemed to them to be lacking in impressionism. Rewald records it as follows:

Denis and his friends had found that impressionism had a "synthetic tendency, since its aim was to translate a sensation, to objectify a state of mind; but its means were analytical, since color in impressionism was merely the result of an endless number of contrasts." Cézanne, however, by revealing a structure beneath richly nuanced surfaces, went consciously beyond the appearances which satisfied a Monet. To the younger painters his work offered a solution of the problem of "preserving sensibility's essential role while substituting conscious reflection for empiricism."[58]

Cézanne represented one of the new directions painting was to take; there would be others. Beyond this, comment upon that statement would be superfluous.

THE "OFFICIAL" SCHOLAR: A SURVEY OF CERTAIN RESEARCH IN AMERICAN FOREIGN POLICY

By RICHARD HUMPHREY

Department of State, Washington, D.C.

THE responsibility for formulating the foreign policy of the United States is shared with the Chief Executive by the Secretary of State. Since omniscience is required of neither of them by the Constitution, they discharge their functions through delegation. The existence of the Department of State is an outward and visible sign of that delegation.

There are, therefore, many heads concerned in the framing of American policy, as there are many hands in the execution of it. The mere number and complexity of the problems involved are not in themselves, however, the exclusive reason for this delegation of responsibility. Foreign relations, additionally, is a field for "experts," in the sense that no man can hope to master the intricacies of more than a relatively small portion of its ramifications. The best judgment of the many must produce the synthesis which, well founded or ill, becomes the body of doctrine and practice governing America's world relationships.

The method of evolving foreign policy is more largely deductive than inductive. A Monroe Doctrine, a Good Neighbor Policy, or a Marshall Plan is seldom arrived at from studied contemplation of general principles. It is of the first importance that the policy-framers be in possession of all the facts necessary to the correct evaluation of their problems, which must rather be derived from the correct evaluation of particulars. Although the accumulation of data is probably no more than the beginning of wisdom, the need for basic and accurate information as a starting point in this analysis is no longer called into question, if, indeed, it ever was, by those whose policy decisions fundamentally affect us all.

Of recent years the research scholar, to a very considerable extent the historian, has come to play an increasingly prominent role as an "expert" in the process of accumulating the basic data and assembling the pertinent information which are the foundation of intelligent foreign-policy formulation. He occupies today a place of some importance in the Department of State, seldom as the man who recommends what should be done, but certainly as the man who must advise as to what has been, through the whole wide gamut of circumstances related to a pending issue. He has become a breaker of ground in the elaborate process of policy-framing which culminates in judgments indorsed by the Secretary of State and the President.

The historian has, besides, another function to fulfil for the department. Into his hands is intrusted the task of preparing for publication the record of American diplomacy, which constitutes the account of the department's stewardship to the people of this nation. His competence in this job is hardly less important than his *expertise* as a historical adviser. The record of the discharge of public responsibilities must, in a democracy, be made available for all the people who will to examine and pass judgment. That record must be compiled by honest and able men. It was for the fulfilment of this function, in point of fact, that the department first employed professional historians on its permanent staff.

With emphasis varying at the several stages of its evolution, therefore, the Department of State's historical research program has been directed basically along two channels: (1) the publication of the record of American diplomacy as a contribution to public enlightenment and understanding and (2) the assembly and analysis of broad masses of historical data which provide part of the background against which current policy determinations are made.

Expert research resources in the field of historic American diplomacy do not, however, exhaust the information needs of the department's policy-framers. As everyone knows, the experience of the second World War enormously elaborated what has come to be called "intelligence" activity within and without the Department of State. This arm of modern American foreign policy devotes substantial resources to scholarly analysis and research on the general problem of the policies of *other* nations and states as they affect our own.

The evolution of the concept "intelligence research" stemmed, in very large measure, from the efforts of General William Donovan's wartime Office of Strategic Services, the greatest part of whose research resources transferred under Executive Order to the Department of State following the termination of World War II hostilities. The President observed, in his letter to the Secretary of State of September 20, 1945: "The [above] transfer to the State Department will provide you with resources which we have agreed you will need to aid in the development of our foreign policy, and will assure that pertinent experience accumulated during the war will be preserved and used in meeting the problems of the peace."

There are, then, two principal reservoirs of qualified research talent at the command of the Secretary and of his subordinate officers who are responsible for active participation in the policy-formulating process: (1) the historical research staff, which must produce evidence in the broad field of United States diplomatic policy from the founding of the republic to the most recent policy cable, and (2) the intelligence research staff, which must assemble and analyze all obtainable data bearing upon the political objectives, the economic, cultural, and other conditions and situations in other states throughout the world, as they bear upon American policy problems. Taken together, the researches of these staffs provide part of the frame of reference within which the "action" officer operates.

To the research scholars, the "action" officer (or "policy" officer, or "country-desk" man) stands in the relation of client. It is his problem that sets the bounds, and the pace, of the research which is undertaken. The research is performed in the interests of his informed judgment. He, not the research scholars, is responsible for the decisions. It is their function, not his, to assemble the evidence. The other major client of department research is the public, though the end-objective is fundamentally the same— enlightened judgment on the problems and issues of foreign policy. Some of the problems and processes of research for these two sets of clients are the object of the examination which follows.

A general overview of the policy-framing pattern of operation within the Department of State is a necessary prerequisite to a correct understanding of the relation of scholarly reseach to it. In examining this pattern, it is necessary to bear in mind that the department (from obvious necessity) approaches its problems of policy from two basic points of view. Very broadly indeed these may be regarded as (1) "bilateral" problems of a country-to-country nature, as United States relations at a given time with a specific foreign state, and (2) "multilateral" problems, which cut across country-to-country or area-to-area issues, as international trade programs, United Nations Organization relationships, and broad projects, such as the "Marshall Plan" of American assistance to a number of co-operating states.

At the right arm of the Secretary of State sits a group of top-level staff experts, known as the Policy Planning Staff, with responsibility for advising him and the President on the total implications of current American policy. This group specifically does not "operate" or make day-to-day decisions as to what American policy on a given issue shall be. It must, rather, maintain an attitude of cloistered reserve, in so far as that is possible, and insulate itself against the demands of immediate problems in order to plan on a long-range and comprehensive basis.

The Policy Planning Staff is perhaps the most important corporate consumer of departmental research. In preparing its "position papers" and broad recommendations to the Secretary and the President, it has need of competent research advice and assistance. Like the action officers in the department, this staff body cannot devote the requisite time to conducting its own research and assembling its own background evidence.

Planning Staff recommendations, when indorsed by the Secretary of State and the President, are implemented by the operating officials. In point of fact, the recommendations themselves are usually the product of joint effort on the part of the staff and those officials who must make the day-to-day decisions in the name of the Secretary.

In order to arrive at informed judgments, the action officer or operating official needs to know at least three things: (1) the relation between what he must decide and policies previously laid down or currently adhered to; (2) the relevant political, economic, and other conditions prevailing in the countries likely to be affected by his decision (including his own); and (3) the probable effect of his decision, whether he decides to hew to the line of established policy or, by departing from it, to create new policy. As a consequence, his judgment is contingent upon intimate knowledge of the background policy patterns and issues within which he operates (both current and historical) and of probable reactions at home or abroad, official or unofficial, to his treatment of a given problem.

To provide the policy officer or, at the highest level, the Secretary and the Policy Planning Staff with the necessary background and foreground knowledge, the department makes available the researches of scholars.

It is necessary to emphasize that such "official" researches are characterized by their own peculiar requirements, a fact fundamental to an objective evaluation of the work of the scholar in the department. First, the product desired by the policy-framer is likely to embrace comprehensive subject matter; second, it must be conceived and executed under conditions normally requiring maximum speed of production; third, it must embody all obtainable data relevant to a central issue or group of issues; and, fourth, it must be presented to the officer faced with decision in concise and usable form. One may say, indeed, that these characteristics are reasonably general wherever official research is undertaken, whether in the Executive or the Legislative branches of the government. The corollary is, perhaps, obvious. Research in the Department of State necessitates analysis which is as comprehensive in its coverage, and as objective, as research on the same or comparable subjects by the private scholar. Normally, however, it must be conducted under adverse time conditions and presented in a form which is determined not so much by the subject matter as by the immediate needs of a specific action.

Factors vital to the methodology of the official researcher, some of which are quite extraneous to the experience of the private scholar, condition the official research product. These factors complicate the task enormously and, in fact, require that the scholar in the department (or in government generally) superimpose new emphases upon his technical training and such native ability as he may possess. To justify himself, he must bring to his job (or, where pertinent, develop): (1) complete technical competence and the broadest possible knowledge of his substantive field; (2) ability to isolate quickly the central issues of a research problem, the limits of which have been established by the issue before his client, the action officer; (3) aptitude for exhaustive and authoritative scholarly exploration of the central issues with a minimum of diversion to related, though momentarily less important, problems; (4) ability to present findings effectively in terms of the needs of his client; and (5) capacity to produce all required data within time limits which bear no necessary relationship to the complexities of the problem examined.

These are not limitations altogether familiar to the academic scholar striving to "advance human knowledge" (or, less pretentiously, his own) through his investigations. He can afford to follow the basic data through tortuous and time-consuming channels and publish the results of his research after months or even years of labor. Although he may well add to the sum total of knowledge, national policy seldom awaits the product of his pen. For his "brother in service" such unhurried and exhaustive exploration is a luxury. His project would not have been undertaken, had it not been needed to help resolve issues which do not temporize.

The point need not be labored further at this juncture. Related considerations will be discussed more fully in connection with the scholar's role in official publication. Suffice it here to say that, in evolving, during the past decade in particular, a comprehensive research-for-policy program, the department has attempted to recruit scholars possessed of the qualities just outlined. It seems fair to say that a research program of stature has begun to mature and that the Department of State has succeeded in securing competent scholars to support it.

The generalizations adduced thus far have had to do chiefly with what might be termed the "rationale" of departmental research. The picture can be illuminated further by some examination of historical research for policy and for publication and of intelligence research for policy, as they are actually conducted in the Department of State today.

The antecedents of the present historical research program have deep roots in the department's history. As early as 1789, Secretary of State Thomas Jefferson saw to the founding of an institutional library, and something like an ordered collection of diplomatic correspondence and related papers was begun.

The employment of scholars to undertake research for departmental policy or for publication is not, however, a phenomenon characteristic of the nineteenth century. It should be kept in mind that the size of the department well down through World War I reflected the fact that its officials were expected to carry the relatively simple business of foreign affairs "in their heads." The day of governmental "briefing" was not to arrive until the need was more imperatively recognized. The memory of living men could encompass the cardinal issues of American diplomacy, or at least it was thought that this was so, and it must be admitted that there were significantly fewer issues than at present with which harried officials had to cope. Selective specialization in the tasks of department officers had not been necessitated by the great complexities in world affairs so familiar to the last generation or two. Consequently, such historical research as was conducted by scholars in the department prior to World War II was intended primarily for publication.

Collection and publication of diplomatic correspondence was first officially undertaken at the onset of the Civil War, in 1861. The first volume of the series now entitled "Foreign Relations of the United States" was published in 1862, the papers included having to do with the events of the previous year. The series was undertaken, it is important to note, by regular members of the department staff, each of whom had other duties to perform as his principal function, not by research experts. Over sixty years were to elapse before it was regarded as necessary and appropriate to assign this responsibility as a full-time task to qualified scholars.

A major change in the policy of compiling "Foreign Relations" took place in 1924. It was then decided, for the first time, to recruit professionals to prepare the diplomatic papers for publication. From this time onward the "Foreign Relations" staff was drawn increasingly from academic circles, and the function assigned to the scholars was recognized as of full-time importance. In point of fact, this was the first time that a *staff* of scholars was recruited by the department for any permanent function.

It is worthy of more than passing note, of course, that the talents of individual scholars of distinction had been employed by the department prior to this time, as, indeed, they were to be again and again. Francis Wharton, a member of the department's legal staff, had edited the six volumes of *The Revolutionary Correspondence of the United States* in 1889. John Bassett Moore turned his hand to the "Foreign Relations" volumes of 1898, and later (as a private scholar) revised the *Digest of International Law* prepared in the legal office of the department by Wharton. Gaillard Hunt was the department's historian of World War I. Hunter Miller began his monumental *Treaties and Other International Acts of the United States of America* in 1929. Commencing in 1937, Green Hackworth prepared his *Digest of International Law*.

Nevertheless, it is submitted that these men command attention rather in their capacity as individuals than as participants in a conscious program of departmental research. Their work had much to do with departmental acceptance of and respect for the research concept, but the tasks they undertook were isolated, by and large, from the main stream of the department's consciousness.

From the very inception of the scholarly "Foreign Relations" program, the department was confronted by the problem of the "inclusiveness" of the series. The introduction of expert methods and criteria of compilation made this the more inevitable, and, as the documents of foreign affairs grew more numerous with the passage of time, the problem became increasingly acute. Clearly, all other considerations aside, publication of the complete archives for each year in the more recent periods represented a quantitative absurdity.

Prior to World War I, a single volume sufficed to encompass the record of a year's diplomatic activity. Thereafter, the number of volumes required to cover the same categories of papers tended to increase. While the department was aware that the greater the inclusiveness of the volumes, the less the opportunity to prejudice the record through omission, the sheer weight of documentation available in recent years tended to erode the principle. Between 1912 and 1933 the number of diplomatic papers received and indexed annually rose from about 125,000 to over 1,200,000. By 1947, comparable statistics ran well over 2,000,000, despite the fact that much information, previously transmitted by papers which ultimately found their way into "Foreign Relations," was by this time transmitted by other means.

Other problems than mere multiplicity of documentation confronted the compilers, however. The solution of these problems made increasingly imperative sound canons of selection. In the forefront of these difficulties was the fact that publication of diplomatic correspondence relating to matters still current often presented very nearly an insuperable obstacle to pending negotiations. On the other hand, since a given negotiation may well be affected by relatively remote antecedents, the problem could not be solved by mere delay in placing related documents before the public. Consequently, it became necessary shortly after World War I, as the critical judgment of department scholars began to bear upon this problem for the first time, closely to define and isolate the fundamental principles of selection for the "Foreign Relations" series. Moreover, it was thought well to make public the conclusions arrived at.

Secretary of State Kellogg approved an order on March 26, 1925, which, basically unmodified, constitutes a kind of "charter" for the preparation of "Foreign Relations" to this day. Under the terms of this order, omissions of the following kind are recognized as legitimate and necessary in the published record of American diplomacy:

a) To omit matters which, if published at the time, would tend to embarrass negotiations or other business

b) To condense the record and avoid needless details

c) To preserve the confidence reposed in the department by other governments and by individuals

d) To avoid needless offense to other nationalities or individuals by excising invidious comments not relevant or essential to the subject

e) To suppress personal opinions presented in despatches and not adopted by the department. To this there is one qualification, namely, that in major decisions it is desirable, where possible, to show the choices presented to the department when the decision was made.

On the other hand, the order went on, "there must be no alteration of the text, no deletions without indicating the place in the text where the deletion is made, and no omission of facts which were of major importance in reaching a decision. Nothing should be omitted with a view to concealing or glossing over what might be regarded by some as a defect of policy."

The department desired to indicate, through the publication of the foregoing canons of selection, that thenceforth the published record should reflect the maximum documentation consonant with the public interest as it saw it and the sheer physical limitations imposed by the bulk of available papers. Thereby it accepted responsibility for making decisions, in its own best judgment, within the framework thus laid down. The department was aware that there would be those who would not agree entirely with the principles and that everyone would recognize that department officials would determine what was "in the public interest" and what was not. There was no escaping either responsibility, however, once it became evident that publication of the "entire" diplomatic record was an illusory goal.

Reflection upon the mechanics and objectives of diplomacy can hardly fail to make clear the fundamental problem raised by continuity of diplomatic negotiations, in so far as it relates to publishing the related documentation. It is the concern of diplomacy to facilitate good relationships between states—to maintain them where they already exist in the particular and to establish them, if possible, where they do not exist. Within this broad mandate, American diplomacy must uphold and further the interests of the United States. No foreign office, certainly not the Department of State, can afford the kind of "open" diplomacy presupposed by concurrent publication of its working papers. No citizen would really wish that it could. To state these facts is to reiterate a truism—a truism, however, which is frequently obscured by an entirely different issue.

The Kellogg order was meant to emphasize that the department would not withhold from public view documentation which might disclose defects in United States policy. For the suppression of this kind of information no justification can be found, and the department has sought none. Although it will not publish papers which will embarrass the conduct of the public business, it will not refrain from publishing papers which would embarrass merely the department.

The increasing complexity of international relations during the past decade has given rise to another basic problem in compiling "Foreign Relations" for this and subsequent periods. In an operational sense, the conduct of America's international affairs is no longer the sole concern of the Department of State. One need but reflect momentarily on the ramifications of the control of atomic energy, world-wide economic programs, occupation problems, transportation and communication relationships, and even cultural exchanges, to recognize that important diplomatic responsibility is shared these days with other agencies of government, great and small. A Hoover Commission task-force report of January, 1949, stated: "Within the executive branch there are 59 departments, agencies, commissions, boards, and interdepartmental councils under the President, of which the work of at least 46 (including the State Department) involves some aspects of the conduct of foreign affairs."

This being so, it is equally clear that the "record" of foreign relations knows no longer a single repository. The Department of State cannot, certainly, lay claim to the complete record. It cannot, therefore, pretend in the future to publish it. The student of foreign affairs in the years to come will have to seek out his documentation in many places.

Even the briefest survey of the department's problems in publishing diplomatic documentation must take account of the dichotomy of interest in what is published which exists among those who appear to depend most heavily upon the "Foreign Relations" volumes.

Although the record as printed in "Foreign Relations" proves of distinct value to the department's own policy officers, outside scholars can, I think, rightfully be regarded as its principal clientele. Among these, chief interest is displayed by the historians and by the international lawyers. These two groups differ sharply in their documentary needs, a circumstance which constantly haunts the compilers.

Two points of illustration should suffice. Although both the historians and the international lawyers agree that the gap between events and the appearance of the published record of them should be narrowed (currently it stands at about seventeen years), they do not agree as to how much. The need of the international lawyer for diplomatic documentation is much the more immediate of the two. Judge Hudson remarked a few years ago that he had less objection to being proved wrong by documentation inaccessible to him at the time of writing than he did to waiting fifteen years for the proof. His colleagues in the profession have pointed out many times that current adjudication should be based upon the very record published much too late to affect it. As a consequence, the needs of this group cannot adequately be served by official publication which does not reflect almost immediately the course of events covered.

The historians, on the other hand, can better afford to postpone their analyses for the appearance of the papers, although even they can point out with some cogency that the existing publication rate does not comport with their professional responsibilities in an atomic age. The fact that both groups agree in protesting delay is more important than that they disagree in the particular as to how much delay is tolerable. The reasons for the delay, therefore, bear examination.

Of first importance in this connection is the fact that the extent of the publication gap in "Foreign Relations" is not determined by principle. The department has not taken the position that a fifteen-to-seventeen-year publication lag is desirable or diplomatically necessary. Indeed, it has struggled for years to reduce the gap. Despite the struggle, the department has not been able to hold its own.

The reasons are transparent. At no time in recent years has the department commanded sufficent research resources to cope with the increasing complexity and quantity of the papers to be analyzed. While war, for example, added to the difficulties of the task, increased staffs for scholarly government projects very naturally received no priority in congressional appropriations committees for the duration of the emergency. With the cessation of hostilities, the Congress, again quite naturally, strove to reduce the expenses of government throughout the executive establishment, and the scholarly projects suffered the same cuts sustained generally. Too much, therefore, must be attempted with too few.

Of at least equal concern to the editors of "Foreign Relations" is the difference in emphasis between the two professions as to what categories of papers should be published. Since the department must begin with the assumption that, at best, only a relatively small, representative selection can be compiled, this problem becomes of first importance. By and large, the international lawyer appears much more interested than the historian in documentation of immediate relevance to legal proceedings or current legal questions. The publication of treaties and other international instruments, for example, together with all related papers, appears to him as a *sine qua non*. The historian tends to regard such documentation as but part of a much more generalized mosaic. In the competition for space in "Foreign Relations," he would sacrifice these papers to broader coverage. The answer to this type of dilemma has thus far not been found in terms of the "Foreign Relations" series. Rather, the department has attempted to publish separately in various forms the more narrowly specialized documents of foreign policy.

Unique in the annals of scholarly department publication is a project now under way for editing and printing the archives of the German Foreign Ministry. During the penultimate stage of World War II, British and American forces captured many of the archives of the Third Reich and of the preceding German governments. Among these were found over four hundred tons of papers originating in the Foreign Ministry. The Department of State and the British Foreign Office concluded that the possession of these documents entailed both a responsibility and an opportunity —a responsibility to make this rich historical collection available to scholars of German diplomacy throughout the world and an opportunity to counteract, through positive means, a series of postwar German apologetics in the tradition of *Die grosse Politik*.

In consequence, the two governments concluded an agreement in June, 1946, adhered to by the French government in April, 1947, which contemplates publication of twenty or more volumes of German Foreign Office and related papers in the original German and a similar number of volumes in English, which it is hoped will contribute to the enlightenment of scholars and laymen both within and outside Germany regarding the course of German prewar and war diplomacy. The first regular volume in this series was published in July, 1949.

The participating governments were aware from the start that official publication of these archives by Germany's former enemies was open to suspicion as mere propaganda. To assure to the greatest possible degree public confidence in the scholarly objectivity of the proposed edition, it was agreed that the selection and editing of these papers should be the joint responsibility of government scholars and of eminent nonofficial historians temporarily employed for this specific project. Moreover, each government placed principal editing responsibility in the hands of the outsiders. At the outset the editors-in-chief were Professor Raymond J. Sontag, for the United States, Professor John Wheeler-Bennett, for the United Kingdom, and Professor Pierre Renouvin, for France. Professor Sontag has since returned to his post at the University of California and has been replaced by Professor Bernadotte E. Schmitt. The department editors have, further, had the benefit of continuous consultation with an advisory committee made up of such distinguished American scholars as William Langer, Carlton J. H. Hayes, Sidney B. Fay, Hajo Holborn, Conyers Read, and Guy Stanton Ford.

As soon as possible after each volume in this series emerges from the press, there will be made available to scholars generally the whole body of documents from which the particular selection was made. In the United States, microfilm copies of the original archives will be deposited in the National Archives, thus enabling scholars to carry their researches as far beyond the scope of the official publication as the available documentation will allow.

It is perhaps worthy of note that Dr. Sontag, in a paper presented at the annual meeting of the American Historical Association in December, 1948, called atttention to the scrupulous observance by the department of its policy of noninterference with the editorial policies of the joint editorial staff. Certainly, it is true that those responsible for "administering" the project within the department have endeavored assiduously to provide it with maximum resources and have been content to leave the editorial policies in the hands of the editors. Whatever light may be thrown upon *American* policy by this publication will be regarded as wholesome, no matter where, upon occasion, that light may fall.

The published output of the Department of State has broadened substantially in recent years. This fact is attested to not only by such undertakings as the German war documents project but also by the increase in nonserial documentary issuances and in expository pamphlet material. These publications, produced in part by the historical staff, are widely distributed through department distribution channels and through the Superintendent of Documents.

Acceptance of a broader publishing responsibility than that assumed by the mere issuance of documentation came slowly. Perhaps more than any other Executive agency, the department was reluctant to undertake publication which, in its choice of areas of policy to be illuminated as well as in terms of "interpretative" exposition of policy, could be regarded as a rationalization of its position. Not the least of important potential sources of criticism on this score was the Congress and its appropriations committees, constantly vigilant to prevent expenditures of public funds in ways which could be interpreted as departmental "lobbying."

On the other hand, traditional American distrust of "secret diplomacy" found more and more ardent champions even in Congress as America's foreign responsibilities enlarged during and after World War II. It became increasingly clear that published explanations of policy were essential to an informed public opinion. The department recognized that an informed public provided a more reliable ally in its day-to-day decisions than a public left in ignorance; and so it embarked during World War II upon a program of publishing many times more extensive than anything previously contemplated.

From a policy point of view, the difficulties of encompassing an adequate and objective documentary program were writ large and compounded by the broader perspective of expository publication. The problem of identifying what "should" be said with what "could" be said loomed ever more acute. Acceptance of full responsibility for this type of decision, however, has become part of the department historian's lot.

Although historical research in the Department of State prior to World War II was undertaken primarily with a view to publication, the last decade has witnessed the parallel expansion of the program of research analysis planned to meet the needs of policy-determining officials within the department. The greater part of the studies and analyses produced under this program is confidential, or classified, and does not normally meet the public eye. Some of the studies, however, are released to publication channels when they have served their original purpose within the department and can be declassified. The focus of departmental historical research has turned inward as well as outward during most recent years, therefore, and a basis for a research-for-policy program has been laid.

Among the factors that gave rise to this program should be noted, first, the enormously increased tempo of world events which characterized the period of the 1930's and, second, the impact of World War II itself. Both these factors broadened the department's functional base in many directions. Despite the fact that many other agencies of government entered the operational field of foreign relations during the period, the department was faced with determining policy (in some measure) for virtually all these activities. As everywhere else in government, this proliferation of responsibility severely restricted the usefulness of the general policy officer, whose breadth of background had hitherto been sufficient to cope with most of the current policy problems. In his place appeared the "expert," the specialist in an area or a substantive problem of policy, and it became necessary to provide these men with sources of basic information required in their own day-to-day operations.

The magnitude of the new departmental responsibilities was, in a measure, attested to by the increase in the department's staff during the course of the recent hostilities. The size of the department in Washington before and at the close of the war is illustrative. By 1938 the total personnel had grown to 963. In March, 1946, after the department had absorbed certain of the functions and personnel of agencies which had emerged during the war, the figure stood at 7,623. The significance of these figures lies in the extension of functions that are reflected. The new staff engages in large-scale economic, information, and intelligence programs of the first magnitude which reflect a vastly more complex era of diplomacy.

In simpler days or throughout much of the department's history, its policy-formulating officials felt little need for professional research assistance. Most of these officials, operating within a framework of country-to-country relationships which were predominately bilateral, kept informed principally through the medium of incoming cables and other communications from the rest of the world. A fair proportion of these officials were foreign service officers temporarily detailed to Washington. While in the department they tended to preside over the affairs of posts in the foreign area in which they had most recently served. General background and knowledge of this area were deemed sufficient for the purpose of analyzing the problems which came before them in Washington.

The crisis decade preceding World War II and the war itself so greatly enlarged the field of substantive knowledge required of the policy-framing officers that they were less and less able to keep abreast of the facts essential to the performance of their tasks. Moreover, with foreign policy rapidly maturing in the direction of the multilateral, it became increasingly important that all officers, faced with day-to-day decisions, be thoroughly briefed on all past policies of the department which related to issues currently before them. Some of the processes by which policy is formed have already been noted. The problem assumes its truest proportions when these are considered against the background of the wider policy horizons which have marked the most recent period. Generally speaking, the areas of research information most necessary to the policy officer have become (1) the historical background of American diplomacy and (2) the factors (political, economic, social, and cultural) affecting the foreign policies of the other states of the world. The department's policy officers have been provided with research services in both these fields. Taken together, they form a frame of reference for the solution of present problems.

The historical research studies have the longer departmental history of the two. Ever since, following World War I, the department employed professional scholars to compile its documentary record, their services have been utilized from time to time to produce historical analyses for intra-departmental use as well.

Until the most recent years, however, such studies and analyses were an adjunct of the compiling and publishing program. At best, they were a part-time responsibility of the professionals, whose chief function was to prepare the record for publication. It became clear during the war and subsequently that the problem could no longer safely be handled in this way.

In consequence, over and above the professional staff maintained for compiling the diplomatic documentation, the department now supports a small group of historical scholars who analyze past problems of policy and produce special research studies for the guidance of the makers of today's decisions. This group is broadly subdivided into two parts, one of which deals primarily with studies of United States relations with particular countries or areas and the other with problems of policy not susceptible of strict geographical analysis. The studies of both groups are used both within the department in day-to-day operations and without the department in its publications program. Studies which today may be confidential, may tomorrow be released to the public and thus serve a double usefulness.

The impact of this type of research can perhaps best be illustrated by citing examples. The major postwar international conferences, in success and in failure, are milestones in the diplomacy of our immediate times. Among the technical officers assigned to these conferences are those who must, in one way or another, be responsible for conference documentation. Whenever possible, a historical research officer discharges this responsibility. His efforts benefit the department in many ways, not the least of which, in the case of such conferences as those convened from time to time by the Council of Foreign Ministers, is analysis of the complete documentation of each conference which may serve as a guide to the next. Among the most important "briefing" documents for the delegation to the Council of Foreign Ministers in Paris in May-June, 1949, was a series of volumes entitled *The Council of Foreign Ministers' Minutes and Records of Decisions,* Vol. IV: *The Moscow Session* (1947) (or Vol. V: *The London Session* [1947]). In the extensive official use of these volumes one finds the most intimate kind of connection between the policy of today and the experience of yesterday.

The "outgoing" or publication aspect of research on such conferences as the Council of Foreign Ministers is reflected in such papers as *The Austrian and German Problems in the Council of Foreign Ministers,* published by the Department of State in June, 1948, and constituting a survey of two of the seminal problems at issue between the postwar Great Powers.

Straight background documentation and analysis, for use within the department, tends to be classified and cannot, in that form at least, be released to the public. Examples of this type of research may be found in the *Minutes and Records of Decisions of the Council of Foreign Ministers,* cited above, and in such studies as *Agreements Reached at the Cairo, Tehran, Yalta, and Potsdam Conferences: Implementation and U.S. Policy,* produced in September, 1948. On the other hand, broad survey of the background policy issues involved may be prepared especially for publication, as previously noted, or for the use of department officers making speeches or otherwise assisting in the public information program. Among the latter may be cited *The Coming Session of the Council of Foreign Ministers* and *U.S. Policy and the U.S.S.R.,* both prepared in the spring of 1949.

The range of these policy analyses is, of course, broader than may be illustrated solely in terms of international conferences. Scattered, almost random, illustrations may perhaps prove most useful in this connection: *The Support of Free Governments in American Policy and Practice, Freedom of Information in American Policy and Practice, American Policy on Establishment of Relations with Foreign Countries, The Provision Regarding Monopolies in the "B" Mandates under the League of Nations, United States Relations with Argentina, United States Relations with Spain, The Calvo Clause in American Policy and Practice, The United States Position Respecting Argentine-British Claims to the Falkland Islands, American Recognition Policy in Regard to Changes in Latin American Governments by Revolution or Coups d'État, 1929–1948, The Negotiation of the Treaties of Peace with Italy, Rumania, Bulgaria, and Hungary,* Part I: *Economic and Related Articles and Economic Annexes, The Negotiations Leading to the Anglo-American Soviet Statement on Commercial*

Policy of December 6, 1945, and *The St. Lawrence Seaway and Power Project: A Chronology of Important Developments.*

The logic of such a program of research analyses is difficult to contest. It need not be proved, I think, that logic alone accounts neither for the program nor for its acceptance by the department. The history of research in government, not unlike the history of research in industry, involves slow adaptation to aids and techniques less essential to the decisions of simpler days than to the complexities of our own. For the policy-formulating officer of the department the test has been quite pragmatic—to the extent that research has demonstrated its usefulness to him, to that extent he would subscribe to it, make use of it, and support it as a necessary tool in his own trade. Although some policy officers of consequence rely but infrequently upon the product of research, it would appear more significant that many who do, depend upon it consistently. In any case, the demand for research studies far exceeds the staff resources to supply them. Strict priorities, as a result, have been set up as between projects; and to this extent it must be confessed that an integral, long-range research program is still a dream for the future. If weaknesses in an operation can ever be viewed as wholesome, it can be supposed that this is a wholesome weakness. It might even occasion real alarm if the research resources so far outstripped the demand as to make elaborate program planning feasible.

It would appear that historical research programs of this character are not common among the foreign offices of the Great Powers today. Excluding Soviet Russia from this generalization for reasons which will be readily appreciated, it can safely be noted, for example, that neither Great Britain nor France conducts similar researches in a regularized way in their respective foreign offices. On the other hand, the British Foreign Office (at least) does conduct a program of research roughly comparable to that which in the Department of State is characterized as "intelligence."

The term "intelligence," in foreign-office parlance, often tends to mean all things to all men. Certainly, the Department of State recognizes that it is seldom precisely defined. In relation to a specific type of research, however, it can be taken to indicate, broadly, the production of needed information concerning the policies of other nations in their international relationships, and particularly of the factors conditioning those policies. Two basic processes are involved in the derivation of this information: (1) its procurement from abroad and (2) its analysis. The second of these processes represents a research activity, and the Department of State employs a considerable corps of qualified scholars to analyze and evaluate the current intelligence information which it derives from its sources within and without the department.

The nature of the intelligence operation in its broader aspects severely circumscribes what may be said about it. So far as intelligence research and analysis are concerned, however, it can be noted that the research technicians operate in collaboration with policy officials presiding over the principal countries or geographic areas of importance to the department and, as well, prepare analyses in "functional" fields which cut across geographical boundaries. In this respect, an obvious parallel will be noted between the frames of reference within which the historical scholars are at work and those which delimit the tasks of the intelligence analysts. It is intended that the research of both groups, taken together, should provide a groundwork of information essential to the policy officers responsible for the long-range planning of American foreign policy as well as for the day-to-day decisions.

Close working relationships must be maintained, of course, between the department's intelligence forces and comparable activities elsewhere in the federal government. Chief among the agencies with which the department actively collaborates are the Central Intelligence Agency and the Department of National Defense. These relationships cut both ways. The department both receives from and contributes to the other interested agencies. In the field of intelligence, par excellence, the major executive establishments with foreign affairs responsibilities cannot afford isolation from one another.

One may pertinently inquire whether the relatively elaborate research apparatus of the present-day Department of State actually plays the role which its blueprints reflect. To this there can be no categorical answer. Research and analysis for policy, whether of the historical or of the intelligence variety, is a relatively new function in the department. It must win its way by proving its utility to policy officials dealing with problems whose complications can hardly be described as "academic."

Perhaps the best evidence of the validity of the respective research programs is the evidence of demand for their services. Here all judgments are relative, but it can be asserted without qualification that the research products of both groups are increasingly utilized and that neither operation is satisfied with the adequacy of its staff resources. The whole research process is markedly evolutionary in character, and it would appear that this is as it should be. The justification of any "service" operation is, at bottom, quite pragmatic. When such operations are of obvious utility, they live and expand; when their utility becomes questionable, they wither and, quite properly, gradually disappear. At present, there is every indication that the department's research services need no theoretical justification, and it is to be hoped that their usefulness to American policy-makers can continue to receive ever wider recognition.

JOHN WESLEY AND THE AMERICAN REVOLUTION

By WILLARD M. WALLACE

Wesleyan University

JOHN WESLEY'S attitude toward the American Revolution has been the subject of scathing criticism and stout defense. Generally, opinion has been determined by whether one is an American or an Englishman and, if an Englishman, whether one has been brought up in the Whig or the Tory tradition. Perhaps the least happy writers have been those Americans of Methodist persuasion, for their explanations have not infrequently been couched in an apologetic vein. Actually, of course, the importance of Wesley's attitude, as well as the difficulties which it evoked on both sides of the Atlantic, transcended the bounds of sect or nationality. Wesley was a great man, possessor of a keen mind, a classical scholar of no mean repute, an indefatigable preacher whose influence extended throughout England and the American colonies, and a friend and confidant to noble and commoner alike. Perhaps more than any of his contemporaries, he could also be aptly called the keeper of England's conscience. Certainly, in his day England could boast no man more alive to social ills or more energetic in endeavoring in his own way to alleviate them.

The difficulty in Wesley's attitude toward the American Revolution is that he exercised the proverbial prerogative of women and wise men: he changed his mind. In the first part of 1775 his views were quite clearly favorable to the Americans, though it is possible that in his heart he shared the opinion of his brother Charles, who remarked in March to a friend, "I am of neither side, and yet of both."[1] At any rate, John Wesley wrote to the prime minister, Lord North, that, in spite of his "long-rooted prejudice" against the Americans, since he was brought up to believe in "passive obedience and non-resistance," he could not avoid thinking "that an oppressed people asked for nothing more than their legal rights, and that in the most modest and inoffensive manner that the nature of the thing would allow. But waiving all considerations of right and wrong, I ask, is it common sense to use force toward the Americans? These men will not be frightened; and it seems they will not be conquered as easily as was first imagined —they will probably dispute every inch of ground; and if they die, die sword in hand."[2] In an almost identical letter to the Earl of Dartmouth, he pointed out, even as to North, the uneasy temper of large masses of the people within England and the danger in leaving the country exposed to possible invasion by foreign enemies.[3]

Had Wesley persisted in this view, which in a number of respects was less pro-American than antiwar, he would not have exposed himself to the bitter denunciation which presently arose. But Wesley wrestled with his principles and loyalties and lived unhappy days. Then Samuel Johnson, wielding an acidulous pen upon the Americans, published his *Taxation No Tyranny: An Answer to the Resolutions and Address of the American Congress.*[4] It appeared as a kind of heaven-sent revelation to Wesley. Accordingly, in the fall of 1775, he wrote his *Calm Address to Our American Colonies,*[5] an article so remarkably similar to Johnson's essay that a number of people raised the cry of plagiarism. One editor went so far as to print Johnson's and Wesley's essays in parallel columns to show the similarity. Suffice it to say that the great pundit of the day, who was scarcely the man to let such an incident pass without reply, had he chosen to take offense, was immensely pleased to have so distinguished a convert to his views. He wrote to Wesley, expressing his thanks "for the addition of your important suffrage to my argument on the American question. To have gained such a mind as yours may justly confirm me in my own opinion."[6]

In his *Calm Address* Wesley examined in some detail the vital question of representation. He was quite put out by the American allegation that "he that is taxed without his own consent, that is, without being represented, is a slave."[7] Wesley retorted that he, himself, had no representation in Parliament, that he was also taxed, yet that he still considered himself no slave. Furthermore, nine out of ten in England had no representation or vote but were hardly slaves; certainly, they enjoyed "both civil and religious liberty to the utmost extent."[8] The difference between liberty and slavery was that an Englishman could go whither he wished and enjoy the fruit of his labors, while the slave had no such privilege. For those who did not know what slavery truly was, Wesley, with a touch of irony, pointed to America, where the very people struggling for their alleged liberty were masters of the Negro, "fainting under the load, bleeding under the lash."[9]

Wesley was a believer in what has been called "virtual representation," according to which members of parliament represented not merely their own constituents but Englishmen at large.[10] To Wesley it was absurd for the colonies to claim that their lack of representation nullified the right of the government to tax them. If parliament could not tax them because they were not represented, neither could it make laws to bind them. This power, he asserted, the colonies had never disputed, since they had "always admitted statutes for the punishment of offenses, and for the preventing or redressing of inconveniences; and the reception of any law draws after it, by a chain which cannot be broken, the necessity of admitting taxation."[11]

The colonies, moreover, inherited all the privileges which their ancestors possessed, but no more. Colonists were the descendants of men who either had no vote or relinquished it by emigrating to America. Hence the people of America now had exactly what their ancestors left them: "not a vote in making laws, nor in choosing legislators; but the happiness of being protected by laws, and the duty of obeying them."[12] The colonists, therefore, by giving up their right in one legislature, had not acquired the right to set up another. True, they might possess a right to privileges granted by charter but only in so far as those privileges were consonant with the British constitution.[13]

Wesley was hardly a revolutionist in his political thinking! He subscribed to Johnson's dictum:

All government is ultimately and essentially absolute, but subordinate societies may have more immunities, or individuals greater liberty, as the operations of government are differently conducted. An *Englishman* in the common course of life and action feels no restraint. An *English* colony has very liberal powers of regulating its own manners and adjusting its own affairs. But an *English* individual may by the supreme authority be deprived of liberty, and a colony divested of its powers, for reasons of which that authority is the only judge.[14]

In this conception of parliamentary supremacy over the colonies, Wesley and Johnson were by no means alone. The revolution of 1688 was regarded by a considerable body of opinion as having established parliamentary supremacy over the colonies as well as over England; hence there was no dearth of critics of the American view that the colonies were dependent solely on the crown.[15] Apart from rights specifically reserved to the colonies in their charters, defenders of parliament saw little validity in arguments questioning parliamentary supremacy. There were those, of course, who vigorously attacked such a contention or who were willing to compromise. Chatham considered taxation not to be a part of "the governing or legislative power."[16] Edmund Burke and Lord Effingham held that parliament should attempt to requisition supplies from the colonies rather than tax them; Burke, in particular, urged that America be left to tax herself and England remain content to bind America by laws of trade.[17] Chatham, James Macpherson, William Knox, and Adam Smith were not unwilling to see the American colonies represented in parliament, while, individually, Richard Price, Granville Sharp, Major Cartwright, and William Adam actually drew up blueprints of federation.[18] But plans by English friends of America or by Englishmen who were more critical of the government than friendly to America had little effect upon the government itself. It resolved to stand by its point of view. Parliament was supreme—it could quote Blackstone on that; hence parliament could tax the colonists.

But, granting that John Wesley had good company in his views as embodied in his *Calm Address,* had he not executed an about-face in his position on the American question? Superficially, this is true; and his shift shocked friends of America quite as strongly as it encouraged friends of the government. Wesley, however, was quite frank in confession. When Caleb Evans, a Baptist clergyman of Bristol, hurled furious charges of inconsistency, as well as of plagiarism, Wesley countered by reprinting his *Address* and remarking in the Preface: "I was of a different judgment on this head, till I read a tract entitled, 'Taxation No Tyranny?' But as soon as I received more light myself, I judged it my duty to impart it to others. I therefore extracted the chief arguments from that treatise, and added an application to those it most concerns. I was well aware of the treatment this would bring upon myself: but let it be, so I may in any degree serve my King and my country."[19] Wesley's subsequent treatment of Evans' arguments evoked almost as much heat as his original *Address*. One of Wesley's chief opponents in religion, Augustus ("Rock of Ages") Toplady, less concerned about Americans than in keeping alive his hatred for Wesley, printed a tract entitled *An Old Fox Tarr'd and Feather'd,* in which he began with this notable contribution to English literature: "Whereunto shall I liken Mr. John Wesley? I will liken him unto a low and puny tadpole in divinity, which proudly seeks to disembowel a high and mighty whale in politicks."[20]

What Trevelyan describes as the "hailstorms of wild calumny, and unsavoury abuse"[21] to which Wesley was exposed stung him, but he stood his ground. As we have already seen, he rejected the charge of plagiarism by having acknowledged Johnson's pamphlet as his inspiration. He denied the accusation of venality, either as a servant of the government or, in answer to Horace Walpole's vituperation, as a suppliant for the patronage of the Earl of Dartmouth; in his own words, "I attend no great man's table."[22] As for his having altered his views, this he freely acknowledged, but the frank and open confession did little to allay the criticism that gathered about his head.[23] Still, whether people agreed with him or not, they read what he had written. He said that "within a few months, fifty, or perhaps a hundred thousand copies, in newspapers and otherwise, were dispersed throughout Great Britain and Ireland."[24] Obviously, what John Wesley believed to be true was regarded as important by thousands of English folk, great and simple. If he had changed his mind about the troubles in America, others might want to do likewise; there is little evidence, however, that he convinced many of the Whigs.

But, although Wesley may with good warrant, and by his own admission, be charged with having changed his mind, there is some reason for believing that his inconsistency was merely superficial, that, fundamentally, he was consistent with principles and views held for years. He was ever a lover of law, order, and peace and a sturdy hater of their opposites. In his *Free Thoughts on the*

Present State of Public Affairs, written in 1768,[25] he deplored the attacks upon the king and his ministers; the petitions by such people as colliers and keelmen, who were so presumptuous as to consider themselves judges of measures taken by the government; and the irresponsible criticism both within and without parliament which might well usher in the rule of King Mob. Toward John Wilkes and his friends he evinced great scorn and no little fear.

Similarly, in his *Thoughts upon Liberty,*[26] in 1772, he deplored the popular excitement about the king and the government as being a threat to civil and religious liberty. Reasonable men should realize that civil and religious liberty already existed, and they should not, therefore, be swept away by the torrent of "general infatuation" inundating the land. Wesley thought he saw the true focus of attack, the king:

> How long have the public papers represented one of the best of Princes as if he had been one of the worst, as little better than Caligula, Nero, or Domitian! These were followed by pamphlets of the same kind, and aiming at the same point,—to make the King appear odious as well as contemptible in the eyes of his subjects. Letters succeed, wrote in fine language, and with exquisite art, but filled with the fall of bitterness. "Yes, but not against the King; Junius does not strike at him, but at the evil Administration." Thin pretence! Does not everyone see the blow is aimed at the King through the sides of his Minister?[27]

A royalist, a redoubtable supporter of law and order, Wesley dreaded what might happen to the liberty that England cherished if popular agitation in behalf of John Wilkes, or any such individual, got out of hand. Wesley saw neither his life nor his property jeopardized by king or parliament. The menace was by "good patriots," something far worse:

> Hark! Is hell or Bedlam broke loose? What roaring is that, loud as the waves of the sea? "It is the patriot mob." What do they want with me? Why do they flock about my house? "Make haste! Illuminate your windows in honour of Mr. Wilkes." I cannot in conscience: I think that it is encouraging vice. "Then they will all be broken." That is, in plain English, Give them twenty shillings, or they will rob you of five pounds.[28]

Wesley saw the people, "that 'many-headed beast,'" roaring for a kind of liberty quite different from civil and religious liberty. He wrote bitterly:

Many want Indian liberty, the liberty of cutting throats, or of driving a brace of balls through the head of those ugly-looking fellows, whom they cannot abide the sight of. Many want the old Highland liberty, the convenient liberty of plundering. Many others there are who want the liberty of war, of borrowing their neighbors' wives or daughters; and not a few, though they do not always avow it, the liberty of murdering their Prince.[29]

Wesley had a well-developed apprehension of mob potentiality. And certainly few men have had better opportunities for judging the capacities of a mob than Wesley. For years he, Charles Wesley, George Whitefield, and their fellow-workers in Methodism had faced angry hordes of people. Sometimes these mobs acted on their own; more often gentry, magistrates, or business people provided the motivation; and, occasionally, even Anglican clergymen entered the lists, as in the case of the Rev. George White, who, armed with a horse-pistol, organized and maneuvered his roughnecks against Wesley as might a division commander.[30] In the mob attacks against the Methodists, particularly about mid-century, when the violence was greatest, preachers were stoned, stripped, and thrown into water in mid-winter, blinded, and even killed. Their homes were entered, their furniture hacked to pieces or stolen, and their houses torn down or burned. Methodist women and children were torn from their beds and abused. Pregnant women were kicked and so badly treated that miscarriages and death often resulted. Wesley himself, like so many of his co-workers, never flinched and often, through sheer force of personality, reduced a mob to an orderly crowd. But that is not to say that he did not fear a mob or did not hate the intolerance responsible for its action or did not deplore the demagoguery which whipped a mob into being. He now condemned the increasing use of the mob in America, even as he had denounced its use in England against Methodists and in behalf of John Wilkes. For the Boston Tea Party and John Hancock he had scornful words. Hancock he considered a smuggler acting in flagrant contravention of the laws, and the tea party he regarded as outrageous in its breach of the peace and its destruction of property.[31]

In his *Calm Address to the Inhabitants of England*,[32] written in 1777, a period in which, as a patriotic Englishman, he had swung all the way over to the side of the government, his aversion for mob rule and his wrath at the lack of respect for law, order, property, and freedom of expression knew few bounds. He wrote with a burning pen of conditions in America:

There is no civil liberty. No man hath any security, either for his goods or for his person; but is daily liable to have his goods spoiled or taken away, without either law or form of law, and to suffer the most cruel outrage as to his person, such as many would account worse than death. . . . Do you not observe, wherever these bawlers for liberty govern, there is the vilest slavery? No man there can say that his goods are his own. They are absolutely at the disposal of the mob, or the Congress. . . . Those who have the disposal of his substance, who have the disposal of his liberty, have the disposal of his life also, and of this they have given recent proofs.[33]

The treatment of American Loyalists was receiving full publicity: the destruction and dispossession of property, the baths of tar and feathers, the painful rides on a rail, the hangings, and all the varied category of intimidation, humiliation, and torture. To Wesley such measures were of a piece with the treatment early accorded the Methodists in England, while the disregard for decency and restraint corresponded to the atrocious attacks upon the government by Wilkes and his supporters.[34] It is clear that Wesley had journeyed far from his gentle reproaches to America in his *Calm Address* and his assurance that the "designing men, the Ahithophels" were not in America but England.[35]

Fundamentally, in addition to his consistent love for law and order and his fear of mob rule, Wesley also showed consistency in his love for peace. War had ever seemed to him an unworthy instrument, while internecine war was a very horror. In his *Seasonable Address to the Inhabitants of Great Britain,*[36] composed in 1776, when he may have thought some possibility of reconciling the factions still existed, he wrote feelingly of the "awful contest" in America.[37] "A kingdom divided against itself is an evil, of all others," he said, "the most dreadful."[38] He pleaded for calm reason on both sides to bring to an end the melancholy dispute, with its destruction of property, its suffering, and its waste of life. If the conciliatory tone of this address was lost, a year later, in his *Calm Address to the Inhabitants of England,* it was largely because he wanted to rally support to the government, with the object of extinguishing the fires of war with the utmost expedition. The only way now remaining, unfortunately, was a speedy triumph for British arms over those "in open rebellion against their lawful Sovereign."[39]

Politically conservative, pacifically inclined by conscience and inclination, loving the law, and abhorring mob rule, Wesley could scarcely have been expected to sanction the turn of events in America. Yet, judging by the furor raised by his *Calm Address* of 1775, that is precisely what many English friends of America had thought he might do. Or, at least, they had not anticipated his opposition. Obviously, they had failed to evaluate him correctly. They had not perceived that, among other things, he was a thorough patriot. Certainly, his fear that other powers might take advantage of England's distraction, if it were not quickly ended, was amply justified. And this patriotism, which led Wesley to address pamphlets to the people of England and Ireland during the war, induced his enemies to charge him with being a pensioner of the government. But this neat little "human gamecock," as Leslie Stephen described him, was nothing if not sincere; and, if his pamphlets brought aid and comfort to the government, he wrote not from a mercenary motive but because he was a respecter of law, a lover of peace, an invincible Tory, and a stalwart patriot.

On the other hand, Wesley had many of the faults of the government leaders, including their shortsightedness. Like Johnson, he was a man of positive opinions and was, perhaps, influenced too closely, and quite adversely, by the characters of those who opposed the government.[40] It has been said that he could not endure Charles James Fox, possibly because Fox was a gambler. Certainly, he had the greatest contempt for John Wilkes. Edmund Burke provoked him to sarcasm, and on at least one occasion Wesley wondered why parliament should permit a statesman whom he had revered, the Earl of Chatham, to continue to speak in a pro-American, antigovernment vein. His comments about other men are illuminating. On Rousseau, Hume, and Machiavelli, whose ideas he considered menacing to the existing system, the vials of his wrath flowed over. Rousseau was "that prodigy of self-conceit . . . a shallow but supercilious infidel, two degrees below Voltaire," whom he alluded to as "that wretched man." Hume was "the most insolent despiser of truth and virtue that ever appeared in the world," while Machiavelli was the "first-born of hell." Conversely, he respected and profoundly admired George III, no doubt, as Bishop McConnell has suggested, because George was a man of prayer and showed favor repeatedly to Methodism.[41]

Wesley's opinions and attitudes were those of an enlightened or, more accurately, a humanitarian Tory. Yearn after their souls though he might, he had little faith in the political ability of the masses. Throughout his life he considered the majority of the people neither the wisest nor the best part of mankind, and more than any other form of government he dreaded democracy, with the people as its ultimate source of power. Democracy, pushed to the extreme to which he felt Richard Price, the Unitarian, was tending, meant anarchy. In fact, Wesley used historical argument in asserting that "there is most liberty of all, civil and religious, under a limited monarchy, there is usually less under an aristocracy, and least of all under a democracy."[42] Change, if it was to occur, should be of an evolutionary character; heaven, even a heaven on earth, was not reached in a single bound. Meanwhile, one should trust one's political betters, support king and country, and have faith in God.

But, though a Tory in politics and therefore unfriendly to the revolution being effected in America, Wesley was not a complete standpatter. Harold Laski's criticism that Wesley's preaching made workers more inclined to acquiesce to, rather than resist, conditions of the day may be true, for Wesley could not have tolerated action by the workers; it was only too likely to lead to mob violence. On the other hand, Wesley did not hesitate to condemn the lucrative slave trade; courageously opposed the enclosure movement, which enriched a few at the expense of the many; denounced the distilling interests; urged that the national debt be discharged and the people given work; and castigated luxury as wasteful and morally inexcusable while thousands suffered want. He was thus keenly alert to evils of the day and by no means stood four-square with the principles of die-hard Toryism.

It was unfortunate, however, that his political conservatism was of such an unbending nature. As embodied in the *Calm Address* of 1775, it raised up a host of foes to Wesley in England.

Moreover, the *Calm Address* was prevented, undoubtedly in part by the exigencies of war, from accomplishing its mission, since, according to Wesley, "the ports being just then shut up by the Americans, I could not send it abroad as I designed."[43] But Robert Southey accounted in another manner for the failure of the *Calm Address* to reach America. Said Southey: "Such, indeed, was the temper of the Americans, that a friend to the Methodists got possession of all the copies . . . which were sent to New York and destroyed them, foreseeing the imminent danger to which the preachers would be exposed, if a pamphlet so unpopular in its doctrines should get abroad."[44] Even so, people in America were not long in discovering Wesley's views, with the result that, throughout the war, overzealous patriots made life very difficult for many Methodists.[45]

It would have been perfectly natural, therefore, if Methodist leaders in America had taken sharp issue with Wesley. Fortunately, Francis Asbury, the outstanding worker in the American field, stood by his spiritual chief. In a most charitable entry in his *Journal* Asbury wrote:

> I received an affectionate letter from Mr. Wesley and am truly sorry that the venerable man ever dipped into the politics of America. . . . However, it discovers Mr. Wesley's conscientious attachment to the government under which he lives. Had he been a subject of America, no doubt but he would have been as zealous an advocate of the American cause. But some inconsiderate persons have taken occasion to censure the Methodists in America on account of Mr. Wesley's political sentiments.[46]

Asbury himself was loath to follow the example of such English missionaries to America as Thomas Rankin, George Shadford, and Martin Rodda, who left for England rather than support the colonies.[47] Asbury's conscience told him that there still was a work for him to do. One consequence was that, by 1778, he was the only one left of the ten English or Irish-born preachers who, in 1773, constituted the first American conference.[48] Hence in the personnel of the leading Methodists in America the war had brought about a marked and decisive change.

In fact, as a result of the conflict of loyalties, so many Anglican clergy in America left their parishes, voluntarily or otherwise, and so obnoxious had the Anglican church become in many people's eyes because of its supposed association with crown policies,[49] that Methodism in America actually grew during the war; it even seems to have thrived on the rough treatment accorded it in certain quarters. At the conference held in 1773, 10 ministers and 1,166 members were reported, but, at the time of the conference of 1784, the number had increased to 83 ministers and 14,998 members, most of them in the middle and southern colonies.[50] It is significant, too, that, though opposed to disestablishment in 1776, American Methodism was a separate establishment in 1785, thus becoming part of the tradition of dissent, particularly moral dissent.[51] And Methodists, officially at any rate, have never lost their "come-outer" spirit as embodied originally in Wesley's exhortation to Methodists to "be singular or be damned."[52] In spite of Wesley's rather grudging acceptance of the success of the Revolution in America, a revolution effected by "a very uncommon train of providences"[53] for which he had little liking, the increase of his flock must have been something of an assuagement to his disappointed patriotism. At any rate, through the virtual ordination of his assistant, Thomas Coke, as superintendent of the societies in America, he proceeded with vigor to re-establish contact with Methodists on this continent.[54]

Though one may deplore (if one is an American) the old gentleman's position in regard to the Revolution, he was less of a turncoat than he appeared to many of his era. He was actually more consistent with his principles and loyalties than he himself realized. Possibly a more valid charge of a change of mind was his initial shift from what was basically a Tory point of view to a Whiggish sympathy for the Americans. As we have seen, Wesley was not long in repudiating such political heresy and soon became as redoubtable a government supporter as that pompous autocrat of the "Cheshire Cheese," Samuel Johnson. Nor was Wesley's shift back to Toryism less sincere in its motivation than his early sympathy for the Americans was genuine. One might lament with Francis Asbury that he had ever entered the field of political discussion, but Wesley was a fighter and scarcely the man to shrink from an issue which engaged his deepest loyalties and sentiments. Thus did this "brand plucked from the burning," as he chose so often to allude to himself, stand by his king and his country. Thus did he rally to the defense of English liberty as he conceived it and do battle against those who he thought might despoil it. Let change be orderly and reasonable, let the law prevail, let there be peace, and let the work of the Lord flourish—these sentiments he dearly cherished; these sentiments he would uphold against all opponents. It was scarcely his fault that mightier forces than his voice and pen could muster wrought the defeat of the cause for which he strove so valiantly.

THE IRISH REPUBLIC

By Susan M. Lough, *Emerita*

Westhampton College, University of Richmond

A DRAMATIC series of events in recent years has brought into the foreground of world affairs the tangled skein of Anglo-Irish relations and revived many half-forgotten controversies. The Anglo-Irish Treaty was agreed to by Irish delegates and British ministers in 1921. A constitution for the south of Ireland was drafted the following year. By virtue of the treaty and the constitution, there was set up a new and rather anomalous political entity designated as the "Irish Free State." The status of a Dominion in the British Commonwealth of Nations had been offered to the new state and accepted. Since 1922 executive authority has been exercised by successive prime ministers. Mr. William Cosgrave held office for ten years and was succeeded by Mr. Eamon de Valera, who served as prime minister for sixteen years. This long tenure of office seemed to savor of monopoly; so there came a reaction. Mr. de Valera's party was defeated at the polls in 1948, and there is at present (1952) a coalition government in which Mr. Costello is prime minister.

In November, 1948, Mr. Costello introduced into the Irish Free State Dail Eireann a motion to repeal the External Relations Act of 1936. The abdication of Edward VIII in December, 1936, had given Mr. de Valera the opportunity to throw overboard all the remaining clauses of the 1921 treaty which concerned domestic jurisdiction of the crown in the Irish Free State and the king's authority over external affairs. There was much unfavorable comment in Dublin, inasmuch as Mr. Costello's pre-election speeches had quite definitely stressed his acquiescence in the political status quo of the two countries. There was no political mandate for repeal, though it is quite true that members of the Dail Eireann had frequently questioned Mr. de Valera as to the status of the Irish Free State.

The constitution of 1937, implementing the External Relations

65

Act, declared Ireland to be an independent, sovereign, and democratic state, recognizing the authority of the crown in such external affairs as accrediting ministers and ambassadors. "Are we a republic or not a republic?" was the question asked by Mr. Dillon in one of the very controversial sessions of the Dail Eireann. Mr. de Valera's answer a few days later was diplomatic. It consisted merely in the reading of copious extracts from all of the available dictionaries sent over by the obliging and much amused custodian of the adjoining National Library. Definitions of a republic were, however, not wholly satisfactory to Mr. Dillon. He did not have to wait very long for the answer to his pertinent query. Mr. Costello's announcement of his intention to repeal the External Relations Act was made rather casually during a visit in Canada. Press comment in England was critical of this method of dealing with a policy which concerned both countries. There had been, for example, no formal consultation with members of the British cabinet. The Irish Free State Dail Eireann passed the act of repeal of the External Relations Act in November, 1948.

The second of the dramatic episodes of these two years was the formal proclamation of the Republic of Ireland. At midnight of Easter Sunday, April 17, 1949, a huge crowd assembled in Dublin's main thoroughfare, near O'Connell Bridge, to hear high dignitaries of state formally announce the birth of the Irish Republic. Twenty-one-gun salutes, fireworks, and illuminations of all sorts were a part of the midnight ceremony, not only in Dublin but in many other parts of the country. All day Easter Monday there were further celebrations in Dublin, beginning with a service of intercession in the Pro-Cathedral of St. Patrick. After this, there was a military parade and at night various social festivities. Rulers of foreign lands and ministers of state of the dominions in the British Commonwealth of Nations sent felicitations to the president of the Republic of Ireland.

These two spectacular events in November, 1948, and April, 1949, necessitated formal recognition by the British government of the legal status of citizens of the Republic of Ireland resident in England. The Act of External Affairs of December, 1936, had renounced the authority of the crown in all matters affecting internal affairs in the Irish Free State. It stated clearly, however, that, as a member-state of the British Commonwealth of Nations, the Irish Free State accepted certain specified rights of the crown in external affairs. It apparently did not jeopardize the rights of Irishmen resident in England as English citizens.

The constitution of 1937 implemented the Act of Repeal and stated that the Irish Free State was an independent, democratic, sovereign state. By virtue of the Statute of Westminster the External Relations Act had legal validity. As a result, however, of Mr. Costello's Act of Repeal, followed up by the proclamation of the Republic of Ireland on Easter Monday, there devolved upon the British government the necessity of taking cognizance of a new situation. Irishmen in England were uncertain as to the implications of the Act of Repeal. Were they citizens or foreigners after Easter Monday, April 18? British ministers deemed it imperative to give some assurance to Ulster. Leaders of public opinion in Belfast were apprehensive. Did the title "Republic of Ireland" foreshadow encroachment upon the territorial integrity of the six counties of the northeast?

These two problems were discussed in the British House of Commons early in May. As a result of much controversial debate, there was introduced the Ireland Bill on May 3. The question of Irish residents of Great Britain was generously dealt with in this bill. They were not to be classified as foreigners. They retained all the rights and privileges of English citizens. Needless to say, Mr. Shaw was pleased. Press comment in England on these clauses of the bill was rather amusing—"They cry for the moon and they get it." "Up the Republic." "The Irish get away with it." "They have the best of both worlds." Meantime, the lawyers realized that the legal status of Irishmen in England was not fully covered by the House of Commons Ireland Bill. And what about the Dominions? Will they be as generous as Westminster?

The second group of clauses of the House of Commons Ireland Bill are more controversial and produced widespread discussion in both England and Ireland. The purpose as stated is: "To recognize and declare the territorial integrity of northern Ireland." In 1920 the six northeastern counties had accepted an arrangement which gave them home rule and severed relationship with the south of Ireland. In the intervening years there had developed closer political and economic ties with the United Kingdom. There had also developed increasing separateness and hostility to the policies of the Irish Free State. The resulting partition was an accepted fact in the north but was execrated by statesmen of the south.

Conservatives at Westminster approved the policy of the Labour government, but a large group of members of the Labour party in the House of Commons expressed open hostility. Some of these refrained from voting, and others voted against these clauses. In England press comment was, on the whole, favorable. The implications of the clauses concerning Ireland were provocative and aroused instantaneous hostile reaction in the twenty-six counties of the new republic. The constitutional position of Ulster had been defined in the Government of Ireland Act of 1920. Partition seemed in those years of crisis and civil war the only possible solution. It has been denounced for thirty years by Irish leaders in Dublin. Partition as defined in 1920 and reaffirmed in 1949 was the creation of the British government. Ulster was an occupied country.

It is not surprising, then, that in Ireland there was demand for action. Inquiries in the Dail Eireann were numerous and insistent. On May 10 Mr. Costello was asked if he had protested to the British ministers against the clauses in the Ireland Bill guaranteeing the integrity of Ulster and thereby perpetuating the crime of partition and if, further, he would indicate to the British government that such a step can only be regarded as an affront to the Irish nation. Headlines in every newspaper in the south of Ireland protested British interference. It was imperative to act quickly. And so, on May 10, Mr. Costello rose in Dail Eireann to introduce a motion of protest. He recalled in his introductory speech memories of that earlier Irish parliament in which Henry Grattan had protested the right of the British government to make laws for Ireland: "The British have learned nothing in these hundred and sixty-nine years. . . . They are guilty of ignorance and stupidity . . . . Apparently they will give nothing except to an Ireland that has become a nuisance to itself and to Great Britain." The motion of protest was then introduced and was seconded by Mr. de Valera. It consisted of a series of clauses and an amendment of some significance.[1]

It was, of course, obvious that measures must be taken to give effect as far as possible to the motion of protest against the House of Commons Ireland Bill. A Mansion House all-party antipartition conference was set up and a committee appointed to make plans for public meetings and such further action as seemed desirable. Much stress was placed upon the necessity of informing public opinion abroad as to the significance of recent events and enlisting the support of overseas friends of the new republic. A mass meeting arranged for by the Mansion House committee was held May 13 in O'Connell Street, near the monument of the great Irish statesman. Speeches were made by Mr. Costello, Mr. de Valera, Mr. MacBride, the brilliant minister of foreign affairs, and by many other ministers and members of Dail Eireann. The purpose, of course, was to assert the determination of all parties to end partition. Many expressions of intense indignation against the British government were voiced by the assembled crowd. Partition was created and is being maintained by Great Britain, and by this bill now being debated in her parliament she is seeking to consolidate it, was the thesis of Mr. de Valera. Mr. Costello stated that, if the facts of partition were brought home to public opinion abroad, there is no fear of what the verdict would be in the international court of justice. Mr. MacBride characterized the bill as a tragic blunder. Other speeches were of like tenor. Of some significance was the statement that British interference would unite all parties in Ireland in a world-wide crusade which would sweep partition into oblivion. During these speeches there was almost continuous vociferous applause, and, because of the far-reaching influence of the wireless, the propaganda effect in all parts of the country must not be ignored.

Students of Irish history, observing these almost hysterical demonstrations, must seek to find the answer to the Irish riddle. How does it happen that in this little far-western island, so remote in many ways from the clashing ideology of the continent, there are such bitter conflicts, such passionate outbursts, such apparently irreconcilable viewpoints? "Partition today is indefensible," stated Mr. MacBride. Its effects are utterly demoralizing. Between the six counties of the northeast and the Irish Free State there is a long straggling boundary line. Smuggling is endemic. Such a frontier is provocative of incidents which fan to a high flame the indignation of people on both sides of the border. Mass meetings in Dublin to protest against partition are not phenomena of recent months. For thirty years there has been a strong undercurrent of hostility. Recent events have simply intensified the campaign to put an end to such intolerable conditions. Partition is indefensible.

Public opinion in England is more in accord with the statement of Mr. Lloyd George when the third Home Rule Bill was introduced in 1912, "that the people of Ulster are a homogenous group whose political allegiance is to England. Their cultural heritage and historic traditions separate them from the people of south Ireland." This divergent trend began to be clearly apparent about 1886 (when Mr. Gladstone introduced the first Home Rule Bill). Not only political but economic ties strengthened the entente between the more industrialized Scotch-Irish of the six counties of the northeast of Ireland and their English neighbors. Cultural separateness was fostered by the Gaelic League and the Celtic literary renascence. Educational propaganda emphasized the teaching of Irish in the public schools of the south of Ireland. National legends were revived, and a newborn sense of Irish nationality began to be a factor in the cultural life of the country. Arthur Griffith built up the Sinn Fein party as a movement espousing withdrawal of Irish members from the British House of Commons and complete political separation of the two countries.

During the last thirty years an intensive educational propaganda based upon the teaching of Irish in all the national schools and the obtaining of a certificate in Irish as a prerequisite to the professions widened the gap between north and south. Such propaganda is increasingly an obstacle to good relations. The religious question is, of course, a very serious obstacle to unity. The majority of at least four counties in Ulster is Presbyterian or Anglican. There are also some members of other Protestant denominations. In the cities there are quite a number of Catholics. In two counties of Ulster membership in the Catholic church is larger than that of any other denomination, and it is often asserted that there is a Catholic majority. The affinity of Catholics in the north is with their co-religionists in the south.

In the Irish Free State there has been a quite preceptible in-

crease in the number of Catholic convents and schools. It is probable that there was a significant exodus of nuns from France
in the first decade of the twentieth century and that many of these
found a haven in Ireland. Religious affiliation coincides with political viewpoint. Economic patterns in the industrial northeast
are not in harmony with the more backward industries of the
south. All these factors have contributed to heighten the tension
and to create an irresistible demand for the elimination of what
seems to be the last barrier to the realization of the dreams of
Wolfe Tone and Patrick Pearse.

The student of Irish history is baffled as he seeks to find some
rational explanation for the outbursts of hostility in Dublin and
Belfast. The tragedy is that the answer to the Irish riddle at the
present moment is largely emotional. It is the resultant of animosities which developed during many centuries of British rule or
misrule in Ireland. A study of some half-forgotten chapters of
Anglo-Irish relationships may provide the solution of a baffling
problem. Divergences such as exist today have deep roots. The
strong monarchy concept of the Tudors meant for Ireland a more
efficient administration and the ending of disorders in the Irish
lands beyond the Pale. Irish countries were to become English
counties, with the full paraphernalia of coroners, escheators, and
sheriffs. Brehon law and Irish tanistry were doomed to extinction.
Quite naturally, Irish pride took alarm, and Irish rebellions created new problems for the English government. A brief survey of
Tudor policy seems to reveal that moment in the tangled web of
Anglo-Irish relationship in which there appears the parting of the
ways and the beginnings of the cultural and economic divergencies which are of such vital significance today.

English and Irish historians quite frankly admit that, during
the first three hundred and fifty years after the so-called "conquest" of Ireland by the Anglo-Norman barons and Henry II,
there was but little success in solving the problem of effective and
orderly government. The conquest was but a half-conquest and
therefore endlessly provocative. Misrule and wild disorder in Ireland were inevitably the result of the clash of the clan system and
Brehon law versus the ill-controlled feudalism of Norman and
Angevin barons. A century later, waning feudalism was replaced

in both countries by the royal courts of justice, local courts, parliaments, and local government. At the end of the fifteenth century there was an attempt through Poynings' law to bring Ireland more directly under the control of the English crown. Some fifty years later Henry VIII was recognized as king of Ireland. Both these measures foreshadowed a more vigorous program. The "Wild Irish" beyond the Pale must accept English civilization.[2]

The new policy resulted in a plan for establishing plantations. The O'Connors and O'Mores and later other clans were driven out of the Leinster lands lying west of Dublin. English counties equipped with the usual mechanism of civil administration, i.e., sheriffs, coroners, and escheators, were provided for and the Irish customs and the Brehon law quite hopefully set aside. For a full century and a half the plantation system was endlessly repetitive. During the reign of Elizabeth there were large grants to court favorites. With the extension of English control there came a mounting tide of Irish hostility to the encroachment of these adventurers. Rebellions were frequent and were followed up by attainders and extensive confiscations. English occupation alternated with Irish recovery. The Butlers and the Desmonds were bitter rivals in Munster. Both families played politics and kept the south in constant turmoil. The great Irish Earl of Clanricarde was practically independent in Connaught. He was friendly to the English government in Dublin but failed utterly to curb the wild passion of his turbulent sons.

The most interesting experiment of the Elizabethan half-century was that of extending into Ireland the system of presidencies which had been so successful in Wales and the north of England. Elizabeth's very able vice-deputy, Sir Henry Sidney, had been president of the council in Wales for many years. In 1567, while on a visit to London, he obtained the consent of the Queen and Privy Council to the establishing of presidents and councils in Munster and Connaught.[3] Ulster at this time was comparatively quiet, so the idea of an Ulster presidency had been put aside. But even with the approval of the Queen and the Privy Coucil there was much exasperating delay. Owing to the illness of Sir John Pollard, the first appointee, the Munster project was delayed for months. In June, 1569, the presidency system was launched in

Connaught, and Sir Edward Fitton was appointed by the Queen as president. Sir Rafe Rookeby was appointed as first justice of the council. The deputy and Privy Council of Ireland were given instructions to select a suitable man of this country (Ireland), learned in the laws and with a knowledge of the Irish tongue, to be second justice and a suitable person to be clerk of the council.[4]

The presidency plan was to have a resident governor in each province who would be responsible to the deputy and council in Dublin with sufficient authority for minor emergencies. Unfortunately for Connaught, the first president was ill fitted to handle the somewhat difficult problems which presented themselves upon his arrival. The presidency system at the outset met with an opposition so vigorous as to indicate that Irish leaders in all parts of the country realized the full implications of the new policy. The situation in Connaught was complicated by the doubtful legitimacy of one or both of the sons of the chief lord of the country, the Earl of Clanricarde. According to Irish law, this question made little difference. Succession would be settled by the common method of tanistry or election or, if need be, fought out by the brothers personally. To such a settlement the presence in Connaught of a president with martial powers and judicial authority for the holding of sessions and hanging of malefactors was an unlooked-for obstacle.[5] And so, in spite of their rivalry, both brothers united in antagonism and open hostility to the presidential system and the extension of English influence which its presence foreshadowed.

To make matters worse, Sir Edward Fitton failed to deal tactfully with the religious prejudice of the province. Eventually he was besieged in Galway and waited despairingly for the reinforcements sent by Sir Henry Sidney from Dublin. Meanwhile, the young Burkes plundered and spoiled the country.[6] Fitton's ill-fated presidency came to an end in 1572, and for an interval of several years the question of Connaught's government was obscured by other problems. Sir Nicholas Malby was sent over with extensive military authority in 1575, and, because he was ultimately successful in quelling the disorders of the country, the title of president was revived in his favor and the pet project of Sir Henry Sidney tried out again in Connaught. This time it met with greater success. During the Desmond intrigues and the turmoils of the decade which followed the final departure of Sir Henry Sidney, Connaught was in good order and its president was able to intervene successfully in behalf of the hard-pressed officials in Munster. On the whole, therefore, the presidential enterprise of the Elizabethan period was of somewhat questionable utility. That the system had possibilities of solving the peculiar problems of that most difficult half-century of Irish history is unquestionable.

The Tudor strong monarchy concept as embodied in the appointment of presidents and councils in Munster and Connaught gave notice to all the Irish earls and their adherents that the old regime was a vanished institution. The Brehons and Brehon law could no longer be accepted in any part of the country. All the rebellions of the last three decades of the sixteenth century were the outcome of Irish awareness of what was involved in the Tudor presidencies. Religion was also a factor in these latter years. Jesuit intrigues and Spanish gold had more or less effect. The English queen sent over men and money. The great Desmond rebellion came to an end in 1583. Attainder and confiscation brought colonization on a hitherto unprecedented scale. Confused titles involved endless litigation. One fact, however, can be established without question. English landlords had come into the provinces of Leinster, Munster, and Connaught to stay. They occupied half of two western counties in Leinster, half of four counties in Munster, and scattered estates here and there in Connaught. Many of the English landlords were court favorites and adventurers. Some of them had fought in the Desmond wars and expected payment in land. Others had shadowy titles from some Anglo-Norman ancestor. Many of the Irish whom they displaced had been killed in the Desmond rebellion or in that final series of revolts in the last decades of the sixteenth century. Attainders and confiscations brought it about that few of the great Irish leaders remained in the country. Some of their adherents remained as a tenant class. The English adventurer of these decades found Ireland too turbulent a land for peaceful settlement. Intermittent raids drove many of them back to England. Their occupation of Irish estates and the allocation of lands in Connaught to the Irish whom they displaced in Leinster and Munster involved great confusion as to land titles and the perpetuation of injustice to the Irish claimants in the seventeenth century.

Unforeseen circumstances brought it about that the system of confiscation and clearance in the province of Ulster was very effective. The last of the O'Neills had enlisted the support of all the great Irish leaders in Connaught and in Munster. The final rebellion of the sixteenth century was national in scope. At last, Elizabeth sent over men and money in abundance, and the Irish war was fought to a finish. A few months after Elizabeth's death many of the great earls left the country, and there came an opportunity for attainders and confiscations on a great scale. Much of Ulster was half-empty and desolate, so there was projected the Ulster plantation, so momentous in its significance, not only then but in later centuries. To a thrifty Stuart king it seemed wise to encourage large numbers of Scottish and English settlers to take possession of lands so often in dispute between O'Donnells and O'Neills and so often raided by island Scots. James I was generous in his grants to his Scottish subjects, and every possible effort was made to publicize in England the new venture.

It seems clear, then, in retrospect that Irish attainders and confiscations in the Elizabethan era initiated that phenomenon of later centuries, English landlordism in the south of Ireland. It also brought about the beginning of the Protestant ascendancy in Dublin. It gave to the west counties of Leinster and the provinces of Munster and Connaught vast depopulated areas and deprived the Irish earls and their adherents of the estates which their families had occupied for centuries. The flight of the earls left Catholic Ireland without leadership. The administration at Dublin was utterly unable to control the situation. Civil war in England between parliamentarians and Stuarts and independents increased the confusion and chaos in Ireland. The arrival of Cromwell in 1649 gave the Ulster exiles some prospect of redress and eventually many of them recovered their lands. Cromwellian victories in the south brought new adjustments and also complications. The Cromwellian veterans must be satisfied with extensive land grants. But, meantime, Charles I had issued the so-called "Graces" in order to win support of Irish Catholics against the parliament.

The confusion of land claims and land titles became indescribable in the mid-decades of the seventeenth century. After Cromwell came the Stuart Restoration and revival of the Graces. With the Restoration came concessions to Catholics and new grants of land to adherents of the Stuart cause.[7]

It was inevitable that the Catholics of Ireland should rally to the cause of James II in the last decade of the seventeenth century. Not until the victories of William III's armies in the north and south and the signing of the Treaty of Limerick did the Catholics give up hope of regaining their lost heritage and re-establishing themselves in Leinster and Munster. After the Treaty of Limerick some twelve thousand Irishmen left the country of their birth and sought service abroad. This was the tragic exodus of the

> Wild geese rising on clamorous wing
> To follow the flight of an alien king.

As a result of Cromwellian confiscations and the Restoration failure to provide redress for their adherents, the great bulk of the lesser Catholic landowners had been displaced. The Williamite victories deprived Ireland of its great families and thus left the greater part of three provinces to be occupied by English settlers. Land titles were chaotic, and there was, of necessity, endless litigation. Legal claims based upon concessions to Catholics in the Treaty of Limerick were rendered void by conflicting claims of Cromwell's veterans and the Stuart adventurers of the seventeenth century. As for the "old inhabitants," the native Irish who remained in the country, they were assigned the less productive lands in Connaught. Ireland thus came to have three regions of utterly dissimilar cultural and historical background. Legal subtleties were invoked all too frequently for the benefit of English landlords. A bitter sense of injustice would be handed down from one Irish generation and bring about unhappy reprisals in future years.

For all students of Irish history there survives but one concept of the eighteenth century. Mr. Lecky characterized the penal laws as a policy which degraded not only the race but the nation. An Irish statesman has described these laws as a machine of elaborate contrivance for the degradation of a people and the debasement in them of human nature. For the penal laws dealing with religion and education the Protestant ascendancy in Dublin was largely responsible. They controlled a parliament which met but once in every two years. They were imbued with hostility against the Catholic Irish and thus deliberately adopted a policy intended to keep them a subservient class. For the second group of penal laws the British government must bear the blame. An articulate mercantile group had great influence at Westminster. They were fiercely jealous of competition and so enacted laws discriminating against Irish industries, trade, and commerce. These laws affected all parts of the country and were disastrous to the woolen trade, especially in Ulster. Penal laws concerning religion enacted in Dublin were discriminatory against both Catholics and Nonconformists in Ulster. They were, however, less effective in the Protestant north than in Munster or Leinster.

During the greater part of the eighteenth century these degrading laws were more or less effectively enforced in the south of Ireland. They were directed mainly against the Catholic clergy and limited their activities as priests and as teachers. The Catholic clergy could not give instruction of any sort. Catholic gentry could not send their sons abroad for education, nor could they have them taught at home. Landownership and land purchase were restricted, and preference in inheritance of land owned by Catholics was given to any one of the sons who had forsworn Catholicism. The effect of this upon character and family loyalties was tragic. English landlords were the dominant group in Munster and in Leinster and were, of course, in control of both houses of the Dublin parliament. There could be but slight lessening of the severity of the penal laws during these years of English landlordism and Protestant ascendancy. Irish hostility to their English oppressors was fanned to high flame in these years of adversity.

The first sign of change came to the oppressed land in 1782. Conditions in Ireland were intolerable. News of the success of the American Revolution brought a gleam of hope. English statesmen read the writing on the wall and evinced some readiness to make concessions. These were too insignificant and too late to stem the increasing demand to shake off, once and forever, control from Westminster. The immediate result was the repeal of Poynings' law and the obtaining of legislative independence. Some reforms were now put upon the statute books. Unfortunately, however, there was a great lack of enlightened leadership in these years. Henry Grattan, who was so largely responsible for the measure of independence obtained in 1782, did not take office. A rudderless parliament seemed to drift. Discontent was widespread, and a sense of bafflement and frustration was apparent. So much had been expected and so little achieved.

These days of indecision turned the thoughts of men abroad. French revolutionary philosophy seeped in, and men began to talk of *liberté, égalité, fraternité*. Vision of a united Ireland, shaking off the oppressive rule of England, filled the minds of such men as Wolfe Tone and Edward Fitzgerald. Presbyterian volunteers in the north and Catholics in all parts of the country hastened to pledge support. A republic was proclaimed, and for the moment it seemed as if success was in sight. Misfortune, however, dogged the footsteps of the leaders. The French expedition arrived too late. Wolfe Tone was arrested and executed. A like fate befell many others. In years to come Wolfe Tone and the heroes of 1798 were names to conjure with. Patrick Pearse in 1916 and Prime Minister Costello in 1949 called upon Irishmen in all parts of the country to fight for the ideals of Wolfe Tone. The Republic of Ireland proclaimed on Easter Monday, 1949, is the realization of the dreams of the men of 1798.

After the failure of the legislative union and the Irish independence movement, English statesmen came to the conclusion that the Irish parliament must be abolished and the turbulent country ruled directly from Westminster. Legal technicalities were strictly observed, and the Irish parliament was persuaded to vote for its own extinction. Pledges to abolish Catholic disabilities were one of the means used to effect this purpose. Bribery and corruption were freely used, and the Act of Union provided for Irish representation in both houses at Westminster. There could, however, be no finality in a union so repugnant to the great majority of the Irish people. Chronic misrule during the years between the Act of Union and the accession of Queen Victoria seem to justify the statement that in no country of Europe was there a worse form of government. Pauperism and ignorance, illiteracy and crime, were a tragic commentary on the hoped-for beneficial results of the union.

For Irishmen in the early decades of the nineteenth century there were two great objectives: first, to repeal the union and, second, to obtain fulfilment of the pledges of Catholic emancipation. The very effective leadership of Daniel O'Connell and the organizing of hundreds of thousands of Irish peasants made possible in 1829 the enactment of an Emancipation Act which rendered tardy justice to Irish Catholics. But the first objective was not realized for many long decades. Scores of leaders plotted and planned but failed to achieve repeal of the Act of Union. In the final analysis, responsibility for failure must be assigned to the great orator and emancipation leader, Daniel O'Connell. During the thirties the great struggle in England was for the franchise. Daniel O'Connell gave freely of his talents to the objectives of the Whig leaders and momentarily pushed aside the repeal issue. He was without doubt the embodiment of all those qualities of leadership which Irishmen most admire. But in these tragic mid-century decades young Ireland looked in vain to O'Connell for guidance. It seems clear that the Irish leader was not willing to pay the price or ask young men to make the supreme sacrifice in order to achieve repeal. And so his leadership waned in Ireland, and younger men took up the challenge. The Young Ireland group was impatient and critical. Economic tragedy had stalked across the land. Ignorance of Irish affairs at Westminster and maladministration in Dublin led to failure in dealing with successive crises. Many Irishmen were members of the British House of Commons, and so each decade saw a more articulate demand for the ending of misrule in Dublin. Commission after commission was appointed to study conditions in Ireland and report specific abuses. In these latter years of the nineteenth century the land question was the most serious grievance. Absentee landlords left the management of their estates in the hands of agents. Evictions were everyday occurrences. Mean one-room huts or hovels were occupied by ignorant, illiterate, pauperized peasants. Irishmen of a somewhat better social status belonged to a tenant class whose tenure of land was precarious. They had no protection in law against the landlords and no incentive to increase productivity or make improvements. Only in Ulster was there a better system of land, usually known as the "three F's"—fair rent, fixity of tenure, fair compensation. Visitors in Ireland give a vivid picture of the poverty and mendicancy of the peasants in the southern and western counties. M. de Beaumont, a quite observant French traveler, was appalled at conditions in Ireland. He attributed much of the poverty and misery to the indifference of the English landlords, whom he characterized as a *mauvaise aristocratie*. A distinguished economist of this period thinks that the ignorance of English statesmen, who had never visited the country, was largely responsible for these bad conditions.

Famine and pestilence are the topics of a tragic chapter in every history of modern Ireland. Desolation such as comes after invasion of a country by hostile armies brooded over the land. The failure of the potato crop, which was the staple diet of thousands of peasants, brought starvation and death in all parts of south Ireland. The human misery of these days is as difficult to comprehend and visualize as that of the concentration camps in Germany in recent years. Sheer unadulterated human misery brought at first little awareness in England of what was happening in every village in the south and hence slight effort to deal with such an appalling condition. Emigrants flocked to the United States and Canada by hundreds of thousands, taking with them not only the fatal pestilence of the country from which they fled but bitter, burning hatred of an English government which took no steps to prevent corn ships leaving Irish harbors in the starvation years. When the real situation became apparent, there were vigorous efforts to provide relief. Millions of pounds were spent on charity and public relief works. It is said that at one time three million people were being fed by relief agencies. But the survivors could not forget the thousands who had died by the roadside in the early years. It is certainly true that the population of Ireland decreased from over eight to six and a half million in five years and steadily declined even further in the next few decades. In one year a hundred thousand left the country. English charity could not atone for the misrule of past decades. English government must come to an end. New leaders took up the challenge and fomented anew the spirit of revolt. Across the Atlantic in the sixties the Fenian movement gave evidence of an Irish-American response to the call of the motherland. In the minds of the older men who remembered the dead and the dying on country roads there developed a passionate hatred of England destined to bear tragic fruition in years to come.

The turning of the tide in Anglo-Irish relations seems to coincide with the first ministry of Mr. Gladstone. Much reading had convinced the great English statesman that gross injustice had been done to Ireland. The first problem seemed to be land tenure. Attainders and confiscations in the sixteenth and seventeenth centuries had been followed up by large-scale plantations. Scottish "undertakers" in the north and English adventurers in the south had acquired vast estates. Many of the descendants of the latter were the *mauvaise aristocratie* described by M. de Beaumont in the early nineteenth century. They were friendly to the English government and spent more time in England than on their Irish estates. All of that must come to an end. But, unhappily, there must intervene nearly three-quarters of a century before the final chapter could be written. Land acts, crimes acts, land-purchase acts, land commissions, are the alternative schemes, until in 1938 the record of unhappy memories is completely erased by Mr. de Valera's annuities settlement.

Mr. Gladstone's four ministeries were responsible for many efforts to find the solution of Irish problems. To a very limited extent he was successful. The Home Rule Bill of 1886 was the answer to the insistent clamor in Ireland for repeal of the Act of Union. Possibly this measure of justice for Ireland was premature, in view of ill-informed public opinion in England. And at this juncture there appeared that small cloud on the horizon— the opposition and apprehension of Ulster. Some thirty years later it was a thunder cloud of serious dimensions which wrecked the Home Rule Bill of 1912 and at a later date led to the substitution of a quite different measure.

At this moment (1886) in Anglo-Irish affairs we begin to see clearly the divergences which had resulted from the Ulster plantation. Extensive grants of land to Scottish Presbyterians in the days of James I had initiated the separation in culture, religion, and political attitudes which has created the Ulster problem of today. During the eighteenth century English penal laws were discriminatory against all parts of Ireland. Thus the north and the south drew together, and Wolfe Tone organized the Volunteers of Ulster in the abortive war for independence in the last decade of the eighteenth century. After the Act of Union there came a change in the economic pattern of Ireland. Ulster became more highly industrialized and developed the woolen and the linen trades and also a prosperous shipbuilding center in Belfast. The land-tenure and agrarian customs of Ulster were admirable as contrasted with conditions in the south. There is much evidence of an extensive system of education, due largely to private enterprise, supplemented by public grants under the auspices of the Kildare Place Association in Dublin. There was in Ulster a less distinct social gap between landlord and tenant and less friction between the successors of the Scottish and English adventurers and servitors and men of Irish birth. The partition issue of today has to a large extent ended that harmonious relationship. There was in Ulster a larger group of small farmers and also a much larger industrial middle class. Landlord and tenant were not aligned against each other as Protestant English and Catholic Irish, as in the southern counties. Mr. Lloyd George's statement in 1912 that the people of Ulster are a homogeneous society and that, in their cultural traditions, their loyalties are English was only partly true. This was, of course, gratifying to many English statesmen, but to the group of Irish Nationalists, such as the Redmonds and Mr. Healy, the intransigence of Ulster in 1912 and 1920 was the death knell of their hopes for Irish unity.

Developments in the nineteenth century had intensified Ulster's divergence from the Nationalist pattern. Belfast had doubled and trebled its population. It had become a flourishing metropolis, and its linen and shipbuilding industries gave employment to thousands of workmen. So Ulster would resist the separatist movement, and Ulster would fight. Many Conservatives in England echoed Mr. Carson's phrase, "and Ulster would be right." The results were the Ulster Covenant, the drilling of volunteers, the gun-running at Larne, and the Curragh incident. Mr. Redmond, hoping in vain to get Ulster support, made one concession after another. But the die was cast, and the partition of today, which Irish Nationalists characterize as indefensible, seems to be inevitable. Perhaps it is a tempest in a teapot. But teapot storms may effect world affairs in a quite unpremeditated fashion.

The outbreak of the first World War brought for the moment in Ireland, as in Russia, a lessening of friction and unity of action in a common effort. All too soon, however, inexcusable military blunders jeopardized this momentary enthusiasm and fanned high once again all the old animosities. The truth of the many accusations against the British War Office is difficult to prove or disprove. All-important is the rankling sense of injustice in the minds of Irishmen, whose sons were fighting and dying in the mud-lined trenches of the western front.

Meantime, the Gaelic League and the Celtic renascence were reviving the legends and heroic deeds of Irishmen in a far-distant past. The literary and cultural heritage of Ireland came alive again on the stage of Dublin's famous Abbey Theatre. Many leaders began to realize that, in the last resort, physical force was the only solution. Sir Horace Plunkett's Irish Agricultural Association had brought about better agrarian conditions and taught Irishmen to rely on their own resources for a solution of economic grievances. A vigorous labor party was denouncing the almost criminal indifference of the Dublin corporation to the widespread mendicancy and pauperism of the slums. It was said at this time that one-third of the population of Dublin was living as family units in one-room tenements. Vice, immorality, and disease were rampant in many sections of the city. The very effective leadership of Mr. Tom Connolly brought these conditions before the public in scathing denunciation of an English administration which tolerated ignorance and inefficiency in high places. Ireland was, it seemed, a pauper country, but Irish leaders recalled the report of the Childers committee and accused England of starving Ireland to pay the imperial debt. As a result of the union in 1800, it had been agreed that Ireland must contribute to the payment of the imperial debt. The assigned proportion was utterly inequitable, and, as a result, Ireland had been overtaxed all through the nineteenth century. And, furthermore, an excessive amount was paid out in Dublin for pensions and sinecure positions. Intolerable social conditions were the result of low wages and widespread unemployment.

During 1915 and 1916 there developed a new tenseness in Anglo-Irish relations. There was irritation in England as a result of the slackening response to the insistent demands of the War Office for volunteers to fill the gaps in the depleted Irish regiments of the western front. There were numerous incidents and provocative speeches in both countries. On July 15, 1915, there took place a great funeral procession through the streets of Dublin, and at the grave of O'Sullivan Rossa, one of the notable Fenian leaders of the nineteenth century, there was delivered a passionate, provocative oration by Patrick Pearse, the son of a rather obscure Dublin schoolteacher.[8] On this memorable occasion the bitter denunciation of England by the young leader was a clarion call to action. It fanned to high flame a spirit of hostility and hatred which found a ready response in the minds of Irishmen and foreshadowed the unhappy events of the next decade.

The sequel came on Easter Monday, 1916,[9] when a group of young men, whose best-known leaders were Pearse and Connolly and Clark, initiated a movement of revolt by seizing the central post office and other public buildings in Dublin's main thoroughfare. There followed "seven mad suicidal days." They were but a handful, perhaps three hundred all told, but they launched a revolt which eventually brought repeal of the Union, complete separation of the south of Ireland from English authority, and the proclaiming of the Republic of Ireland on Easter Monday in 1949. It is not surprising that the most popular serial in Dublin during the Easter week celebrations of the birth of the republic was the Easter rising of 1916. The leaders in 1916 were, however, rebels, and they had to pay the price. Military reinforcements arrived from England to restore order in the beleaguered city. English government in Ireland had broken down. Military authorities took charge. Then followed secret trials and delayed executions, which lasted for nearly two weeks, while men and women waited in fearful suspense. In these days the tide of public opinion changed completely. As Ireland's greatest poet wrote, "In that Easter week a terrible beauty was born." Patrick Pearse at Glasnevin had pledged Irishmen to free Ireland and by the manner of his death had made it impossible for Irishmen to forget that pledge. In his memorable words, "Ireland free must be all Ireland."[10] There would be no peace with England until Ireland with its islands and territorial seas was completely free. That is the challenge of today. The aftermath of Easter week was the initiating of the great crusade for repeal of the Union. After 1916 there seemed no hope of solving the Irish problem by constitutional methods. England was facing the great crisis of intensified German offensives and was deeply concerned over depleted manpower. American assistance at this juncture was imperative, and American public opinion was swung this way or that by Irish-American influence. Conscription in Ireland was talked about in 1918 but not put into effect.

After the Armistice in November, English ministers took cognizance again of what was happening in Ireland. There was an increasing tendency to resort to military coercion. The continuance of castle government from Dublin meant anarchy and turbulence in all parts of the country. The English Black and Tans were eventually sent over, and Anglo-Irish warfare began to be a sad story of atrocities, reprisals, and more atrocities, in a vicious cycle. Meantime, an effective Sinn Fein group of leaders took over the Mansion House in Dublin, called an election, set up a Sinn Fein parliament, and proclaimed a republic. Mr. de Valera was elected president; courts of justice were set up in country districts and functioned efficiently. Financial assistance was sought in the United States and much popular support given to the Republic of Ireland. Mr. de Valera was successful in floating a large Irish-American loan through public subscription. It was also highly desirable to gain support for the Irish independence movement at the coming Versailles Conference. What Mr. Wilson one time called the great metaphysical tragedy of the twentieth century had led millions of men to acclaim the doctrine of the self-determination of small nations. Ireland's grievances were much in the foreground on the eve of the peace conference.

Meantime, in Ireland the situation was chaotic. South Ireland was ostensibly a republic. Ulster was vociferous in opposition to any solution which jeopardized her allegiance to England. The Home Rule Bill of 1920 in somewhat ironic fashion gave autonomy to the six counties of northeast Ireland. This solution was wholly unacceptable to the Nationalist and Sinn Fein group of the republic. Out of such conflicting viewpoints it was difficult to find a compromise solution.

The answer seemed to be foreshadowed by the visit of King George V to Belfast for the formal opening of the Ulster parliament and in his urgent plea to the peoples of Ireland to put aside personal hostilities and to work together for peace. Mr. Lloyd George seized the opportune moment and followed up the king's speech by an invitation to Mr. de Valera to take part in a conference at Downing Street. Protracted and sometimes acrimonious negotiations followed, but finally Mr. de Valera appointed five Irish delegates to meet with a cabinet committee in London.

Out of this Anglo-Irish conference in 1921 there emerged the Anglo-Irish Treaty and the Irish Free State of the years between 1922 and 1948. For many Irish statesmen this is the first milestone in the pattern of an independent Ireland. In the clauses of this treaty there is much that is controversial. Ireland was not yet a sovereign, democratic, independent state. Ulster, by a strange paradox, had accepted the Home Rule Bill of 1920 and was recognized as an integral part of the United Kingdom of Great Britain and Northern Ireland. This was a solution most unacceptable to the delegates of the London conference and was very reluctantly acquiesced in. From the point of view of Irishmen since 1920, partition is the creation of the British government. It is, of course, the crux of the Ireland Bill introduced in the House of Commons on May 3, 1949, and the occasion for the vigorous protest in the Irish parliament in the following week. In the Anglo-Irish treaty of 1921 the oath of allegiance to the crown was insisted upon by the British ministers and reluctantly agreed to by the Irish delegates. Quite controversial also was a group of clauses concerning the retention of certain Irish harbors by the British government. Other questions caused less difficulty, and the treaty finally received the signatures of all the delegates. It seemed to be a great triumph for Mr. Lloyd George.

In conformity with the treaty, the constitution of 1922 was drafted, and the new government was launched on a perilously difficult journey. There were many immediate problems. The boundary of Ulster was not defined in the treaty, so a boundary commission was appointed and finally agreed to a frontier, distasteful both to Ulster and to the Irish Free State. About four Ulster counties there could be no question. There were two others in which there was a large number of Irish Catholics, possiby a majority. But Ulster, like Czechoslovakia, must be a viable political and geographical entity. The frontier compromise was quite unacceptable to both the north and the south. Another adjustment, arrived at in 1923 and 1925, concerned the financial clauses of the treaty. War damages and pension payments were scaled down, and a lump sum agreed to by Mr. Cosgrave as prime minister of the Free State. There were many opportunities for friction, but, on the whole, there was moderation on both sides and an amicable series of adjustments.

For the Irish Free State during the ten years of Mr. Cosgrave's incumbency as prime minister, there were many difficult social and economic problems. Half a decade of intermittent civil and guerrilla warfare left waste and desolate many flourishing villages and country districts. Debates in the Irish Free State Dail Eireann were centered upon financial estimates, housing, and agricultural subsidies. The Shannon River electricity scheme was initiated in this decade. When completed, it transformed the social life of a vast number of agricultural communities. Ireland was entering a new age.

During these difficult years of social and political readjustment, the opposition of Mr. de Valera to the terms of the Anglo-Irish treaty had a profoundly disturbing effect in the country. Mr. de Valera's contention was that the Irish delegates signed the treaty under duress and with the threat of immediate and terrible warfare ringing in their ears. He further maintained that the five delegates had received instruction not to sign without referring the final draft to the cabinet in Dublin. So Mr. de Valera repudiated the treaty and led the opposition against it, both outside and inside the Dail Eireann for the next decade.[11] The oath of allegiance was for some years a barrier to political action. Mr. de Valera, however, declared the oath to have no legal validity and entered the Dail in 1927. From this more strategic position, he conducted the opposition to the treaty. During these years Mr. de Valera contributed notably to the series of conferences at Westminster which resulted in the Balfour Declaration and the Statute of Westminster of 1931. He was also quite active at Geneva and came to be regarded as the champion of the rights of small states.

Mr. William Cosgrave served as prime minister of the Irish Free State for the ten years during which Mr. de Valera was the leader of the opposition to the treaty. In domestic affairs this was a decade of notable achievement. In the 1932 election Mr. de Valera's party obtained a majority and he was elected prime minister.

During the first six years of Mr. de Valera's tenure of office as prime minister the record of constitutional change is quite phenomenal. Amendments were introduced which abolished the oath of allegiance to the crown, nullified the powers of the upper houses and finally abolished them, and declared the right of appeal to the Privy Council of England incompatible with the measure of independence secured by the terms of the Anglo-Irish Treaty. The next question on Mr. de Valera's agenda was annuities. The Land Purchase Grants between 1893 and 1903 had provided for the buying-out of English landlords in Ireland. In 1921 the Irish delegates to the London conference had accepted the financial responsibilities which provided for paying off the English loans. During Mr. Cosgrave's prime ministership these annuities had been paid without protest. Mr. de Valera's viewpoint as adumbrated in these years became very popular. English landlords had in the first place acquired these lands by a successive series of attainders and confiscations on the part of the English government. Centuries passed. One generation of English landlords was succeeded by another. The British government at Westminster and the Protestant ascendancy in Dublin safeguarded their rights of inheritance. During all the years of the nineteenth century Ireland was taxed unjustly and inequitably for imperial debt payments. A pauperized people had in 1921 agreed to the payments provided for in the Wyndham Act of 1903. The English landlords of the Victorian age were gone. Annuities in the 1930's were a heavy financial burden. To Mr. de Valera they seemed utterly unjust. So his solution was to withhold the annuity payments, place them in a suspense account, and wait for a favorable opportunity to negotiate with the British government. The result was a most acrimonious debate and an economic war sanctioned by irate British ministers. This program was ruinous to Irish farmers and cattle breeders. English reprisals took the form of a 100 per cent tax on Irish Free State exports. Exasperation and indignation were intense in both countries. Meantime, Mr. de Valera urged diversified farming and the diversion of cattle pastures to tillage. Economic self-sufficiency for Ireland was highly desirable but, as an immediate remedy, was not likely to appease the farmers and cattle breeders. Finally, concessions were made which paved the way for a final solution in 1938.

In the first six years of Mr. de Valera's tenure of office the bonds of English control were perceptibly lessened. Dramatic events in England in the latter part of 1936 gave Mr. de Valera the opportunity to take the next step. The Dail Eireann was summoned December 10 for an emergency session. Mr. de Valera introduced an External Relations Act in which he anticipated the constitution and stated a new formula for international relations. A limited and restricted jurisdiction in external affairs was acknowledged. Was such an amendment constitutional? Did it not mean the final and most decisive repudiation of one of the most binding and significant clauses of the Anglo-Irish Treaty of 1921? The constitution of 1922 had implemented the treaty and thus brought into existence the Irish Free State. Mr. de Valera was adamant. The treaty must be thrown overboard. By virtue of Mr. Balfour's declaration as embodied in the Statute of Westminster of 1931, the Dominions were free and autonomous members of the British Commonwealth of Nations. The status of the Irish Free State as a Dominion was implied in the terms of the treaty and in the constitution of 1922. Dominion status implied the right to secede and thus renounce the jurisdiction of the crown in domestic affairs and accept only such relationship in external affairs as both governments agreed to. Mr. de Valera chose an opportune moment for a new interpretation of Dominion status, but there was sharp criticism both in the Dail Eireann and in the Irish Free State. The abdication crisis was surely not the moment for secession. Despite much unfavorable comment, the Act of External Affairs was ratified in the Dail Eireann and became statutory law. It was received in England with some amazement, but its validity was not questioned. The Statute of Westminster undoubtedly gave the Dominions such a right. Prophets of doom looked upon this measure as foreshadowing the disintegration of the British Empire. Recent events in the Far East seem to justify this apprehension. For the Irish Free State this was the second milestone in the progress toward complete and absolute separatism. Since every link with the crown in domestic affairs was abrogated, the existing governor-generalship seemed an anachronism. The office was abolished. In one of the Dublin newspapers of that week there was a cartoon depicting the governor's hasty and rather ignominious exit. The governor-general murmured to himself, "Maybe I ought to have asked for a farewell broadcast." These events of 1936 were in part the realization of the dreams of Irish liberation.

For Mr. de Valera the next step was to fit all these rapid changes into a coherent pattern. The drafting of the constitution of 1937 was achieved in record time. It was imperative to clarify the new relationship of the Irish Free State not only to the British government but also to member-states in the British Commonwealth of Nations. Article V of the constitution states that the Irish Free State is a sovereign, independent, democratic state. In Article XXIX, clause 4, there is a statement to the effect that any executive function of the state in, or in connection with, its external relations shall be dealt with by the government in accordance with the method of procedure of any group of nations with which the state is or may become associated. This statement in the constitution implemented the clauses of the External Relations Act providing for the accrediting of ministers abroad and such customary diplomatic functions.

After the enactment of the 1937 constitution the next question to be dealt with was the long-deferred problem of annuities. For both countries economic warfare was suicidal and had been partially abandoned. It now seemed possible to arrive at a final settlement. At this juncture a committee in London was considering the question of the so-called "treaty ports." British control of Irish harbors was an anachronism, incompatible with the status of a sovereign state. The problem of annuities and of the treaty ports was concurrently dealt with in the London conferences. Mr. de Valera is conceded by many of his critics to have reached the pinnacle of successful diplomacy in these negotiations. It was agreed that British forces should be withdrawn from the three strategic harbors. The annuities question was amicably settled by a lump-sum payment of £10,000,000. Between 1893 and 1903 the

British government Land Puchase Acts had provided loans for buying out the English landlords on the basis of long-term payments, the so-called "annuities." These were now liquidated. There was left but one cloud on the horizon, that of partition. Time alone would provide the solution. Mr. de Valera had consistently denounced the Government of Ireland Act of 1920, which gave a separate government to the six counties of northeast Ireland. At this juncture, however, he saw the wisdom of not forcing the issue. Much had been achieved in the six years of his tenure of office.

World War II and its aftermath brought little change in Anglo-Irish relations. At times there was bitterness and a tense atmosphere. In the face of terrific strain on British shipping, Irish neutrality was proclaimed and, of course, sharply denounced in the English press. After American entry into the war and the arrival of American troops in northern Ireland, there was increased tension. The calm attitude of the English government in these years of crisis made it possible for Mr. de Valera to maintain Irish separateness and independence.

During the war years the Act of External Relations was consistently defended by Mr. de Valera. Apparently it was the last milestone. Every clause but one of the Anglo-Irish Treaty of 1921 had been cast into the discard. Successful majorities for Mr. de Valera's party in electoral campaigns gave evidence of popular approval of his policy. But sixteen years' tenure of office suggested a dictatorship, so in 1948 a reaction set in which brought into office a coalition government and the election of Mr. Costello as prime minister. Social and economic conditions were to a large extent responsible for the electoral defeat of Fianna Fail. There was much unemployment in Dublin and other cities and towns and much labor agitation. There was also much agrarian discontent, due largely to the dislocation of trade and shipping during the war years. Ireland is today a country of small farms in which the use of up-to-date agricultural machinery is difficult and expensive. Much attention has been given in recent years to agricultural improvement and to better techniques in handling export products. Agricultural subsidies are, at best, only a temporary solution. The advent of a labor government in England in 1945 and the adoption of its very comprehensive system of social security have enhanced the discontent of the Labor party in Dublin. Question time in the Dail Eireann is largely devoted to social and economic problems, such as housing, rents, wages, and pensions. There had been much criticism in recent years of the government's failure to deal with these vital domestic problems of the country.

Whatever the explanation of Mr. Costello's election in 1948, one fact emerges. No revolutionary change was foreshadowed in the campaign speeches. Mr. Costello neither sought for, nor obtained, a mandate to overthrow the settlement of 1936. Nevertheless, the significant measures dealt with in the first paragraphs of this paper were taken and aroused widespread comment in both England and Ireland. The External Relations Act was repealed in November, 1948, and the Republic of Ireland proclaimed on Easter Monday, 1949. The final outcome is clear and definite. By unilateral action in successive sessions of the Dail Eireann the Anglo-Irish Treaty is but another scrap of paper. An English kingship first acquiesced in by an Anglo-Irish parliament four hundred years ago has vanished. The dreams of Wolfe Tone and of Patrick Pearse seem to be realized in the events of 1948 and 1949. Possibly the proclamation of the Republic of Ireland is the last milestone. The twenty-one-gun salute seemed to be the knell of English power in Ireland and, for the Republic, the dawn of a new day.

One shadow still darkens the horizon. Partition, declared by Irishmen in the south to be indefensible, is not in any way so regarded in Ulster. The Ireland Bill introduced in the House of Commons reaffirms the point of view of English ministers in 1912 and in 1920. It declares that under no circumstances will the six counties of Ulster or any part thereof cease to be a part of the United Kingdom of Great Britain and Northern Ireland without the consent of the Ulster parliament. It reaffirms the territorial integrity of the six counties. The answer to this challenge is found in Mr. Costello's Motion of Protest, followed up by a great mass meeting in Dublin a few days later and the launching of an anti-partition crusade. What is the answer to the Ulster problem? Sir Edward Carson at one time told a too insistent representative of the press that it would take six months to read up on the Ulster question and six weeks to tell him about it—and then he would not understand. There are many indications that the Ulster question may not be settled for some time. There are different viewpoints, and there are conflicting arguments. Visitors from Belfast are numerous in Dublin in recent years. There is much good food in the shops and restaurants. There are few restrictions, but prices are high. These Belfast visitors see many beggars in the streets of Dublin and look askance at the evidences of poverty and inadequate housing. In northern Ireland pensions and social security services are of the English pattern. The cost is high, but there is less real pauperism. Whether this is good or bad makes little real difference. What Mr. Lloyd George said in 1912 is still true. In Ulster there is a homogeneous society with different cultural and historic traditions and loyalty to England. So Ulster (strange parody) accepted home rule and clings to it with unabated zeal. The genesis of partition lies far back in the dim and distant past. The abortive Tudor plantations and presidencies and the Ulster plantation of the seventeenth century are responsible for the great Irish riddle of today. There are many obstacles to the unity dreamed of by Wolfe Tone and Patrick Pearse. The Gaelic League and the Celtic renascence were instrumental in reviving an almost decadent nationalism. There came about the re-creating of that regenerative pride in Ireland's cultural heritage which has been so significant in recent years.

The study of Irish history inevitably revived bitter and poignant memories of seven hundred and fifty years of Anglo-Irish relations. English landlords have been bought out in three Irish provinces, and the descendants of the displaced "old inhabitants" of the sixteenth and seventeenth centuries are in possession. South Ireland is largely Catholic today. Irishmen of the Free State and of the Republic of Ireland think of themselves as members of a great mother-country with a far-flung spiritual kinship to Irishmen overseas. Separatism in Ireland is largely the resultant of the plantation system of the seventeenth century. So there has come about the intensifying of a divergent viewpoint. To the statesmen of the republic, the House of Commons Ireland Bill perpetuates a crime. Ireland free, "the whole island of Ireland, its islands and territorial seas," is but the echo of the words of the young leaders of the republic proclaimed by Patrick Pearse in 1916. That is the viewpoint in Dublin. Meantime, in Ulster there is loyalty to England. The majority in the six counties are Scottish and English and largely Presbyterian. There is an Ulster parliament and a governor-general appointed by the king of England. Belfast, the capital, is a prosperous metropolis with flourishing industries. This industrial development of the north would seem to be complementary to the economic pattern of the south. Both states would profit from union. But Ulster is apprehensive, and thus there seems to be a stalemate.

Another rather significant obstacle to the ending of partition is the revival of the Gaelic language as an integral part of the educational system of the Free State government and today of the republic. Every effort is being made to preserve Gaelic in such counties as Galway and Donegal, and other predominantly Gaelic-speaking parts of the country. For the last twenty-five years primary-school classes have been taught only through the medium of Irish. In senior schools some subjects are also taught in Irish. This program is fairly successful. In the last four years £250,000 have been spent by the government in compulsory summer courses for Irish teachers. There were established in 1927 six preparatory colleges in the Gaelic-speaking regions of Ireland, and as a result the great majority of the teachers in the Republic are fluent in the language.[12] Knowledge of Irish is a prerequisite to the obtaining of a teacher's certificate and is required for entrance to many of the technical colleges and higher institutions of learning. Irish is heard in the streets of Dublin much more frequently than twenty years ago. It is also heard in the Dail Eireann and at public meetings. The majority of Irish leaders are becoming increasingly bilingual. The emphasis, however, on the teaching and fluent speaking of Gaelic may well bring about an even greater lack of understanding between Ulster and the Republic of Ireland.

Many Irishmen stress today the fact that partition is indefensible. A long, straggling frontier brings about evasions of customs and a moral laxity that is deplorable. In view, however, of age-old divergencies continually intensified by new issues, partition may well be thought of as inevitable. The Irish riddle is unsolved. Is it insoluble?

Epilogue.—The elections[13] of May, 1951, in the Republic of Ireland resulted in the overthrow of the Costello coalition government. Mr. de Valera has been elected prime minister by the Dail Eireann and thus, at sixty-eight, the old soldier who defended Dublin so brilliantly at Bolands Mill in 1916 is back in office. As a statesman of thirty years' experience, Mr. de Valera has possibly a wider viewpoint than in those early years of militant opposition to the English government in Ireland. There are many problems still unsolved. The small fragment of the Irish republican army is a disturbing factor, especially in the two largely Catholic counties of Ulster. St. Patrick's Day and July 12 speeches are provocative of riots in Belfast and in other cities and towns of the north of Ireland. A student of Irish affairs who spent several weeks in Dublin in the summer of 1950 sees no immediate solution of the partition problem.[14]

Mr. de Valera has been for thirty years the implacable foe of the Government of Ireland Act of 1920 and of the Anglo-Irish Treaty of 1921. Quite consistently he has opposed the Boundary Commission settlement of 1925. Partition is the will-o'-the-wisp, the leprechaun, of Irish politics today. Not only national but international politics are disturbed by insistent demands for redress of Irish grievances. Ireland is not a member of the Atlantic Pact nations. According to Mr. MacBride, participation in a defense program would be difficult in a divided Ireland.[15] More recently the Strasbourg Conference of the Council of Europe has been a sounding board for Irish problems. Even in Washington the question of partition has been presented and discussed in somewhat acrimonious fashion. Since Mr. de Valera has been in pseudo-retirement for some three years, it is possible that he re-enters politics with a more philosophical perspective and that the question of partition will be relegated to the limbo of half-forgotten lost causes. Time will tell.

NOTES ON SCOTTISH WITCHCRAFT
CASES, 1590–91

By HELEN STAFFORD

Westhampton College, University of Richmond

IT HAS often been noted that periods of witchcraft persecution tend to coincide with, or follow closely upon, years of political and religious turmoil.[1] After the turbulence of the 1580's in Scottish history a period of comparative calm might have been anticipated. Such hopes, however, would have been idle. Although the last decade of the century witnessed no such events of epic proportions as the fate of Mary Stewart and the defeat of the Armada, unrest, violence, and quarrels of religious, political, and personal nature seemed to multiply. The vigorous and mysterious figures of Angus, Mar, Gowry, Arran, and d'Aubigny might no longer dominate Scotland's politics with such cool confidence; but a new generation appeared, equally restless, ambitious, high-spirited, and enterprising, who managed with ease to sustain the reputation of their country's history as one of monotonous upheaval. What if the young King James VI had now achieved maturity? He was twenty-four years of age in 1590 and had made a discreet choice in taking as wife Anne of Denmark, thus allying himself with a small Protestant country, albeit one somewhat distant from the center of gravity of the great Catholic-Protestant controversy which absorbed the attention and energies of England, France, and Spain. Scotland had been rocked as recently as 1589 by the Brig o' Dee conspiracy of the Catholic earls, Huntly and Errol, with the king of Spain. The storms which harried the fleet bearing the young Danish princess to Scotland in the autumn of 1589 boded ill. The impatient bridegroom, learning that his bride had been forced to turn back and take shelter on Norway's coast, hastened to her in person in October and was absent from his kingdom until the following May. Thus uncertainty ushered in the last decade of the century, a fit setting for the first period of violent witch persecution that Scotland had known.

Belief in witches was, of course, common in Scotland, as in all western Europe in that age. The government had for generations taken cognizance of it. More than a dozen witches had been burned in Edinburgh in 1479 for conspiring the death of James III through the use of a waxen image of that royal personage. A proclamation of 1510 ordered judges in circuit courts to inquire into witchcraft practices. A statute of 1563 had prescribed death for persons professing to be witches and for those consulting such persons. Occasional cases arose, but until 1590 there had been little vigor of enforcement displayed. In fact, the very words of the 1563 statute implied skepticism as to witchcraft. The law stated as its purpose the "avoiding of all such vain superstition in times to come," and ordered that no person "use any manner of witchcraft, sorcery, or necromancy nor give themselves forth to have any such craft or knowledge thereof, therethrough abusing the people."[2]

The skepticism about witchcraft implicit in the above law was lost in the fury which began in 1590. In July, scarcely three months after the king's return from Denmark with his bride, it was known in Edinburgh that some five or six witches had been arrested in Copenhagen upon suspicion that they had, by their black arts, made it impossible for the queen to proceed to Scotland when she had first set out the preceding autumn. It was likewise rumored that they had conspired to prevent the king's return when he personally conducted the queen to his realm in the spring. At the same time, several witches were tried in Edinburgh, chiefly for causing the death of the young laird of Wardhouse by melting a waxen image of him, whereby he "pined awaie by sweate."[3] In April, one Meg Dow had already been found guilty and sentenced to be burned for witchcraft and for child murder; and, in August, Janet Grant and Janet Clark were sentenced to be burned for bewitching people to death, causing illness to some, killing cattle, and summoning the devil.[4] Thus far these Scottish victims betray nothing unusual. It has been suggested that the latter case involving Janet Grant [or Gradoch] and Janet Clark [or Spalding] may have been meant to prepare the way for the prosecutions that busied the king and the council from November, 1590, through June, 1591, but there is nothing that clearly proves this.[5]

On November 28, 1590, the English ambassador in Edinburgh, Robert Bowes, reported that the king and his council were busy with the examination of various witches. "And some of good qualities are like to be blotted by the dealinges of the wickett sorte."[6] Nine days later the matter was still claiming the king's attention.[7] One woman whom he questioned, Agnes Sampson, confessed to practices against the king himself. Over thirty witches were known, and many others were accused. Obviously, there was much material at hand to whet the royal curiosity. James was deeply interested and attended the examination of various persons.[8]

Part of the tale unfolded by these investigations is told succinctly in a pamphlet, *Newes from Scotland,* published in Scotland and in London in 1591. It is well illustrated with woodcuts that portray the alleged witches as rather demure and dignified women, properly and discreetly dressed, not at all the horrible hags with high-crowned hats so common to modern ideas.[9] But the *Newes* is disappointingly brief. It must be supplemented by the records of the trials of the principal witches, printed in Robert Pitcairn's *Ancient Criminal Trials in Scotland,* themselves too scant, since they consist of little more than the articles of the "dittay" or indictment brought against the miscreants.[10] The *Calendar of State Papers, Scotland, 1589–1593,* which includes reports from the English ambassador in Edinburgh to his superior, Lord Burghley, adds some material. The ambassador was interested in the witches and at one point was falsely accused of consulting them for dubious purposes. Likewise, *The Border Papers,* Volume I, contains some material, but the total is not impressive. As many questions are left unanswered as are answered. Apparently much was omitted, for a purpose, and the modern reader is baffled, not only by the mysteries and horrors of the witches' alleged practices and the cruelties perpetrated on these luckless individuals but also by the broad hints of political repercussions, which refuse to tell their whole story.

According to the *Newes,* it began with a servant girl, Geillis or Gelie Duncan, whose activities in healing sickness aroused the suspicions of her master, David Seaton, deputy bailiff of Tranent. Seaton tortured the girl by using the "pilliwinckes" (thumbscrews) and by "wrinching her head with a cord or roape." True to her alleged covenant with the devil, she refused to confess until the devil's mark was discovered on her throat.[11] She then broke down and confessed her guilty association with him and involved many others in her tale, of whom the chief ones were Agnes Sampson, Doctor John Fian, Euphemia MacCalzean, and Barbara Napier. After this beginning, which was to inaugurate at least six months and more of torture, examinations, trials, and executions, Geillis Duncan is little more heard from. It was revealed that she played a trumpet at a conventicle of witches held in the Kirk at North Berwick on All Hallows' E'en (1590), whereupon the king had her summoned to his presence to repeat her musical performance. Her skill may have entertained and interested the king, but it apparently did not gain her freedom.[12] She seemed to be giving testimony as late as April, 1591, and was referred to as being still alive in June, 1591.[13] Thereafter she disappears from history. She may have been executed.

The next figure to command attention is that of Doctor Fian, alias John Cunningham, schoolmaster at Saltpans in Lothian, a lusty fellow whose vocation apparently held fewer attractions for him than his avocations of philandering and witchcraft. He was in great repute among the witches of southeastern Scotland, being known as the "Devil's clerk." Gelie Duncan said he was the only man to attend the devil's readings.[14] The accounts of various conventions of witches at North Berwick and Newhaven usually cite him as present, though by no means the only man there, and taking an active part. His education marked him for special work and honor; he sat close to the devil on such occasions. At a North Berwick convention he "blew vp the duris, and blew in the lychtis," apparently preliminary ceremonies to be performed before Satan would begin the serious part of the meeting.[15] He took part in the meetings and incantations which were thought responsible for raising the storms which interrupted the queen's passage from Denmark and rendered hazardous the king's crossings of the North Sea when he fetched his bride.[16] Evidence of more serious activities can be gathered from the trial of Barbara Napier's jurors in June, 1591, by which time Fian had been dead more than four months. He was said to have been present at the meeting on Lammas E'en at Newhaven between Musselburgh and Preston-pans, where the witches enlisted the devil's assistance to bring about the king's destruction by the wax-image ritual, as well as by poisoning him with a curious mixture of toad, adder skin, and like vile ingredients.[17] He also attended the North Berwick meeting held on All Hallows' E'en, 1590, where the witches in vain importuned Satan for the waxen image of the king.[18]

Fian's story well illustrates the inadequacy of extant records. He was an ill-humored, touchy individual, to whom the devil appeared as he lay on a bed in Thomas Trumbill's house in Tranent, planning revenge on Trumbill for not whitewashing or cleaning his room as had been promised. The devil promised that he should never want and should have the power to obtain vengeance on his enemies if he would enter Satan's service. The devil urged him to set fire to Trumbill's house. On their second meeting Satan put his mark on Fian. Thereafter, the doctor attended many witches' sabbaths and used his powers to open locks, to raise storms, to cause a man to be possessed with an evil spirit, and to foretell how long certain people would live. Although he employed his occult powers to further his philanderings, they were not always successful. Save for his participation in the raising of storms, the details to be garnered from the *Newes* and from his own dittay reveal him as a somewhat lascivious fellow of no great consequence.

Yet his conduct at this final tragedy of his career commands somewhat belated admiration and respect. Tortured with the rope at his head and with "the boots," an instrument which crushed the legs by successive blows of a hammer on wedges, he refused to confess until, at the suggestion of several witches, two pins found thrust under his tongue were removed. His confession, now lost, was said to have been signed in the king's presence. He escaped from prison after Satan was said to have visited him there, although he on that occasion warned the devil that he was forsaking him. Recaptured at the king's orders, Fian repudiated his former confession, and, although he was tortured again, this time with the boots and with an instrument known as the

"Turkas"—pincers which pulled off his nails—he remained unmoved. He claimed the confession had been wrung from him only through fear of pain. He was sentenced to death, apparently both for his deeds and as an example to others, and was strangled and burned on Castle Hill in Edinburgh on a Saturday late in January, 1591.[19]

Agnes Sampson was tried about the same time. She was variously described as "the eldest Witch of them al,"[20] a midde-wife,"[21] and "Agnes Samson (commonly called the wise wife of Keith) [who] was most remarkable; a woman not of the base and ignorant sort of witches, but matron-like, grave and settled in her answers, which were all to some purpose."[22] Her name appears in various forms, Agnes or Annie or Amy, Simpson or Samson or Sampson. She had the distinction of having at least fifty-three items alleged against her in her dittay.[23] She was evidently long practiced in the black arts. Although her confession, as summarized in a paper forwarded from Edinburgh by the English ambassador, says that the devil first appeared to her after the death of her husband, when she was worrying about the maintenance of herself and her children, she had evidently learned some of her skills from her father. He taught her a prayer, a corrupt and metrical version of the Apostles' Creed, which she was to repeat when approached on behalf of a sick person; if she repeated the prayer without stopping, the ill person would live; if she stopped in her prayer, the patient was sure to die.[24] According to the articles of her dittay, Agnes Sampson's activities were many and varied. She had undertaken to heal the sick, sometimes with and sometimes without success. At times she cured people of illnesses allegedly caused by other witches. She could tell how long a patient might live.[25] She had, through the devil's favor, foreknowledge of the Michaelmas storms which prevented Anne of Denmark's arrival in Scotland in 1589 and of the fact that Anne would never arrive unless the king escorted her.[26] She also dabbled with waxen images, having endeavored thus to assist Euphemia MacCalzean to destroy her father-in-law and to aid Barbara Napier against a man named Archie.[27] She aided women in the pains of childbirth by her witch's powder made of the dried joints of corpses.[28] She could charm cattle so that they died.[29] These gifts she obviously used to earn her living. Her powers over the devil her master were not inconsiderable. She could summon him and dismiss him from her presence after he had replied to her questions. He appeared for these interviews in the form of a dog.[30] At one time she even thwarted the devil's plan to carry off a gentlewoman.[31] She had no fear of her master, not hesitating to upbraid him when he seemed slow to live up to their bargain.[32]

Like Dr. Fian, Agnes Sampson suffered death shortly after these inquisitions began. She was evidently tried by an assize and sentenced January 27, 1591, to be taken to Castle Hill in Edinburgh and there bound to a stake, "wirreit" (strangled), and then burned, which sentence was duly carried out on January 28, 1591.[33] "Sche deit maist penitentlie for her sinnis, and abusing of the simple people renuncet the devil, quhom sche oftentymes callit 'Fals decever of God's pepill'; and had hir only refuge to God's mercie in Christ Jesus, in quhom alane sche was assurit to be saif, as that theif quha hang at his right hand."[34]

In Pitcairn's record of Sampson's case, private wrongs and personal injuries made up the bulk of the charges. David Seaton, Gelie Duncan's employer and torturer, was probably the David Seaton whom Agnes, Gelie, and others tried to harm in his person and possessions at their convention at Foulstruthir.[35] Neither Fian's dittay nor Sampson's, as printed in Pitcairn, reveals much that could be labeled treasonable. Matters of state were touched on when it was charged that both had dabbled in the raising of storms to interfere with the voyages of the king and queen.[36] Both had attended an important convention at North Berwick,[37] although, as far as the dittay of either reveals, this North Berwick meeting was merely the usual witches' sabbath, where the devil preached to his followers, who rendered their homage to him in the usual ludicrous fashion of kissing his buttocks, and where several graves were opened and the corpses therein dismembered, the joints being distributed among those present to be manufactured, when dry, into conjuring powder. The *Newes* carried the note that the devil on this occasion inveighed against the king of Scotland, whom he considered "the greatest enemy he hath in the worlde."[38] Sampson confessed to the king some attempt to charm away his life by using a piece of his linen,[39] which project is undoubtedly the one recounted in the *Newes* and there ascribed to an Agnes Tompson, another witch.[40] But the extant records through January and February, 1591, as yet reveal little worthy of the name of high conspiracy. Nor in these records has Bothwell's name been mentioned, although Spottiswood states clearly that Sampson implicated Bothwell.[41] So far, Dr. Fian, Agnes Sampson, and at least eight others had suffered death by fire, while forty others were said to be held for examination and trial.[42] Apparently these first executions were merely a prelude to greater things.

The chief figure in the story as it unfolded in the spring of 1591 was Francis Stewart Hepburn, Earl of Bothwell, a Scottish nobleman of unusal energy and checkered career, in whose veins ran royal, though illegitimate, blood.[43] Bothwell's record was one of heated quarrels and conspiracies. He had traveled on the Continent, had been recalled to Scotland in 1581, and thereafter had figured somewhat in the tortuous factional quarrels. He had been bold and loud in his denunciation of England at the time of Mary Stewart's death and had been an accomplice of the Catholic earls in 1589 at the time of the Brig o' Dee venture. For this last affair he had been found guilty of treason in 1589, but sentence had not been pronounced, the king expressing hope of his better behavior in the future. He had conducted himself well during the king's absence in Norway and Denmark, when he, together with the king's Stewart cousin, the Duke of Lennox, carried the responsibility for maintaining the government of Scotland.[44] But shortly after the king's return the story changed. Bothwell hated Chancellor Maitland, who stood high in the king's favor. His habit of direct and violent action was evidenced in January, 1591, when he forcibly carried from the Tolbooth in Edinburgh a witness in a divorce case, accomplishing this feat at the very time the king and Court of Session were sitting there in another room.[45] This deed implied little respect for the royal presence and authority, an attitude which Bothwell displayed dramatically on several later occasions. Although the *Newes* and the indictments of John Fian and Agnes Sampson omit any mention of Bothwell, his name had evidently been used in the course of the examinations of November, 1590, through February, 1591, and the wonder of it is that he was not committed to prison until mid-April on suspicion of intrigues with witches against the king.[46] From this point the welter of confusion in the witchcraft cases grows more intense. Several prominent witches and their consultants, Euphemia MacCalzean, Barbara Napier, and Richard Graham, were the centers of attention; the name of the English ambassador, Robert Bowes, was dragged into the stir; and, most important of all, Bothwell, in prison from April 16 until June 21, when he escaped, was apparently believed by the king to have tried to effect his destruction by witchcraft. The records are exasperatingly inadequate, but one gains the impression that the king, convinced of Bothwell's guilt, would have been glad to be rid of this troublesome nobleman by sending him into exile.[47] No harsher punishment was possible, since Bothwell had evoked sympathy on all sides, partly because Chancellor Maitland, the king's trusted councilor and Bothwell's bitter enemy, was so unpopular. Many of the nobles refused to attend a convention to try the earl. His escape from Edinburgh Castle was followed by several years of energetic activity on his part, when he seemed to be able to move at will about the kingdom, although he was outlawed as a traitor. His being at large added a further complication when Scotland was shocked at the murder of the Stewart scion, "the bonnie Earl of Murray," by the Earl of Huntly, head of the Gordon clan, in February, 1592; and when the second conspiracy of the Catholic earls, Huntly and Errol, known as the "Spanish Blanks," was revealed about Christmastime, 1592. These later intrigues and maneuvers lie beyond the scope of this paper. Meanwhile, Bothwell twice raided the royal residence in a vain effort to seize the king or kill the chancellor. His first attempt was at Holyrood House in December, 1591, when he gained entrance into the palace but failed to capture the king or the chancellor. His second raid was staged at Falkland in June, 1592, where he had even less success. In July, 1593, however, he gained control of the court and dominated king and kingdom for a few weeks. A trial held at that time acquitted him of the witchcraft charges, but no faith could be had in the impartiality of the justice thus rendered. Bothwell shortly lost his tenuous power. Once again he allied with the Catholic earls, and, as their power waned, he was forced to flee into exile in the spring of 1595, never to return to Scotland. He died in Naples in 1624, a poverty-stricken, broken wanderer.[48]

But what of his alleged witchcraft practices? What information can be gathered about them? The chief points to be gleaned— and the gleanings are decidedly meager—lie in the references to Richard Graham, a famous wizard who testified against Bothwell, found in the *Calendar of State Papers, Scotland* in the correspondence of Ambassador Bowes in the spring of 1591, and in *The Border Papers,* where an account of the earl's trial in August, 1593, is preserved. These, used in conjunction with the scant records of the trials of Dr. Fian, Agnes Sampson, Barbara Napier, and Euphemia MacCalzean, add something to our knowledge; but the sum total is more suggestive than informative.

Richard Graham testified that Bothwell had dealt with him to accomplish the king's destruction. Bothwell, he said, had been impressed by the prophecy of a magician in Italy, who had told him that he should be wealthy and stand high in the king's favor, that he should kill two men, lose the royal favor, and eventually be executed at the king's orders. Since the first prophecies were fulfilled, the earl was taking steps to avoid the last. Hence his frequent conferences with Graham, who, in turn, consulted with other witches. The result was the effort to be rid of the king by raising storms to prevent his return from Denmark. That failing, the witches attempted to poison him by letting some evil concoction fall on his head. Their third effort was to make an image of the king of "waxe mingled with certen other thinges, which should have consumed and melted awaye in tyme, meanyng the Kinge should consume as it did."[49]

In February, 1591, after Dr. Fian's and Agnes Sampson's executions, the English ambassador, Robert Bowes, wrote of the witches' examinations, saying that, to please the king and to win grace, they told many things "farre more strange then trewe." Among such items he noted an attack on himself, an accusation that he, soon after the king's departure to Denmark in the autumn of 1589, had consulted with them in a cellar and had given them gold to use their arts to poison the king and prevent the birth of any heirs. Bowes thought they had been bribed or in some manner secretly influenced to say this.[50] In April, when Richard Graham, "the pryncipall of the witches heere," was revealing evidence even more damning to Bothwell than had previously been found, James VI told the ambassador that Gelie Duncan and others had confessed that Bothwell had intrigued with them, but had then denied it and accused Ambassador Bowes. Graham said that before his examination Bothwell had approached him with the suggestion that he accuse Bowes, saying that, since both names began with *B,* the witches might think it Bowes rather than Bothwell who had negotiated for the king's death. Gelie Duncan persisted in her accusation of Bowes. Graham, however, seemed willing to turn state's evidence against the earl. The ambassador was quickly proved innocent, since the witches' description of his appearance failed to tally with the reality and since he had been absent from Scotland at the time of his alleged dealings with them.[51]

Bothwell's alibi was not so easily established. In his examination in April, 1591, before the king and the council at Chancellor Maitland's house, he admitted acquaintance with Richard Graham for the previous three or four years, but denied vehemently any conspiracy with him against the king. The earl blamed his political enemies for stirring up troubles to prevent his return to power in court and government. He said Graham had once offered him a magic ring, by which he could foretell his future and could discover whether his servants were faithful to him, which ring Bothwell scorned.[52] More than two years later, at the time of his trial in August, 1593, he claimed that he first knew Graham when a friend had asked him to let Graham, an excommunicated person, live within his jurisdiction.[53] Bothwell undertook to ask the king's protection for the sorcerer, but his credit at court was evidently low and he failed to put in the plea. He claimed that Lady Angus had requested him to send Graham to her husband when he lay ill, which service Bothwell twice performed. On both occasions he was present when Graham came to Angus.[54] A chance meeting between Graham and Bothwell occurred at Kelsey and another at the chancellor's house, "where in the presence of me and the chancelor, as we were ryding, he showd us a sticke with nickes in yt all wrapped about with longe heire eyther of a man or a woman, and said yt was an enchanted stick: to which speache I gave smalle regarde."[55] Bothwell certainly knew Graham, but the truth of his alleged intrigue with the wizard to accomplish the king's death is far from manifest. When he was first questioned in April, 1591, he, with habitual boldness, refused to ask pardon of God or king in this matter. He offered to suffer torture along with his accusers that the truth might be known by the confession of one of them. Evidently he relied on his own endurance under torture to outlast that of his enemies. He also suggested that his accuser (apparently Graham) be executed; if the wretch should die without confessing that he had falsely accused Bothwell, the earl would then acknowedge himself guilty and willingly submit to execution.[56] This ingenious suggestion was typical of Bothwell's rash bravado. His opponent would suffer death in any case, while Bothwell would have a chance to survive!

Bothwell attributed some of his ill-luck to English influence.[57] Early in May, 1591, a letter dispatched by Ambassador Bowes to London was intercepted before it reached Berwick.[58] This letter, dated May 5, clearly demonstrates that Bowes used his influence with the king to push the investigation and reminded James of Bothwell's record of intrigue, but it does not prove that Bowes had any hand in instigating the witchcraft charges. He was, however, quite willing to use the opportunity to curb Bothwell's power, since Queen Elizabeth evidently still mistrusted the earl for his violent words in 1587 at the time of Mary Stewart's death, and for his co-operation with the 1589 Brig o' Dee conspirators, who had been enemies of Protestantism and of England and partisans of Spain.[59]

Meanwhile, on May 8, 1951, Barbara Napier, an Edinburgh woman of some standing, wife of the burgess Archibald Douglas, was brought to trial for her practices with witches. The points of her indictment, as printed in Pitcairn's *Ancient Criminal Trials,* contain only two items that implicated her with Bothwell or with treasonable plans against the king. Apparently, when the king rode against the Catholic earls in 1589 or when he was in Denmark, she consulted Graham, "ane Nicromanser and abusar of the people," on behalf of her son, and, at the same time, "sche in-

quyrit att the said Rychie Grahame, gif the King wald cum hame
or nocht." She was also accused of "being att the conventioune of
North-Bervik . . . ," which was actually the serious charge of conspiring the king's death by witchcraft, but she was acquitted on
this count.[60] She was found guilty of consulting with "Annie"
Sampson and Richard Graham on private and personal matters
and was sentenced on May 10 to be "tane to the Castel-hill of the
burcht of Edinburgh, and thair bund to ane staik besyde the fyre
and wirreit thairat quhill scho be deid; and thairefter hir body
brunt in the said fyre, and all hir movabill guidis escheted to our
vse as convict of the saidis crymes." Upon her declaration of her
pregnancy, however, the sentence could not be carried out. She is
thought to have escaped entirely her harsh punishment.[61] Calderwood noted that, since the 1563 parliamentary statute decreeing
death for consulters of witches had never before been put into
execution, "it was thought hard to execute her."[62]

This turn of affairs, Barbara Napier's acquittal on the charges
of conspiring the king's death and her evasion of the death sentence, scarcely pleased James.[63] She was a known partisan of Bothwell and had written a letter of encouragement to him while he
was in prison.[64] Her influence and skill and that of her legal counsel had evidently been so great that she was able to have a rather
favorable jury chosen and to prolong her trial into the early hours
of the morning.[65] The king determined to make a firm stand
against what he thought a miscarriage of justice. It was easier to
attack a woman of lower rank than a man of Bothwell's stature
and importance. Napier's jurors were therefore summoned and
appeared before their monarch on June 7, when he harangued
them in a lengthy oration. Perhaps he was moved to eloquence
by the public rebuke he had received on the preceding day, Sunday, when, "in the morning doctrine" Mr. John Davidson, one of
the Edinburgh ministers, said "that it appeared by the evill suc-
cesse he had in executioun of justice, so farre, that he had not
power over a carline witche, naming Barbara Naper; that he and
his counsell were not assisted by God, and that, because he had
not repented sufficientlie for his former sinnes."[66] The king took
care to demonstrate to the jurors that it was the royal duty to see
the guilty condemned, that he was impartial in this case (*sic*),

and that the jurors had acted in ignorance. They had evidently acquitted Barbara Napier on the serious counts of treason against the king's person because the only evidence against her came from witches. The king had gone to great pains to get the Court of Session to declare that it was lawful to receive the testimony of women, infants, infamous persons, and *socii criminis,* in cases of *lèse majesté* and of heresy, although in ordinary cases such witnesses were not heard. Such infamous persons as witches, he argued, could be admitted to testify in these special cases, since no honest man could know these matters, the evildoers would not accuse themselves, and no act done by witches could be seen.

Further, I call them witches which doe renounce God and yeld them selves wholely to the devill; but when they have recanted and repented, as these have done, then I accompt them not as witches, and so their testymony sufficient. In this I referre my selfe to the ministers. Besides, the inquest is to judge of the qualitie of the testymony and circumstances concernyng the same. Also it may be observed that never any of good lyfe were chardged with that cryme.

The erring jurors, being persuaded to put themselves in the king's mercy, were pardoned by him.[67]

The dittay against these jurors who had sat in judgment on Barbara Napier reveals far more about the witches' alleged plots against the king than any document as yet discussed.[68] The details, based apparently on the depositions of Graham, Gelie Duncan, Agnes Sampson, and other witches, sketch the following order of events:

ITEM. At the time of the king's journey to the Brig o' Dee against the Catholic lords in 1589, Barbara Napier told Richard Graham of a woman's prophecy that "our souerane lord wald gett skaith be ane taid or gangrell" and asked Graham's opinion. He consulted the devil and received the reply that the king would be troubled by a convention of women by the dropping of a toad. Graham said that Napier, Euphemia MacCalzean, and Donald Robesoun would be three of the perpetrators of this deed.

ITEM. At Lammas e'en last [July 31, 1590] after the king's return from Denmark, Barbara Napier met with Agnes Sampson, Euphemia MacCalzean, John Fian, and others, men and women, at Newhaven. The devil, who appeared there as a black man, drew nine, including the four above-named, close to him while thirty others stood at a short distance in another group. Agnes Sampson there proposed the king's destruction and asked Satan's help. He said he would do what he could, but that "itt wald be lang to, because it wald be thoirterit [thwarted]. . . ."[69] He promised them a wax image and in the meantime ordered them to put a foul concoction of toad, adderskin and other vile materials some place where the king passed often in the hope it might drop on him and destroy him "that ane vther mycht haif rewlit in his Maiesties place, and the ward mycht haif gane to the Dewill." Sampson was instructed to make the wax image and give it to the devil to be enchanted, which she did. The devil promised to give it to Barbara Napier and Euphemia MacCalzean at the next meeting to be roasted. Margaret Thomson was appointed to attend to the toad poison procedure.[70]

ITEM. On All Hallows' E'en 1590[71] a convention held at the North Berwick Kirk was attended by Gelie Duncan, Agnes Sampson, Dr. Fian, Barbara Napier, Euphemia MacCalzean, and many others to the number of seven score, of whom about forty were mentioned by name in the dittay. The devil appeared "lyke ane mekill blak man, with ane blak baird stikand out lyke ane gettis baird; and ane hie ribbit neise, falland doun scharp lyke the beik of ane halk; with ane lang rumpill; cled in ane blak tatie goune; and ane ewill favorit scull bonnett on his heid; haifand ane blak buik in his hand. . . ."[72] He mounted the pulpit and called on all to be good servants to him, promising that he would be a good master to them and they should never want. Robert Griersoun, who stood with Fian at the devil's left hand, upbraided him for not giving them the king's "pictour" [wax image] as had been promised. Euphemia MacCalzean had urged Griersoun to make this complaint. The devil said it was not ready at the moment and promised it for the next meeting, which should be held for that purpose. There was still some dissatisfaction at the delay, whereupon the devil promised Napier and MacCalzean that they should shortly have the wax image of the king. Several corpses were exhumed and dissected and their nails and joints distributed among those present to be used for the manufacture of charms. After the vulgar homage customarily rendered to the devil was performed, the assembly dispersed. As proof, however, that these were no supine subjects of the devil might be cited the outcry raised when, contrary to agreement, several were called by their rightful rather than by their assumed names [e.g., Barbara Napier *Naip* and Euphemia MacCalzean *Cane*].[73] Evidently the compact between Satan and his subjects was far from a one-sided affair. Some bold spirits among the company did not hesitate to insist on the strict enforcement of the terms.

So far no mention of Bothwell in any of the indictments, other than to designate the time of Barbara Napier's first questioning of Richard Graham about the king's future as at the time of the king's journey in 1589 against the Catholic earls, when Bothwell was their valuable accomplice, who created a diversion in the south while the king rode northward against them. In spite of the conspicuous absence of Bothwell's name, this "practising" of the king's destruction by the witches was alleged to have been at his instigation.[74]

It is small wonder that Euphemia MacCalzean was found guilty and condemned to death when she stood trial on June 9, 1591, two days after the king's severe reprimand to Napier's jurors. The dittay against her lists 28 items, of which the longest and most detailed and interesting describe her consultations with various witches to further her private purposes, including attempts to destroy her husband.[75] Euphemia, a woman of good birth, daughter of a senator of the College of Justice, was apparently a strong-minded shrew, who, disliking her husband, Patrick Moscrop, sought to poison him within the first year of their marriage. Although his youth and strength enabled Patrick to survive this hazard, his wife continued to make him so miserable that ". . . the said Patrik being wereit of his lyffe, be the daylie truble he had in youre cumpany, wes compellit, for saulftie of his lyffe, to expone him selff to the seais, and to pas to ffrance in youre defalt." Euphemia speeded him on his journey by trying to raise money and sent him off with the blessing, "the ffeind ga with him."[76] Poor Patrick returned from France, only to endure further efforts by his wife to destroy him. Euphemia evidently used witchcraft to lure one Joseph Punfrastoune to succumb to her charms and then, love turning quickly to hate, sought to poison him and to prevent his intended marriage to another. She was said to have consulted witches and to have learned the art of witchcraft herself. Although her personal peccadilloes were lively and dramatic, the king's special interest in her case must have been awakened by her alleged presence at the conventions of witches when his destruction was planned. He wrote to Maitland: "Lett Effie Makkaillen see the stoup [pillory?] tua or three dayes, and upon the suddain staye her in hope of confession. Gif that servis, adverteis; gif not dispatche her the next oulke anis, bot not according to the rigoure of the dome."[77] Her trial did not misfire, as had Napier's, but it was prolonged some days.[78] She was finally found guilty of nine of the charges, including the treasonable ones of conspiring against the king at Newhaven and at North Berwick.[79] Judgment against her was pronounced, and she was sentenced "to be takin to the Castel-hill of Edinburghe, and thair bund to ane staik and brunt in assis, quick, to the death: And all and sindrie hir landis, heretageis, takis, stedingis, roumes, possessiounes, coirnis, cattell, guides and geir, to be forfaltit and escheit to our souerane lordis vse."[80] This punishment was unusual, since it specified that she be burned alive rather than be first "wirreit" (strangled) and then burned.[81] She steadfastly refused to give testimony against Bothwell. Ambassador Bowes wrote: ". . . the sownd of the prayses gyven by many—wishing the end of her lyfe to be rather with the danger of her owne soule then to the perill of their freendes to be accused by her—doth so prevayle with her as there is litle hope of any change in her."[82] Bothwell, who had escaped from the castle several days before her death, was proclaimed as a traitor on June 25, "and that same day Euphane McCalzeame wes brunt for ane witche, but scho newer confest nathing to hir deathe."[83]

Meanwhile, Richie Graham was detained in prison. This was probably done because he was a suspected wizard and because he was a valuable state's witness in case Bothwell could be brought to trial. Had he been permitted to go free, his life would doubtless have been in jeopardy, since Bothwell and his friends never seemed to hesitate to use violence against their opponents.[84]

Bothwell during May and June grew more and more resentful at his continued imprisonment and fearful of its outcome.[85] The trials of Barbara Napier and Euphemia MacCalzean boded ill for him.[86] He apparently feared that charges of counterfeiting and forging might be added to the count against him. But his fortunes were far from being at an extremity. The king himself in a letter to Maitland planned to exile him. Apparently, James was well aware that he could not execute so important a nobleman. Many of the nobles of Scotland, summoned to attend a convention for May 6 to consider the evidence against Bothwell, sent excuses.[87] A party at court was evidently trying to persuade the king to clemency. James, although his dislike of the earl was apparent in his remark that "he would not have so many kings in this realme, neyther should Bothwell be delyvered in tyme and maner as they had promised,"[88] realized that he must be moderate. While he was conducting negotiations with Bothwell through Chancellor

Maitland for the earl's speedy departure from Scotland for Germany or Italy (evidently England, France, and Spain were too close or too fertile ground for further plots), Bothwell suddenly escaped from Edinburgh castle on the night of June 21:

> . . . breaking an hoelle in the rooffe of his lodging in this castell, he passed over the toppe of that howse to a place most easye to dissend, and ther commyng downe, he esscaped oute of the castell at the west port of this towne with one Lowther the servant of the capten of the castell. At the west porte he fownd and tooke his horsse, with the Master of Cathenes, Gylbert Penycowke, and two or thrye moe, and ys nowe departed, as yt is thoght, towardes the sowth partes of this realme.[89]

He said he broke ward because the king meant to give notice of his sailing to an English ship, lying ready to seize him, and because he found "no hope of lyffe lefte to hyme," because of the machinations of his enemies, whom he challenged to combat.[90] From the time of his escape until the spring of 1595, he was to remain at large, eluding the king's attempts to capture him, mocking the royal proclamation issued on June 25, 1591, against him. This proclamation recited his share in the Brig o' Dee episode of 1589, although Bothwell alleged that the king had pardoned him for that.[91] It referred also to the recent suspicion of his dabbling in "Nicromancie and Wichcraft." Escape from the castle before lawful trial argued that he was guilty of that practice, the proclamation asserted.[92]

Thereafter, the stir about the witchcraft episode gradually subsided. Euphemia MacCalzean's execution a few days after Bothwell's escape was the last dramatic incident recorded for 1591. Graham apparently remained in prison until the end of February, 1592, when he, too, suffered death, a poor requital for the service he had performed in furnishing so much evidence of Bothwell's instigation of the witches' activities.[93] Graham asserted, even at his death, that he spoke the truth against Bothwell. The earl continued vehement in his denials of guilt. Shortly before Graham's death, Bothwell addressed a letter of justification to the clergy of Edinburgh, indignantly denying any conspiracy against the king's life, expressing wonder at how anyone could give credence to such a fellow as "deboshed Richie Graham," and ascribing all his troubles to Chancellor Maitland, the "puddock-stoole of a night" who aspired to take the place of an "ancient cedar" like himself.[94] When he temporarily seized power in August, 1593, he insisted on a trial to clear his name, which empty procedure was then duly observed.[95] The acquittal did him little good. He was forced out of court, and in 1594 again joined forces with the Catholic earls, whom he had assisted in 1589. This time the king was more secure on his throne. Eventually, with the support of the Kirk and of England, James was able to force the Catholic earls into exile. Bothwell also fled in 1595, and the realm was forever after free from his restless energies.

The significance of all this is not easy to summarize. The records furnish interesting information about the commonly accepted beliefs and practices of witchcraft, details that reveal prosaic, homely, crude, rather unimaginative, and sometimes disgusting practices. On the political side they are irritatingly obscure. Did Bothwell instigate the practices against the king? It was not incompatible with his unstable nature, but capacity for it does not prove the fact, as one of his clerical defenders was careful to point out.[96] He had little respect for the king, but it is doubtful that he ever hoped to supplant James on the throne, since there were nearer heirs than he. Miss M. A. Murray makes much of the meager hint in the dittay of Barbara Napier's jurors that the witches planned the poisonous concoction to be used against the king, "that ane vther mycht haif rewlit in his Maiesties place, and the ward mycht haif gane to the Dewill."[97] She suggests that possibly Bothwell himself played the role of the devil in the North Berwick Kirk on All Hallows' E'en, haranguing the witches and taking part in their evil plottings.[98] The hypothesis, brilliant, daring, and suggestive as it is, seems open to serious doubt. To be sure, the assembled wizards and witches were apparently persons of low social standing, unlikely to have known Bothwell by sight, on whom such a hoax could have been perpetrated. Yet the large number alleged to have been present on that occasion, seven score, may easily have included persons to whom Bothwell's appearance was known. Moreover, Barbara Napier, Euphemia MacCalzean, and possibly Fian and Agnes Sampson may have been shrewd enough to penetrate the disguise, though, of course, they may have been willing accomplices in such a fraud. And what of

Richie Graham? Was he bribed by the king and Maitland with the hope of his life to testify against Bothwell, as the earl repeatedly asserted?[99] The king's care to see that Graham in prison had "his ordinaire allouaince quhill I take farther ordoure uith him"[100] may hint at that, though Graham's execution in the spring of 1592 would seem to indicate bad faith on the king's part—perhaps to get rid of a person whose continued existence (would he reverse his evidence?) might embarrass the king. Graham's execution may also have been meant to appease the Kirk ministers, angry with the king because of his failure to prosecute the chief murderers of "the bonnie Earl of Murray," who had been slain February 7, 1592. Graham's death weakened the king's cause when Bothwell finally came to trial in August, 1593, during the brief period of his ascendancy. Bothwell's counsel then argued with telling effect:

> It was further approved there by thexaminacions, that Greyme did never accuse Bothwell in any thing till such tyme as he had a warrant under the councelles handes (which were these, therle of Mourton, the Chancelor, the Kinges advocate, Sir John Carmighell, Sir George Hume and divers others), that if he wold speake simply and trewly what he knewe, his life should be preserved, and he should lyve in Sterling castle, where he should feare no mans mallice and have good allowance. After which warrant, then in all his depositions ever after he toucht Bothwell.
>
> To which point Bothwelles counsell did alledge that the Kinges counsell by there owne dede had quitted Bothwell, "for" (say they) "you have promised him-under your handes that if he spoke simplye and trewlie and nothing but the trothe, he should have his lyfe and be manteyned nowe. So that in taking away of his life you have proved his accusations to be untrewe." Ther came in divers honest men of Edenbroughe that were deposed that Richard Greyme said to theme that he must eyther accuse the Erle Bothwell falselye, or els endure such tormentes as no man were able to abyde.[101]

But who was telling the truth? No party seemed to have a monopoly of it. In fact, one doubts that any party concerned in this tale had had long and intimate and loyal contact with "the truth." Clearly, some, if not all, of the witches' testimony was given under torture or threat of torture.[102] And, while it was remarked that, of all the witches who suffered death, only Richard Graham maintained to the end that Bothwell was guilty of evil practices,[103] this in itself proves little. When death came so close to these witches and wizards, who could tell whether they were true to the devil and therefore persistently refused to reveal their compact with him or were sincere in alleging their innocence of any of these practices?

Thus the whole episode remains shrouded in doubts and uncertainties. The fragmentary records excite curiosity and speculation and offer no solution. The absence of some of the most important items, such as the depositions of Fian, Sampson, Napier, MacCalzean, and Graham, in itself may be significant. Bothwell called attention to this when he wrote of his persecutors: "In sign and token that they themselves are ashamed of the iniquity of that process of witchcraft, in my opinion they have destroyed the same, for neither is it extant in the books 'adjurnall' nor to be found out in any 'scrowlis' [drafts]."[104] It is equally plausible that Bothwell's partisans had destroyed the records.[105]

From it all one can venture little in the way of conclusion. A number of luckless individuals met death, and the incident touched off a period of witch persecution which did not abate until 1597. Some of the victims met their end with courage and constancy, whether to God or the devil one cannot truly say. James VI had been given an opportunity at first hand to learn much detail about witchcraft as believed and practiced in his time, information which he used several years later in composing his *Daemonologie*. Many passages in it quite clearly reflect these 1590–91 examinations. But in the light of history, neither king nor Bothwell, the two chief antagonists, comes off well. The king, in starting proceedings against the earl and not finishing, was guilty of, at best, poor timing; at worst, poor judgment. The inability to complete the prosecution may well be attributed to the factious state of the Scottish nobility. John Colville (Bothwell's partisan, to be sure) wrote that the nobility

knew that the King had na just occasioun of greif, nor cryme to allege aganis him, bot onlie at the instigation of Chanciller Maitland, whome thay all haittit to the death for his prowd arrogance usit in Denmarc aganis the Erle Marshall ambassador.

Indeid the municipall law of Scotland beris, That whasoever salbe fundin to consult with sorcerers, witches or suthesayers, thay shall déé the death.

Bot this law was never heirtofore put in practise, and tharefore the nobilitie thoght, that thay would not begin a preparative upon a member of their awin.[106]

It was, indeed, a severe political defeat for the king. Ultimately he triumphed over Bothwell, but the humiliation of this temporary check in 1591 could only serve to make his hatred of the earl more bitter.

Most of those who suffered death seem to have been practicing witches. Quite clearly, Dr. Fian, Agnes Sampson, Richard Graham, and probably Euphemia MacCalzean belonged in that category, as did various other more obscure figures. Barbara Napier, who consulted with witches, though she may not have practiced the black arts herself, possibly escaped with her life. Bothwell certainly did. To be sure, the evidence against him, as against Napier, was primarily for consulting with witches and hiring them to use their art against the king, rather than for directly practicing witchcraft. But to the modern observer it seems a miscarriage of justice for numerous "little people" to suffer torture and capital punishment for practicing witchcraft both on their neighbors and against the king, while a nobleman, secure because of his title, his friends among the nobility, and his popularity, already guilty of the heinous crimes of murder[107] and rebellion against the king, should escape when he may have been guilty of employing these same "little people" for treason against the king.

One last observation seems appropriate. Popular opinion is powerful, as James had frequent occasion to know. A curious comment on the force of public opinion in Scotland can be gleaned from the letter of one William Hunter, evidently an "intelligencer" writing to Lord Burghley from Edinburgh in June, 1591, shortly after Bothwell's escape from the Castle:

. . . and notwithstanding off the heynous crymis laid to his [Bothwell's] chairge, yitt I assuir yowr honour all Scottland doith allow of his libertie, except itt be suche as bearis thair awin perticurlaris. The moist part off the nobill men and hoill comonis ar prevelie on his syd, notwithstanding he is . . . foirfalltitt.

And, further, speaking of the precarious situation of Chancellor
Maitland, who was much hated: ". . . the comon rwmour is rissin
on him, wiche in this cwntrie, whear the pepill ar wndanttitt, is
a verrie evill sygne."[108] Bothwell, if he had come to trial in 1591
and if the evidence against him had been deemed valid, might
have been condemned legally in accordance with the 1563 statute.
He owed his temporary immuniy to several factors, his own "agil-
itie of body and mind," his friends among the nobility, and, lastly,
the force of public opinion. Perhaps James VI, the apostle of di-
vine right and enemy of democracy, had this in mind when he
wrote the *Daemonologie* in 1597 and spoke of the great wicked-
ness of the people as one cause for the prevalence of witchcraft.[109]

LOS ANGELES DIARY

By Elinor Castle Nef

1414 North Benton Way
Los Angeles, California
January 22, 1932

"CITY LIGHTS"

THE Los Angeles theater, which opened with so much éclat last year when Charlie Chaplin's *City Lights* was shown for the first time, is dark. The flamboyant edifice, which was supposed to embody all the latest improvements and, besides, to be the most luxurious theater *in the world,* could not make money enough to cover overhead expenses. As we shot down Broadway this afternoon in our 1931 hired Buick sedan, I saw the darkened entrance, the boarded-up ticket office, in front of which a blind man with a long white beard sat selling pencils. For a moment I seemed to feel beneath my feet the fabulously thick carpet with the ugly pattern, and to be blinded again by the dazzling lights of the foyer, to smell the too strong perfumes as brilliantly overdressed ladies wafted by, while a wizened-looking little Jew in full dress and a high silk hat talked confidentially in audible tones to another fatter Jew in the same elegant clothes and hat. "He ain't got de situvation," he pronounced with gloomy prophetic satisfaction, while an onlooker nudged his companion and pointed out the two men as famous movie producers.

The feature of this remarkable building which I remembered best was the retiring room, where mothers who had brought babies to the show could retire to still their crying or change their diapers without missing any of the picture, for there in the little room were ear-phones which they could slip on during operations and follow the dialogue. This street, then, was Broadway, where on the magic opening night of the theater and of Charlie Chaplin's *City Lights* we had struggled through the massed crowd which stood so long to catch a glimpse of the "stars" as they

119

emerged from their cars and passed under the blaze of the Klieg lights. There they paused to speak a greeting into the microphone to the audience inside the theater and to that far more enormous, scattered, incalculable radio audience who were listening from their front rooms, from all the dingy, grotesque, anonymous little bungalows, which mile after mile border the broad streets and spread out for no reason, without a plan, over the hills in an endless jumbled agglomeration. The crowd in the street was apathetic. When I pleaded with one man, against whom I was jammed, to lean forward and touch the shoulder of the policeman at the edge of the crowd and attract his attention for me so that I could enlist his aid in getting my party and another party which had attached itself to my leadership, into the street and to the entrance of the theater, he only looked at me vaguely and continued to stand. No one demurred or showed any enthusiasm for the stars or any annoyance with me, as, standing on tiptoe, I reached over the heads of the crowd and managed to grasp the Sam Browne belt over the policeman's shoulder and hold it firmly until his attention and assistance were secured. "Where's Mother?" I anxiously asked John, as we stood at last safe on the sidewalk in the glare of the lights. The announcer took up my question and passed it on: "Young lady is asking for her mother," he boomed into the microphone. Aunt Florence, who heard it from her bed, said jokingly to the cook and maids who were listening with her, "Well, that might be Elinor."

As we passed the darkened theater today, I remembered that Hearst, the great newspaper publisher and multimillionaire, had come in with Marion Davies and a party; she shook her blond curls, but showed no anger when it was found that there were not enough seats. I remembered that the uniformed attendant gave to every ticket-holder a box of candy from Stendahl, the Los Angeles picture dealer and candy manufacturer, and I remembered that Mrs. Stevens, a friend of my mother's, had told the Philadelphia lady, in Pasadena for the winter with her husband, that an explosion in the gas main under the street in front of one of these theaters on a similar opening night had been plotted and brought about by angry Communists, who were furious to think that rich people could pay five dollars a seat for tickets to these movie opening nights when they were out of work. We ourselves had read in an obscure part of the paper that the explosion was caused by defective materials or workmanship in laying the pipes and to their undue heating by the Klieg lights.

Our car slowed up for a red light, then started off at the "Go" signal. I began to look at the crowds on the sidewalks and in the street.

January 25, 1932

THE HAT SHOP

In a certain part of Los Angeles there is a street which for two or three blocks runs downhill alongside a small park containing a number of trees and some grass, a few benches, and a small artificial lake. On the park side of the street there are no buildings. On the other side there are two garages, a closed and boarded-up motion-picture theater with a few old advertisements still inclosed in glass cases and the box office sadly broken, a chain drugstore, a sidewalk newsstand with the garish magazines spread out on the sidewalk, a cheap lunch-counter, and two small hat shops. I had set out with the maid after lunch to buy a cake for dinner, as the cook considered herself too indisposed to bake one. While a mechanic in the garage was changing a worn-out tire of our car for a new one, I wandered into the street with the maid in search of a toothbrush. On our way to the drugstore we passed a small hat shop with an array of smart-looking, new black straws in the window. I looked in, pausing a moment, and she looked in. On our way back to the garage, we both looked in again, and I said, "That's just what you need for your new black silk dress. Would you like to go in and try some on?"

We went into a small, nondescript shop. There were a number of hats on long stands in the window; a shelf running along the wall contained a few more; there was a tall mirror and a table before which you sat down to try on hats; there was a hand mirror, two old-fashioned wardrobe cupboards at the back, a square of plain carpeting which took the chill off the stone floor in the middle of the room, a table with nothing on it, a rocking chair painted white, and wallpaper which was peeling off the wall. Pale California sunshine flooded the bare and shabby room. As we opened the door a nicely dressed man with a slight foreign accent to his American-English offered to show us hats. A tall, willowy woman, the only other person in the shop, when I pointed out the hat I particularly liked and indicated that it was for my companion, spoke a few words of rapid French to her husband and brought out two hats which she held up for our inspection. They had had two shops in Paris, one which he stayed in all day while she kept the other, one Rue Lecourbe and one Boulevard de Clichy, he said. I tried to remember the thriving middle-class and artists' quarter, where clean, bare streets run uphill, where there are theaters, Lugné Poë's Théâtre de l'Œuvre, the Grand Guignol, the antiquated and *passé* Moulin Rouge, *boîtes—les boîtes de Montmartre*—little restaurants, small, middle-class, purely French shops, five-story apartment buildings, a bridge over the Métro. The painter Jules Pascin lived in that neighborhood on the fifth floor of a big apartment building with a steep stairway, and from the French door and balcony of his larger studio room with its northeast exposure he could see a perspective of Paris roof tops, houses all about a uniform height, and a long, narrow street crowned by the mosque-like, sugar-loaf domes of the Sacré Cœur. Rue Lecourbe, that is different, a dreary street, where the buildings and the sidewalks and cobblestones look so old and stained and dark you think it could never look bright again; you think the *loge du concierge* can never be aired of the stuffy smell of old and new cooking and musty carpets and hangings and chairs and slept-in bed linen. I have driven or walked over it a score of times when we lived in the Ingres apartment on the Avenue de Saxe behind the Invalides. If she lived near there, she must have rubbed shoulders with me Monday or Thursday morning in the open-air market of the Avenue de Saxe. On the card which topped a neat pile of cards just beside the door was written:

MADAME
before buying your hat
     look
       "Chez" Maria Gérard
       formerly 86 Rue Lecorbe
Paris, France

"The printers made a mistake and left out the *u* in Lecourbe," the man explained, handing me the card, which he saw me looking at with curiosity.

The little maid was handling and turning about a hat. "Try it on," I said, and, smoothing her curly, rather greasy hair, she pulled the hat on awkwardly, simply put the hat on her head without any style or tactful emphasis.

"C'est bien, c'est très seyant, ne trouvez vous pas?" I said, joining with the woman in French remarks. She tried on another hat.

"Vous permettez?" asked the woman eagerly and snatched the hat she had laid on the table. Madame Gérard removed a little knitted sweater she had been wearing over her black dress, with a graceful, rapid gesture smoothed her curly chestnut hair, and, giving exactly the right turn of her wrist, pulled the hat down over her face, then stood very erect with her thin, tan, expressive, sharp face slightly lifted to show the hat.

Immediately an old forgotten picture flashed through my mind. "She's older than I am and yet"—there was a remembered momentary surprise that a wrinkled woman, that is, a not impeccably smooth-faced young woman like myself, should think to sell me a hat by trying it on herself, without any apology for her age, or the pouches under her eyes, or her stout matronly figure, as if she were better looking than I! So I had thought as I turned about in my chair in the elegant hat shop in the Rue de la Paix and watched Madame Berthe turn her head for me to see how good-looking the hat really was. I remember her intelligent, not unfriendly eyes, as she showed me, and gradually, after my first shock at the unsuitability of an older woman imagining hats would look better on her than on me, some inkling of the art of what she wished to teach me, with which she informed her gestures and movements, penetrated to my mind. I remembered the scene perfectly as I looked at the tall, slender Frenchwoman showing the cheap black straw hat in a shabby shop in Los Angeles, and I murmured a few complimentary words about the hat. Her eyes flashed, and she burst out with vehement excitement:

"Madame, je n'ai jamais vu une femme bien chapotée en Amérique" ("I've never seen a woman with her hat on right in America!"). I glanced hurriedly into the glass, gave my own hat a hasty twitch as she proceeded: "Imaginez vous qu'on est obligé de mettre un fil dans tous les chapeaux—un fil blanc," she cried in shocked despair, "pour indiquer le milieu du chapeau—pour montrer comment il faut mettre le chapeau" ("Can you imagine, you have to put a white thread in every hat to mark the center, to show how the hat should be put on").

I remonstrated with her, her husband remonstrated with her. I said, "You shouldn't judge the whole country by Los Angeles." I was seeing that immensely smart, perpendicular, ragged brown feather of Mrs. Waller Borden's hat, visible over the heads of the great crowd of lunch guests at the Council on Foreign Relations when Mr. Harold Moulton spoke about Japan and China. Her husband seemed to be consoled and strengthened, upheld by my stricture against Los Angeles, as if he had often said the same thing to her, only with less assurance, but had doubted when he said it whether there were many people who would agree, had wondered whether other cities were not like this one.

"Has Madame been to New York?" I asked with an accent of sincere incredulity, already sensing the other criticisms and disillusionments which were bursting to be spoken to me because I seemed to understand and could speak French faster than her husband could or at least with a better accent and with some intermingling of Gallicisms. "Has she seen New York? What port did you sail into after all?"

He said: "Of course, we were a week in New York, but it was so cold she was in bed with a cold and I could not take her out to show her anything." And she with a little air of uncertainty and reluctant concession admitted that she thought she would have been very nicely suited in New York. There was a city where she would have pleased herself. If they had set up a shop there, they would probably have found that the customers would know what was smart, what was good. He explained that it was impossible for her to attempt to live in New York, where it was so cold, that the California climate was necessary.

"You don't like America?" I asked in a disappointed tone.

Again he explained, "The American people are the most friendly and hospitable in the world and the most friendly socially, but not to do business with. They are the hardest to do business with, terrible. Imagine, Madame, we came over to this country with forty French hats, beautiful, hand-made hats with beautiful workmanship, only the smartest models which we had brought with us from Paris and real straw, very fine. We got a shop on 7th Street, downtown. And what do you think? Nobody, nobody would buy those hats. Not one hat. They said they were too extreme. They didn't like it because they were too plain. All they wanted was hats with a bandeau on the forehead and a row of flowers." He looked at me with absolute despair.

"Of course," I said soothingly, "they wanted styles that were already two or three years old in Paris."

He said, "The crowns were draped like what you see now—what Reboux and all the French shops are showing still in Paris." He went to a shelf in the wardrobe and brought me a brown turban as light as a feather, made of softest pliable straw, sewn with wise skill and impeccable workmanship, tiny stitches catching the straw and molding it to clever, sophisticated, simple lines. She slipped it on her head—a perfect, elegant hat.

"Of course, if it were new I wouldn't have this bow," she explained of a neat and dapper little bow, "and you realize that this is now a year old. I have just steamed it and put it in condition again." I admired the hat with a little of the warmth it deserved.

He said: "I wish now I had kept all the forty hats. I became so discouraged I sold them for two dollars apiece." Again his voice had its accent of despair and incredulity. "This is the only one we have kept. My wife has worn it a year. It is not one of the best, but what could we do? The people did not appreciate the style, the fine workmanship, or the good quality of the straw. They only wanted hats with high crowns or with lace and a feather and a flower." Their eyes opened in mute incredulity and incomprehension. And again he brought out of the armoire a hat, a purple straw, brought to them to be remodeled for two dollars, with purple lace and a flower. She held the hat up with an air of helpless condemnation. She professed herself at a loss how to deal with it. She made it plain that it was revolting to her to do work which was not as good as she knew how to do, or to modify the good taste she had been taught in order to please people who have no taste.

"At one time, now let me tell you," he said, "at one time I was doing business with a firm in Paris which made hats for the American market. The buyer, a stout New York woman, middle-aged, came to look at our hats. She picked out a nice little hat, very chic, then she said, 'Now can't you put on a ribbon?' But such a ribbon! She wanted a great big bow and a long ribbon like this with streamers. Ridiculous. We thought she was joking. No, she said, otherwise they wouldn't buy. When I showed the hat and explained what she wanted to our *première,* the head girl in the workroom, a very clever girl, she had worked for years for Maria Guy, you know, she laughed and wouldn't believe me when I told her to spoil the hat. And this buyer was no fool either, she knew what was right for herself, but she ordered the other kind for that big New York department store."

I pointed admiringly to a neat little number. "That's a hat you must sell?" I asked with interest.

"Exactly. It is very smart," said the woman. "In Paris I would sell that by the hundred, but here it's too plain. They want ribbons. They want it changed. Turned up more here."

"But why don't you tell them that it is smart this way?" I asked.

"They all have their own ideas. They won't listen. They think they know better than I. If I try to say this hat is becoming; this is very smart; this is a good line, they grab the hat with their hands and take it off their head. 'I know what I like, I know what's right!' they say. What's the use of trying to say anything?" She looked at me intently as if she had reached the really important part of her story. "Madame," she said, "they come into my shop and try on every hat two, three, four, a dozen times before they buy a hat worth $2.75. But that would be all right, I shouldn't mind if they ended by buying the right thing, but after taking all this time they buy the wrong hat. Do you understand? If even they bought a good hat, something that made them look nice or went with their dress, good-looking or becoming, or suitable, but after all their time and my time wasted they buy the wrong hat." I felt the justice of the criticism.

At that moment two women, a mother and daughter, paused to look into the window.

"*Tiens*—See, see," cried the tall Frenchwoman. "Madame,

allow me to present to you Pola Negri." She gave a flourish of the hand.

"Yes, can you believe," her husband explained to me, "this girl thinks she resembles Pola Negri. She has often told us she has been mistaken for Pola Negri." He glanced at me with a look which seemed to say, "Being used to the ways of the world, by this time nothing surprises me." The girl was short, rather thick-set, with a straight nose and dark eyes, not a particularly pretty face, and too much rouge. Her age was about thirty-four or thirty-five years. She wore a well-made, close-fitting brown straw turban, molded to her head and becoming, with a red and gray and blue plaid coat trimmed with black fur. They stood looking in the window, and then, apparently discovering a hat they had not yet tried on, they turned to come in the door.

"They made half a dozen trips to buy that brown hat at $2.75," said the Frenchwoman vehemently. "Now you'll see." I stood back against the wall, talking to the man as the two women entered and began to try on hats—the new one they had not tried on at their last visit, and the others they had tried on. The French milliner greeted them with requisite cordiality, which they appeared to accept as their due, without in turn making any special effort to show friendliness to her or to her husband. They both tried on the new hats. The girl looked very well in two rather dapper little hats. She removed her coat and showed a perfectly good-looking dress which bore no relation either to the hat or the coat which she wore; it was a nice-looking green dress. She tried on several hats which looked well. Then the girl reverted to the tip-tilted hat trimmed with a vivid pink velvet ribbon, a cluster of blue flowers, and a pale pink gardenia. At this point the husband went forward again as he had done already once or twice.

"Yes, I like this all right," vouchsafed the girl, "only I would like this flower to be deep pink like the ribbon."

"Very well," said the Polish-American husband, "let us order for you a deep pink flower, we will be glad to do so, it will only take until tomorrow, we will be glad to do so." The girl took the hat off, gave one more look around. The woman removed the hat in which she had been walking about the shop, and they both put on their own hats; they said nothing; they gathered together their bags and gloves and started out the door without saying thank you and with an air of being well within their rights, as if they were amused by the eagerness of the shopkeeper and his wife.

"We'll be back again," they promised magnanimously.

The door swung to behind them; they made their way on up the street. The mother had on very long skirts, the daughter had on a dress which reached just to the middle of her thick calves.

"If there is anything in the world I cannot abide," said the Frenchwoman, "it is fat legs. Those terrible fat legs." As we stood looking out, several unlovely types passed walking up the street.

"Imagine I have to look out at that all day. Oh, no, Madame, it is too much. Girls in evening dresses in the daytime with no stockings, wearing sport coats."

January 1932

THE SYRIAN LINEN SALESMAN

"As shoppers, Americans won't take advice," the Syrian linen salesman said. "They are obstinate, they think they know what they want. They think they are good shoppers, but they aren't. Going shopping to them, that means shopping around. In the old country if a woman went out to buy a piece of silk, she felt it with her fingers, and held it in her hand or used a match to it—some trick her mother taught her. When the salesman had put three or four pieces of silk before her, she knew which was the best. Now, if a woman goes in to buy a piece of silk and they show her several pieces, she doesn't know which is the best. They tell her this costs fifty cents a yard more than the other, and she thinks if she takes the piece that costs more she has bought something better. Or they say this is Mallinson's Pussy Willow, and she is satisfied. She buys it even if they show her something twice as good. She buys by name. American women will take up a lot of time, go to several stores in order to be sure to get the best and cheapest, then in the end they will buy something that is not good. They buy the wrong thing and pay more for it than they should, because they are all tired out."

"Why don't they take advice?" I asked.

"Because they think they know what they want. They are obstinate. Some woman comes perhaps from Iowa, another from Boston, one perhaps from Cairo, or Ireland, or Germany or Czechoslovakia. It takes many years to learn what is right. Ten, twelve years," he said.

"Why is it," a French milliner the other day complained to me, "people will not buy the right thing—they always want something changed? 'It would be all right perhaps if this flower were not such a pale pink,' they say."

"Because of the great variety of persons who come to this country each with their different ideas," the Syrian linen salesman said, "nobody makes any money here now except the big stores and the eating places. The big stores on their cheap articles, the eating places, and the ten-cent stores." I asked why that was.

"Because there is too much competition," he said.

"Do all these small shops lose money?" I asked.

"Yes, they either lose money or they lose their time," he said, "or if they make a little money they use it for rent or for living expenses. For instance, a couple buys a small business for say five thousand dollars, then after a year or two they will sell it for maybe four thousand."

"What happens then?" I asked.

"Well, somebody else buys it. These small businesses are always changing hands. Look at Wrigley's fortune," he said. "What is that he made it on—not even the best gum. In Lebanon in Syria, there is a gum the young boys chewed for fun, much better than that. They always said to the young boys, 'Do not chew it or your moustache will grow crooked.' But think of the American public buying that gum, it is not even the best gum." He named a gum he thought was better, "the flavor lasts longer," he said. "They do not know what is good. They buy by name. Look at the cigarettes. Kind to your throat—it soothes your throat." He gave a laugh. "My professor at college in Beirut said the right thing. He said if God created man to smoke, he would have made a hole in the top of his head for the smoke to come out. Yes," he said, "I just started to smoke last year, a few cigarettes a month, just because I got tired of everybody talking about how I never smoked, you know."

February 20, 1936
"STAGE DOOR JOHNNY"

We drove to town last night to a small ten-cent movie theater on South Broadway, to try to see *Stage Door Johnny,* an old single-reeler of Charlie Chaplin's, a film made about twenty years ago. When we arrived at the theater, the ticket girl informed us the film had already been shown and would not be shown again.

"Couldn't you run it off for us again?" I asked, showing my disappointment.

"You'll have to ask the manager," she said, "there right behind you on the sidewalk." She pointed to a thin, gray-haired little man, neatly dressed in a cheap, gray suit.

But no amount of gentle, reasonable, or impassioned pleading could induce him to run the film for us. Although we offered to pay extra and to tip the operator generously, although he admitted that it took only six or seven minutes to run, and that one feature was still running, to be followed by another soon, the last of the evening. Although he did not deny that it would be easy to slip the Chaplin short in between the two features and that the theater was half-empty, anyway, he made one excuse, then another. He explained that the delivery man would be calling for the film "any minute." "Probably some other theater is waiting for it right now for a midnight show." He'd love to do it for us, but "Union operators are very strict, you know, lady." He made his excuses one after another as if he didn't mean them, or expect me to believe them.

The ticket girl put up a placard "Box Office open at 9:00 A.M." The money in two bags was rushed by an attendant into a side room off the outer lobby, while a tall, unshaven man with bad teeth loitered in the entrance, eyeing us and grinning intermittently. The glass box office was closed, the ticket girl said a smiling, impartial good night and went home. The ticket girl had remained carefully impartial. French bystanders often take sides, I thought.

The manager emerged from the side room, and the tall, unshaven loiterer, his hand very obviously on a gun in his back pocket, accompanied him down the street.

Two boys removed the large placards advertising the day's features. One of them told me the man who called for the films wouldn't come until after twelve and would let himself in with his own key. The lights over the marquee were switched off.

A scattering of the audience began to come out of the theater at the end of the first feature. Poorly dressed elderly couples, a Chinaman in a leather coat, a bell-boy still wearing his uniform, one or two Mexican families, the boys with the collars of their thin suits turned up for warmth, some young people. All walked aimlessly and slowly, looking sad, and at a loss. We sat on the fender of a shabby old car parked exactly opposite the box office and waited for John to come back. He had gone to the nearby post office, which is open all night, to buy stamps and mail letters, while we stood talking with the manager, I pleading, my companion looking noncommittal. Presently the owner of the car arrived, the tall, unshaven fellow who had accompanied the manager when he left the theater.

It's interesting to watch people come out of movie houses. Two hours later, when we came out of one of the big expensive, downtown theaters, after seeing *The Petrified Forest,* the slightly better-dressed, slightly more prosperous crowd emerging from the theater mostly in silence had the same listless walk and faces. I overheard one woman say: "Leslie Howard is always pretty good in those kind of half-crazy parts."

John and I praised the film, which is "forceful and compact," sincerely written, and beautifully acted, seeming, for all the dramatic tension, real and probable and dealing in values which are not material. I have never seen a gangster before who excited pity rather than envy or loathing. Our companion made only one comment:

"I wonder what the American Legion will think of the way it poked fun at the Legion?"

"Heavens, that! That wasn't serious, it was the smallest part of the film. You mean the part about the father dressing up in his uniform and going to the meeting. The Vigilantes, they called them."

"Oh, it was thinly disguised, the blow was blunted."

"How about the intellectuals, it pokes fun at them, doesn't it?"

"But how do you think the Legion will like it?" he repeated, as if their opinion were what mattered about the film.

"They can't take it?" I said slangily. "Can't the Legionnaires be grown up and take it? In France, in a French play they poke fun at everything, especially the French."

I felt relieved, thinking of France as an oasis. Oasis of freedom? Mirage? Only last week Léon Blum, the deputy, was attacked by a gang of Camelots du Roi as he was driven home from the Chamber of Deputies. The Action Française, every day, incites royalists to violence. Will France change? Become like Germany? Like America?

I thought of the two audiences we had seen. Were the audiences sad and listless because they have seen so many bad films? Are the films bad because the audiences are so apathetic, because they cannot tell good from bad, truth from sham? How can one expect people to develop standards of taste, I wondered, if they must carefully hold judgment in abeyance until they know—for instance—"what the Legion will think"?

We slid smoothly over the hills and down, in our splendid car —last year's Buick—driving home through the broad, half-empty streets, past ramshackle bungalows elbowing each other on yawning embankments or seeming to sink into the soft, untidy earth. Large, flimsy, temporary-looking markets, still open at midnight and picturesquely gay with their displays of fruit and vegetables, caught one's attention, or brightly lit, empty gas stations, or enormous billboards depicting larger-than-life-size, highly colored people and objects impervious to the weather and the hour. We drove swiftly over excellently paved streets through the city littered with houses whose hideous architectural disparity we no longer observed, through some older streets lined with old palms or acacia trees, where small wooden bungalows in close sequence are set off by lawns embellished by bushes and flowers. When a traffic light stopped us, a boy or elderly man would step up to the car and offer us for a few cents tomorrow morning's newspaper, the future entertainment and opinions of the people who live in those houses and visit the movies.

There is something about the disposition and grouping of streets and houses, churches and public buildings, shops and public squares in a French town, I thought, which conveys a more intense sense of life, of the reality and continuity of authority. The authority is old, the buildings are old. You can recognize a post office. Restaurants are where they should be. Eating habits are orderly. Everything speaks of old habits, of patterns of conduct slowly devised, handed down from generation to generation, and shared by everyone. A pharmacy is a pharmacy, where people go to buy pills, bandages, remedies, not to telephone, buy cigarettes, pick up magazines, drink a soda or a cup of coffee, eat a sandwich or a plate of meat and gravy, listen to the radio, or take chances on a gambling game. The people make their own every foot of the town, walk and meet and talk on the streets; they stop on the streets, which are more than thoroughfares. There the streets unite the people in their living, here they interrupt living. If this must be, since the coming of the motorcar, then let us follow Le Corbusier and lift the streets above the earth, away from the city, let them be *autostrades,* impersonal, efficient, raised highways. Where are the symbols of our common life, I wondered, glancing at a huge, brightly colored billboard. The advertisements, the gas stations. And authority is transmitted by the traffic lights, vested in the newspapers.

Americans—*easy to fool, hard to convince,* I said, inventing an epigram to describe my friends—most of my friends—and acquaintances, and those strangers who are my compatriots, movie audiences, newspaper readers, voters, buyers, radio listeners.

"I suppose they imagine," said John, "that by being hard to convince, they make up for. . . ."

"For being easy to fool!"

"Bad reasoners vehemently given to opposition," I said, quoting Swift.

As we drove along I thought of the little manager who talked to me indifferently on the sidewalk in front of the cheap movie theater on South Broadway. He did not hesitate for a moment in his blank refusal, he would not stop to consider my request. His imagination remained untouched. He did not indicate the slightest impulse of sympathy for us as his fellow-men—either for our eagerness or for our disappointment—he showed not the faintest curiosity as to our interest in Chaplin. I can hear a Frenchman with a slightly amused, superior smile stopping in the middle of our discussion or business to ask skeptically: "Quoi, vous l'aimez tant que ça?" "Vous y tenez tellement?" marveling moderately, possibly disagreeing, yet understanding very well. He would look us over with a spark of interest, size us up, give advice, express his opinion of Chaplin in general and of this film in particular. He would probably make a mental note to reconsider for his own pleasure Charlie's merits. He would rapidly turn over in his mind the circumstances; weigh the convenience or inconvenience of obliging us; make a rapid reckoning of the gain which would accrue; satisfy himself as to the truth of our statements and the reasonableness of our request. And if he consented, it would not be because the favor was asked by someone famous or rich or influential; he would consent almost as readily for us, or any other anonymous individual. Nor would the interview be a barren, literal exchange, there might be a joke, some bit of philosophy expressed. Each might learn from the encounter.

What about the little American manager? Was he too lazy to undertake the simple arrangement? In his tiny, half-empty theater, to depart by six or seven minutes from his routine? Afraid of being told on? Of losing his job? Had he not sufficient independence in his job to make such an unimportant decision on his own initiative? One knew from looking at him that his flat and lame refusal was not based on any moral grounds. He would do wrong fast enough, I thought. Besides, we were not asking that he do wrong, it would only have required a slight deviation from routine. And what would that require? The patience necessary to listen to an argument; the ability to judge circumstances as they arise on their merits, to make readily small adjustments (to readjust one's plans); the possession of sufficient independence to make decisions on one's own account—not all decisions, some decisions —and certainly some feeling of security in his job, some confidence in his relation to his employer or superior officer and in that man's reasonableness. All these things, I think, the Frenchman would possess.

5650 Dorchester Avenue
Chicago, Illinois
May 4, 1936

In America, when motorists pass a man on the road asking for a lift, or see peculiar-looking people apparently in trouble with their car, they pass by quickly—step on the gas good and hard—turning away their eyes, refusing help or sympathy, because, after all, it may be a holdup. Several of our friends have been held up this way; you read about it daily in the papers.

The cheap little manager with his lame excuses was thinking of the cash, perhaps? Getting it safely away with the protection of his tall, unshaven bodyguard?

Worrying about danger, safety, makes one forget the rest of life. In some countries people must worry about their safety far more constantly than in others.

While I thought about the cheap little manager, I was thinking also about the saleswomen, the delivery boys, the floormen in stores, who go to the movies, read the papers, listen to the radio, who are unable to make the smallest spontaneous action, are made stupid in the rigidity of their routine. Impervious to reason they are, I thought. I was thinking of this, because in Los Angeles there is a most excellent big department store where stupid rules are honestly broken every day. Once when I was on my way to catch a train I stopped at this store to make a purchase, all the saleswomen were busy with customers, so the floor man waited on me himself, he took the stocking boxes down from the shelves behind the counter and found me the required size and color, he completed the sale expeditiously. In another emergency I telephoned after the store had closed to inquire for a delivery which had not yet arrived. The night watchman who answered the telephone informed me that if the handbag I had bought to carry the next day, Sunday, with my new costume on an expedition to the desert did not arrive within the next hour or two he would telephone to someone in the handbag department to come downtown and select another handbag for me which would be delivered without fail that same evening. In a big organization they behaved the way I had become accustomed to observing people behave in a small place. In Bullocks the employees have zest, a flash of life, a look of common sense in their eyes. I don't say common sense because we repeat it so often tritely about the French, I mean it. Reasonableness. I experienced this twenty times in that one store, and was amazed.

"We're still on NRA rules here, you know," one saleswoman told me contentedly, "although Mr. So and So, the manager, doesn't want it known or talked about. People might become antagonized."

"Is he a democrat, or something, then?" I asked.

"I dunno, but we're still on it, and we like it fine," she volunteered. She stood there behind the counter, she wasn't waiting on me, or hoping to sell me anything. Someone else was waiting on me. She overheard a compliment I paid my own saleswoman whose patience and perseverance I praised. My saleswoman had finally found if not the article I asked for, anyway a satisfactory substitute. The other woman, without a customer for the moment, was listening, and she addressed me gratuitously from a desire to explain and give the reasons. In France I had become accustomed as a daily occurrence to being spoken to gratuitously when the remarks, not sales talk or selfish propaganda, were made to convey interesting information for a disinterested motive or for sheer love of communication and conversation, but I was delightfully surprised to find this aesthetic motivation operating in a Los Angeles department store.

Just now I said reminiscently to the nice young student who was typing this for me, "You know, it still makes me indignant, indignant isn't the word, thinking of that little manager."

"Oh, I know, it sounds as if you'd driven quite a way to get there!"

"It's not that only. He'd do wrong, it was written all over him that he'd do wrong. Besides this wasn't wrong, you know."

"Perhaps, then," said this young woman wisely, "that is why, if he'd do wrong, he had to be so careful about the little things."

In America when they're doing something they oughtn't to be, they're doing somebody dirt. The little manager wouldn't be doing anybody any harm by doing something irregular, by running the six- or seven-minute Chaplin "short" again, if indeed he should not have repeated it anyway in the last show, if indeed he had not deliberately dropped it from the program in order to get away earlier, or for some other reason I had no means of knowing.

I believe the American conception of conduct is more like the German than the French. (The American idea: It must be wrong to break a rule.) To me this episode raises one of the crucial questions of modern times; these people who break the rules honestly, reasonably, they are wiser than animals, they are more human than machines. With a machine you can turn on and off the electricity, switch on and off the radio; but a man can exercise judgment, can hesitate and change his mind, and consider the circumstances. I described this all to my painter friend, Laura Van Pappelendam, who suggests it's like the difference between a camera and an artist. The artist can select, can make judgments in his painting all the time, a camera cannot.

Monsieur Sée, the French historian, had been ill and kept indoors in his house in Rennes, for fifteen years. One spring day a dear friend persuaded him to venture out for his first drive in her closed limousine. They drove to a little town he had visited twenty-five years before. Nowadays there is a rule that no automobile may be allowed to enter the town. But when the lady explained to the guard at the gate the circumstances of Monsieur Sée's illness and his outing, the guard let their automobile enter the town, he made an exception to the rule. The French recognize this practice, have a witty phrase to describe it: *interdit mais toléré.*

Somehow I would like to make clear that this is not something done only for the rich. A friend of mine said, "No poor person would think of asking for a movie to be run over." "No, nor any rich person either," I replied. Consider this, then, just an illustration of a man's exercising his human judgment, to perform a kind act.

THE ROLE OF THE HOUSE OF COMMONS IN BRITISH FOREIGN POLICY DURING THE 1937–38 SESSION*

By MARION L. KENNEY

Wilmington, Delaware

MR. CHAMBERLAIN'S DECISION

THE role of the House of Commons in British foreign policy during the 1937–38 session of Parliament can be briefly stated—it was essentially that of the Greek chorus. The tragic hero was Neville Chamberlain, who destroyed himself and very nearly destroyed his country by his virtues and his faults. The chorus alternately defended his acts and gloomily foretold the horrors in store, but it was powerless to stay him from his course. In the Greek tragedies there is always some transgression or weakness in the hero which initiates the train of disasters, and the tragedy is the more poignant when, as in *Oedipus Rex,* the sin is unwitting. A similar poignancy is felt in Neville Chamberlain's tragedy, for he never understood wherein his fatal transgression lay. The sin he committed was not against France, or Abyssinia, or Spain, or Czechoslovakia, or Russia, but against the spirit of his own nation. In the twentieth century the proper part of the British House of Commons is not that of a Greek chorus, impotent to influence the decrees of fate. It is important to discover how it could have been relegated to such a role and how Neville Chamberlain came to play the part of the tragic hero.

As early as the spring of 1936, he seems to have reached a decision to secure for himself a dominant position in the formulation of British foreign policy. Through a combination of chance and fanatical determination, his goal was achieved and was dramatically signalized two years later by the resignation of his Foreign Secretary, Anthony Eden, on February 20, 1938.

* Part of a doctoral dissertation prepared under Conyers Read at the University of Pennsylvania and slightly adapted for the purpose of this article.

138

The importance of Mr. Eden's resignation did not lie in his own importance as a political force, but in the fact that it gave Mr. Chamberlain, in addition to the ultimate responsibility for foreign policy which he properly bore as Prime Minister, the possibility of controlling the day-to-day conduct of foreign affairs. This was a serious misfortune because of Mr. Chamberlain's readiness to adopt methods of personal diplomacy which isolated him from the House of Commons and played directly into the hands of Hitler and Mussolini. These methods could less easily have been employed during Mr. Eden's incumbency at the Foreign Office.

Mr. Chamberlain's tendencies were the more dangerous because of certain aspects of parliamentary democracy in Great Britain. By the 1930's it had come to be accepted that the House of Commons ought to participate in foreign policy in three ways:

1. It should hold the government to their duty of executing mandates given by the nation.
2. It should evaluate the necessity or desirability of any contemplated departures from the terms of these mandates.
3. Once the House was satisfied that a new course ought to be adopted, it was the duty of Members to impart their conviction to the public through speeches within the House and by various means outside in the constituencies.

It will be seen that Mr. Chamberlain's concept of his duty as Prime Minister and of his obligations to the House of Commons conflicted directly with these parliamentary axioms, which, however, were so universally believed by the country as a whole to be in effect that the assumptions upon which they rested were never questioned by any important segment of the citizenry. Actually, the first possibility had gone by the board in the 1935–36 session, with the wreck of the sanctions policy, and the last two were always largely contingent upon the willingness of the government to bring them into operation. If a Prime Minister has his party and cabinet well in hand and is fortified by a large majority of docile back-benchers, he need not give the House of Commons any real opportunity of evaluating a new policy. He can, instead, employ a formidable array of obstructive devices to postpone taking the House into his confidence until his new policy has been brought to a pitch that makes it psychologically impossible to force him to reverse it. Under Mr. Chamberlain the hard necessities of his appeasement policy gradually accelerated over a period of months and, by April, 1938, it was airborne and out of range of parliamentary control or even influence. The international situation had by that time become so critical that responsible statesmen of all parties were unwilling to bring on the kind of major, country-wide political upheaval which would have been necessary for reversal. Thenceforward, the closing of ranks against the gathering storm took first place in the minds of all who now agreed with Mr. Churchill that war was inevitable. When one remembers what national unity meant in 1940 in France and in Britain, it is hard to say that they were wrong—Munich or no Munich. This, however, does not exonerate Mr. Chamberlain, for he need not have gone on to Munich. He chose the position around which the closing of ranks had to occur.

There are indications that Mr. Chamberlain's decision to take over control of foreign policy was precipitated by the combined effect upon the prestige of the Conservative party in early 1936 of the Hoare-Laval fiasco, the sanctions controversy, and the reoccupation of the Rhineland, the resulting impression being catalyzed in his mind by the necessity he was under, as Chancellor of the Exchequer, for preparing a rearmament budget. It is fair to say, too, that the spectacle of a world rearming was a severe shock to his faith in progress. During the bitter debates of the 1937–38 session he often taunted his opponents with lack of realism; but he himself was long a victim of the illusion that mankind is wholly rational and that, if a rational argument could be brought effectively to the attention of Hitler and Mussolini, they would be moved to act in the direction of enlightened self-interest. He believed, and acted upon the belief, that in war there are no winners. This seemed so obvious and fundamental a truth to him that he never was able to understand that the European dictators' acts issued from completely different assumptions. At any rate, whatever his reasons, it is clear that, once his attention was seriously given to the dangerous international situation existing in the spring of 1936, he let nothing stand in his way—least of all, ethical considerations.

At the time when Mr. Chamberlain made the decision to give more attention than formerly to foreign policy, the cabinet had been studying a series of ominous dispatches and reports from British diplomats stationed in Berlin.[1] Presumably one such dispatch had led Sir Robert Vansittart to support Sir Samuel Hoare in his decision to sign the Laval agreement in December. This attempt to strengthen Britain's position by terminating the quarrel with Italy misfired, and Sir Samuel had to resign as Foreign Secretary. He soon returned to the cabinet, however, and thereafter formed part of a nucleus opposed to basing British foreign policy upon adherence to the League of Nations. After the reoccupation of the Rhineland, these men began to get the upper hand, and their position was greatly strengthened by Mr. Chamberlain's assumption of leadership.

There was now begun the long-drawn-out attempt to urge the government of Czechoslovakia to make concessions to the Sudeten Germans.[2] It was confined at first to recommending a settlement of the minorities question per se, as is shown by a letter from the British Minister to the Foreign Office, dated April 12, 1938:

In Mr. Eden's despatch No. 17 of March 12, 1937, which reached me shortly after my arrival in Prague, I was informed of the attitudes which His Majesty's Government had then decided to adopt towards firstly, Czechoslovakian relations with Germany, and, secondly, the Sudeten German question. With regard to the former, their conclusions may be shortly summarized by saying that they were not prepared to offer any advice, and still less to attempt any sort of mediation. With regard to the latter, I was instructed to continue to urge the importance of a far-reaching settlement, but for its own sake, and not because it might facilitate an agreement with Germany.[3]

The writer of this letter, Mr. Basil Newton, went on to say that his duties had been altered by the Prime Minister's speech of March 24, 1938, restating British policy in the light of Anschluss.

Thus, so long as Mr. Eden held office, British instructions to the Minister at Prague were in accordance with the spirit of the League of Nations and with the minorities provisions of the peace treaties. Only after Mr. Chamberlain had secured unrestricted control of foreign policy in February, 1938—for the new Foreign Secretary, Lord Halifax, never offered any effective opposition—

did intervention in Czechoslovakian foreign relations become official British policy.

In the two-year interval between the spring of 1936, when Mr. Chamberlain made his decision to engage more actively in the determination of British foreign policy, and the spring of 1938, when he actually achieved dominance, several major changes resulted in a serious deterioration of British national power. For some of these, Mr. Chamberlain bears a heavy, though not an exclusive, responsibility. By 1938 bad management of British rearmament had given Germany a much greater lead in the air and on land than she had possessed in 1936; France had been exposed to her enemies, isolated from her friends, and reduced by bullying and by her own internal weaknesses to a position of complete diplomatic subjection to Britain's leadership. Britain, already weakened diplomatically by loss of relative military power and by the diminished diplomatic importance of France, was rapidly dissipating her own diplomatic resources by an open policy of appeasement, which was carried to the point of antagonizing Russia and chilling relations with the United States.

THE POLITICAL SITUATION IN 1938

The possibility open to Mr. Chamberlain of wielding almost absolute power was an indirect result of Disraeli's famous "leap in the dark" which initiated the real political democratization of Great Britain in 1867. By 1938 the increased size of the electorate had brought with it an elaboration of party organization and increased election costs for the candidates, which, in turn, enabled the central offices of all parties to insist that candidates must, if aided by party funds, stand by the platforms laid down in party councils. Doctrine and discipline became rigid.

The party leader was very important—in the Conservative party he was the most important single element, and it was generally accepted that he would continue to function until he chose to resign. In the period we are considering, the Labour party was led by Clement Attlee, successor to the pacifist, George Lansbury, who had been ousted in 1935 after an attack by Ernest Bevin. Mr. Bevin had demanded that the pary should support the principle of collective security even if it led to the use of force, and he won his point. By the spring of 1938, however, collective security had already been abandoned by the government in favor of appeasement. Even if ultimately successful, as promised by Mr. Chamberlain, the new policy was attended by terrifying dangers. At the time of Mr. Eden's resignation these dangers had become so apparent that the Communists were encouraged to make renewed bids for a popular front which would include all those who were opposed to appeasement. It was thought briefly that a general election was a possibility, but a Labour party manifesto was issued which rejected the suggestion of a united fight by the Opposition parties. It was declared that a majority, even if obtainable, would leave the Labour party at the mercy of its allies; alliance with the Liberal party was dealt with by the manifesto in terms of friendship and respect, but the dangers of co-operation with the Communists were recounted with some bitterness.

In the House of Commons as it existed after the 1935 general election, the Liberal party had fewer seats than corresponded to its popular vote, and so, in accordance with the traditional spirit of fair play in the House, Liberal Members were allotted a larger proportion of debating time and enjoyed more importance than might be indicated by their numbers. Sir Archibald Sinclair was the party leader, but Lloyd George spoke frequently for a wing called the "Council of Action."

The government, since the defection of Ramsay MacDonald from the Labour party in 1931, had been in the hands of a coalition called the "National Government," which had long since become essentially conservative. Their majority had been much reduced by the general election of 1935, but it was still so large as to be impregnable in the absence of some profound change of opinion among the Conservative Members on the back benches. Several factors militated against a change of this sort within the House in 1938. Some of them were related to the following circumstances.

The vote increment due to plural voting in the 1935 election was about 5,000,000, and the Conservative party had won the election by no more than 2,000,000 votes. Since the plural rights were possessed chiefly by small tradesmen, lawyers, accountants, and doctors, a change in the attitude of any considerable number of the holders of the right might spell defeat for the Conservative party if an election were to be precipitated by a vote of no confidence. This group in the main voted against Labour in 1935, but, if given the opportunity in 1938, it was thought to be much less likely that they would do so again. The plural voters comprised a class in English society which, though it might and did feel friendly toward individual Germans, had a long and honorable tradition of humanitarianism and sympathy for the "underdog." The increasingly convincing display of Nazi brutality between 1935 and 1938 might not have changed enough of these votes to defeat the Chamberlain government if a general election had been called in 1938; but it was fairly certain that there would have been reversals in many constituencies, which would have unseated many a government back-bencher. The trend was plain, for by-elections had already reduced the government's majority by 12, and, what was more significant, margins had been reduced in practically all contested elections won by Conservatives—in many cases, substantially.

It is a peculiarity of the British system that this increasing dissatisfaction with the government had the practical effect of diminishing the restraints upon the Prime Minister within his own party. Given the trend against the government in the country, few back-benchers wished to risk losing their seats by failing to sustain a vote of confidence, and so bringing on a general election.

The individual Conservative Member must not be thought of as entirely selfish. Even if he had begun to doubt the complete wisdom of the Prime Minister's policies, the average government supporter in Parliament was far more doubtful of the ability of Labour Members to deal realistically with the oncoming dangers; on the other hand, if Mr. Churchill's dissident Conservative followers should win control of party policy, few Conservative Members would feel any more secure. The oratory of the Right Honorable Member from Epping (Mr. Churchill's constituency at that time) was admired and enjoyed by all, but many British Conservatives, particularly those within the House, distrusted his judgment for reasons that derived from the history of the Conservative party during the late 1920's and early 1930's.

There had then been serious divisions of opinion within the party, the upshot of which had been that Mr. Churchill's position in the making of party policy had been temporarily lost during the very period when Mr. Chamberlain's influence was coming to the fore. In 1929, when the issue of tariff versus free trade was dividing the party, Mr. Chamberlain gave up his parliamentary seat to take over the chairmanship of the Conservative party with a view to consolidating and strengthening the organization. Thus, at a transitional moment he had occupied a position analogous to that of Stalin under Lenin, and the consequences were similar. When Mr. Chamberlain returned to Parliament in 1931, he had at his back a party organization sensitively responsive to his wishes. In the general election of 1935, this situation was intensified, for by that time his influence with contributors to the Conservative campaign funds had increased tremendously in consequence of his successes as Chancellor of the Exchequer. Each successive budget message had been a milestone along his triumphant way.

It is evident, then, that many of the government's candidates in the general election were something more than merely good party men—they were Conservatives of a peculiar stamp, temperamentally sympathetic with Mr. Chamberlain's outlook and aims. One cannot, however, avoid the impression that, in the country as a whole, among Conservatives outside the party organization there was a larger proportion who shared Mr. Churchill's misgivings concerning the Prime Minister's handling of the international situation than was represented in the House of Commons.

In March, 1938, the *New York Times* carried a dispatch from Ferdinand Kuhn, Jr., which stated that events in Austria and Spain had led many influential right-wing Conservatives and a number of powerful financial quarters to question the entire policy of appeasement. They had suddenly become conscious of Germany's enhanced military position in Europe and the threat to British interests in Spain:

> Yesterday in the midst of the worst depression of the stock market here in many years, a meeting was held at the board room of an important London and New York market banking house at which a complete reversal of the Prime Minister's policy was demanded by nervous financiers. Tonight a bigger meeting of 300 was held in the City with speeches by Harold Nicolson and Robert Boothby, both Government Members of Commons. A

resolution was adopted calling on the Government to act in conjunction with other great powers to sustain the rights and freedoms of small countries menaced by unprovoked aggression.[4]

It seems likely that the terms of this resolution were drafted by men who were aware of the rejection by Mr. Chamberlain of an invitation from President Roosevelt to confer in Washington on the international situation—an incident which will be taken up later in this article. By the time of the meetings reported by Mr. Kuhn, however, it was too late to find solid ground on which to build a new approach to international problems in time to meet the successive steps in the disintegration of the international structure of Europe. By the end of March, Mr. Chamberlain's opponents on the floor of the House of Commons had lost the battle against appeasement and were doomed to the unexhilarating task of mending fences and making good the years that the locusts had eaten. For this reason some of the frankest expressions of opinion on foreign policy, even by the Opposition, are to be found in the speeches on defense rather than in the debates on foreign affairs. The part played by the House of Commons in foreign policy during 1937 and 1938 will, however, be more easily understood if we first examine briefly Mr. Chamberlain's actions in certain matters of which the House was not at the time fully cognizant.

PREPARATION FOR APPEASEMENT

Mr. Chamberlain's first public incursion into foreign affairs occurred early in June, 1936, when he took occasion, only a few days after the Foreign Secretary had assured the House of Commons that there had been no change in the government's position on sanctions, to make a pronouncement upon foreign policy to the 1900 Club which created something of a sensation. He ridiculed the notion of retaining sanctions as "the very midsummer of madness." His diary entry is quoted:

I did it deliberately because I felt that the party and the country needed a lead, and an indication that the Government was not wavering and drifting without a policy. . . . I did not consult Anthony Eden, because he would have been bound to beg me not to say what I proposed. . . . He himself has been as nice as possible about it, though it is of course true that to some extent he has had to suffer in the public interest.[5]

The ethical concepts of a man who could make such a confession and the misunderstanding of his fellow-man revealed in the statement as to Mr. Eden's attitude require no comment. Here we see, naked, and by his own hand, two weaknesses in Neville Chamberlain which at every turn nullified all his great efforts to spare the world the horrors of a general war. From this point forward one can feel confidence in neither his integrity nor his good sense.

The "midsummer of madness" speech, as it came to be called, was followed by a cabinet decision to recommend the formal withdrawal of sanctions by the League—a retreat which confirmed Hitler in his belief, if confirmation were needed after the ease with which he had occupied the Rhineland, that it was time to move in central Europe. Notice was given to the world on July 11, 1936, when Dr. Schuschnigg signed an agreement, of which Dr. Beneš later said:

> This was not only the first but the decisive blow against Austrian independence. It made Nazism a legal movement within Austria and opened the way for shameless intervention by German Nazis in the domestic affairs of Austria and for the creation of the first European Quislings.[6]

It occurred just a month after Mr. Chamberlain's famous speech. By the fall, Nazi pressure was likewise exerted on Dr. Beneš to sign up. The proposal was rejected, and the pressure continued for several months; but in mid-January, 1937, he was informed that Berlin considered the negotiations at an end.

Meanwhile, the question of the return of German colonies had been opened. In August, 1936, Hjalmar Schacht called upon M. François-Poncet in Berlin to warn the French Ambassador that the Führer, haunted by the Czechoslovakian question, "was entertaining the notion of solving it by force if necessary." It was suggested that he might be diverted from precipitating a general war by opening up other prospects—colonies, for example. M. François-Poncet tells us that this bait was proffered to Schacht's friends in Paris but that the resolute opposition of Britain soon quashed the plan and that relations between Germany and France became increasingly discordant thereafter.[7] So long as one could speak of the quashing of a conciliatory plan by resolute opposition on the part of Great Britain, it is clear that Mr. Chamberlain had not attained mastery of the government's policies. The affair probably contributed to his conviction that the control of delicate problems in foreign relations must be brought more completely into his own hands.

Several diplomatic shifts effected in the early months of 1937 represented a step in this direction, and it is interesting to note that the decision to make these changes occurred at about the time that German pressure on Dr. Beneš was temporarily abandoned. The best-known change was the appointment of Sir Nevile Henderson as His Majesty's Ambassador at Berlin. His instructions mark the first clear move in Neville Chamberlain's appeasement policy vis-à-vis Hitler. That Sir Nevile was the channel through which Mr. Chamberlain hoped to reach Hitler personally is fairly evident from the account, in the Foreword to *Failure of a Mission,* of the farewell interview in which Sir Nevile expresses the hope that Mr. Chamberlain will not take it amiss if the new Ambassador should commit a calculated indiscretion soon after his arrival in Berlin. No, indeed, he is assured. Mr. Chamberlain, himself, recently had had recourse to this device with excellent results. Both these statesmen, at this point, seemed to think that the Nazis could be fooled and placated by diplomatic shenanigans, though it must be said for Sir Nevile that he was not long in appraising them more accurately.

The new Ambassador's farewell talk with his chief, Mr. Eden, was clearly on a more distant and formal basis, for Mr. Eden's views on foreign policy were widely different from those of the then Chancellor of the Exchequer. The differences which nine months later led to the break between them have been summarized by Mr. Churchill and may be taken as substantially correct, though Mr. Churchill, like our Mr. Stimson, is frequently restrained by personal loyalties from giving a complete picture:

The Prime Minister wished to get on good terms with the two European dictators, and he believed that conciliation and the avoidance of anything likely to offend them was the best method. Eden, on the other hand, had won his reputation at Geneva by rallying the nations of Europe against one dictator; and left to himself, might well have carried sanctions to the verge of war, and perhaps beyond. He was a devoted adherent of the French Entente. He had just insisted upon "staff conversations." He was anxious to have more intimate relations with Russia. He felt and feared the Hitler peril. He was alarmed by the weakness of our armaments and its reaction on foreign affairs.[8]

Sir Nevile Henderson's departure for Berlin coincided practically with the coronation of King George VI, the retirement of Mr. Baldwin as Prime Minister on May 28, 1937, and the accession of Mr. Chamberlain to this post. After this it was easier, obviously, to counteract Mr. Eden's influence in cabinet decisions and to by-pass him and his department in the conduct of foreign affairs.

Few changes were made in the cabinet, but in retrospect it is evident that those which were made had considerable significance. Especially was this true of the appointment of Lord Halifax as Lord President of the council, an office without portfolio. This appointment enabled him to serve the Prime Minister as a direct representative in foreign affairs much as Ribbentrop served Hitler, before he became German Foreign Minister. In both instances the arrangement permitted the dominant personality in the regime to prepare backstage for basic policy changes, while the Foreign Office was formally enunciating a different policy. Indeed, in studying Mr. Chamberlain's premiership, one is struck by an increasing willingness to imitate Hitler's methods. Mr. Eden, like his opposite number, Neurath, was retained for a time at the Foreign Office but would enjoy less freedom of action than in the past. For him the net result of the cabinet changes was that he lost a friend with Mr. Baldwin's retirement and faced two new opponents of his League of Nations policies. Mr. Hore Belisha,[9] the new Secretary for War, was formidable because of the critical importance of his post and his complete subservience to the Prime Minister; Lord Halifax was formidable because of the prestige adhering to his character and achievements.

This is not the place for ferreting out all the means by which Mr. Chamberlain consolidated his control of foreign policy, but a few instances will be cited in order to reveal the degree of freedom of action he acquired during the early months of his tenure of the premiership. Mr. Churchill, who in *The Gathering Storm* shows himself consistently reluctant to blame Mr. Chamberlain for more than a mistaken belief in appeasement, a somewhat arrogant personality, and for keeping too tight a grip on the funds for military expenditures, presents some interesting testimony:

Mr. Chamberlain was determined to press his suit with the two dictators. In July, 1937, he invited the Italian Ambassador, Count Grandi, to Downing Street. The conversation took place with the knowledge, but not in the presence of Mr. Eden. Mr. Chamberlain spoke of his desire for the improvement of Anglo-Italian relations. Count Grandi suggested to him that as a preliminary move it might be well if the Prime Minister were to write a personal appeal to Mussolini. Mr. Chamberlain sat down and wrote such a letter during the interview. It was despatched without reference to the Foreign Secretary, who was in the Foreign Office a few yards away.[10]

Probably, as on the earlier occasion, Mr. Chamberlain would have said that he "did not consult Anthony Eden because he would have been bound to beg me not to say what I proposed." This friendly overture to the Italian dictator on the part of the Prime Minister was frustrated by some unfriendly piracy in the Mediterranean and by the Nyon Conference, which stopped it. It was not until October that the overture could be followed up.

The early fall months of 1937 seem to have been a period in which German and British foreign policies were crystallizing afresh, but unfortunately the British series of foreign-policy documents so far published do not shed light on Sir Nevile Henderson's activities during his first few months in Berlin. Apparently by September the Nazi leaders had received some sign that interviews with the new Lord President of the council held more promise of success than official contacts through the British Foreign Office. At any rate Göring extended an invitation to Lord Halifax to attend a hunting exhibition on his estate in November. Mr. Churchill has told how Mr. Eden received the news:

> Early in October, 1937, I was invited to a dinner at the Foreign Office for the Yugoslav Premier, M. Stoyadinovitch. Afterwards, when we were all standing about and I was talking to Eden, Lord Halifax came up and said in a genial way that Goering had invited him to Germany on a sports visit, and the hope was held out that he would certainly be able to see Hitler. He said that he had spoken about it to the Prime Minister, who thought it would be a very good thing, and therefore he had accepted. I had the impression that Eden was surprised and did not like it; but everything passed off pleasantly. Halifax, therefore, visited Germany in his capacity as a Master of the Foxhounds . . . and, after some sporting entertainment he was in fact bidden to Berchtesgaden and had an informal and none too ceremonious interview with the Fuehrer. This did not go very well. One could hardly conceive two personalities less able to comprehend one another. . . . Nothing came of all this but chatter and bewilderment.[11]

Meanwhile, German policy was being restudied, and it was finally enunciated by Hitler to Blomberg, Fritsch, Räder, Göring, and Neurath, on November 10. The memorandum of the conference was made by a Colonel Hossbach and is generally called the "Hossbach memorandum." The ideas Hitler expressed on this occasion "concerning the opportunities for the development of our position in the field of foreign affairs and its requirements," were, he said, to be regarded as his last will and testament: "The aim of German policy was to make secure and to preserve the racial community and to enlarge it. It was therefore a question of space." He discussed, first, the possibility of solving Germany's problem through autarky or by participation in world economy, but concluded that neither met German requirements. Conquest of Czechoslovakia and Austria would, however, provide the necessary space. It had to be accomplished by 1943–45 before Germany's military equipment for war had become relatively obsolete. It was quite possible that French internal paralysis or an Anglo-French war against Italy would permit Germany to act as early as 1938.[12] As of November, 1937, he foresaw only two possibilities which would enable Germany to proceed against Czechoslovakia in the near future: if France collapsed internally to the fatal extent of absorbing her army's whole strength for pacification or if, with England, she became involved in a war with Italy, Germany could act "with lightning speed." That France escaped both these dangers, yet Hitler was able to take Austria and Czechoslovakia in little over a year, must be laid at the door of Mr. Chamberlain's diplomacy.

We learn from a memorandum written by Weizsäcker—the head of the political department in the German Foreign Ministry —on the day of Hitler's conference, what Germany aimed at in opening conversations with Great Britain:

> From England we want colonies and freedom of action in the East, from us England wants military quiescence particularly in the West. These wishes are not completely irreconcilable. A point of departure for negotiations can be found and concrete results are of less importance to begin with than the goal of preventing the anti-German front in London from solidifying.[13]

On the very day of the conference and the Hossbach memorandum, the story of Lord Halifax' projected visit broke on the pages of the *Evening Standard* in London. The outcry in the press of both countries and the Anglo-German diplomatic fencing which followed are stories in themselves, but the present interest in this hullabaloo lies in an interview reported by the German Embassy, the essential accuracy of which there seems no reason to doubt.

Dr. Hesse, head of the DNB, the German news agency in London, reported to his government that Mr. George S. Stewart, the Prime Minister's press chief, requested Dr. Hesse to call upon him. Mr. Stewart gave the DNB man certain information which was to be forwarded confidentially and unofficially to the proper German authorities. Three subjects were dealt with, but only that portion relating to the British Foreign Secretary is quoted:

> Chamberlain deplored exceedingly the continued criticism of Eden in the German press, especially the fact that an attempt had been made in German newspapers by responsible publications in fact to represent Eden as in opposition to him (Chamberlain). This was factually incorrect and politically unwise. His policy was also Eden's policy. He had expressly made the remarks concerning Eden in his Scarborough speech as a reply to assertions made in a leading German newspaper some six weeks before. In this connection Stewart referred to a prewar episode, when—apparently at the instigation of the Ambassador, Prince Lichnowsky—a Guildhall address by Lloyd George had been used to indicate to the German public that it could infer the existence of opposition between Lloyd George and Prime Minister Asquith. At that time Asquith had felt called upon to state publicly that the Cabinet was in complete agreement wih Lloyd George's statements. Stewart then added that if the German press continued to attempt to demonstrate opposition between Eden and Chamberlain, this would of necessity cause Eden to be supported by Chamberlain in the same manner as Lloyd George had been supported by Asquith. Such a statement by the Prime Minister, which in the interest of German-British relations, was not desired by Chamberlain, might possibly have an unfavorable effect on those relations. He urgently requested us to influence the German press to refrain from claiming that there was any conflict between the policies of Eden and Chamberlain toward Germany.

The comparison of the existing situation with the relationship between Mr. Asquith and Lloyd George was a fine High Renaissance touch, certainly not lost upon the Machiavellians in Germany. Mr. Stewart then passed to the Prime Minister's reason for sending Sir Nevile Henderson, the normal Foreign Office representative, out of Berlin at the time of Lord Halifax' visit:

> Halifax was, in the opinion of Chamberlain, the most important statesman and politician England had at the present time. He was completely independent and without any personal ambition whatever. Chamberlain had intentionally refrained from having the British Ambassador in Berlin par-

ticipate, because he felt that a direct, informal discussion between Lord Halifax and the Fuehrer and Chancellor was the best procedure in view of the status of German-British relations at this time.[14]

Again we are confronted with Mr. Chamberlain's peculiar inability to understand the diplomatic force of personal probity—as Ambassador, Sir Nevile Henderson would have had to report through his chief, Mr. Eden; whereas, Lord Halifax, as Lord President of the council, could report directly to the Prime Minister, by-passing the Foreign Secretary.

It is well known that Lord Halifax' conversation with Hitler was widely taken as an assent to Germany's aggressions in Czechoslovakia and Austria. Several official versions have been found, and two that have been published disagree on one important point. Hitler began with a reference to Germany's ambitions in Europe, declaring that there were two methods of settling difficulties—by the free play of forces and by the application of higher reason. If the second were selected, it must be understood that it would lead to essentially the same result as would be attained by war. A translation published by the Soviet Ministry of Foreign Affairs in 1948 reports Lord Halifax as having replied

that no possibility of changing the existing situation must be precluded, but that the changes must take place only on the basis of a reasonable arrangement. If both sides are agreed that the world is not static, then they must seek, on the basis of common ideals, to live up to this recognition in such a way as to direct the available energies in mutual confidence toward a common goal.[15]

The version published jointly by the French, British, and American governments in 1949 is not a translation but is the English version sent to Sir Nevile Henderson by the German Foreign Minister. In this version Lord Halifax is reported as emphasizing, in the name of His Majesty's government, "that possibility of change of the existing situation was not excluded, but that changes should only take place upon the basis of reasonable agreements reasonably reached. If on both sides there was agreement...."[16] It will be seen that the initial sentences differ widely. In Aristotelian phraseology, the statement in the Russian document "that no possibility . . . must be precluded" is a universal negative, whereas "possibility of change of the existing situation was not excluded" is very far from universality. Whether or not this discrepancy existed in the original German of the Soviet document and, if so, whether or not it was known and appreciated by any of the British statesmen is not entirely clear. On the whole, it seems likely that there is an error in the Russian translation, because other German documents state without any ambiguity that changes which were not peaceful were known to have been "precluded" by Lord Halifax. There is, however, the further possibility that the Nazis prepared one or more copies with a different wording for certain purposes of their own.

It is plain, however, that the whole maneuver of the visit was purposely so handled from the British side as to bring conviction to the Nazis that Great Britain would go a very long way to avoid war and that not too high a value would be attached to such intangibles as honor and justice. The second point needs to be stressed, because it was the fact that Hitler reached a conviction of its truth at an early stage that enabled him to move so rapidly in 1938, even though neither of the prerequisite conditions specified in the Hossbach memorandum arose—France did not collapse internally, and no Anglo-French war with Italy took place.

A German memorandum of December 20, 1937,[17] enumerates the elements in the changed attitudes of Great Britain and France, pointing out the "obvious progress in the British attitude" with respect to changes in the territorial status quo not only in Europe but in the world. But this same "obvious progress" was disturbing to some of Germany's former friends in Great Britain. On December 6, Lord Londonderry wrote a letter to his friend, Major Gall, which soon found its way to Ribbentrop's desk. Among other things, he spoke of the misgivings he felt after recent visits to Germany:

> You will have seen that there is a very strong anti-German campaign in this country, and in my judgement there is very good reason for it. . . . My efforts for some years . . . were directed . . . at an international policy of disarmament. This should have been the forerunner to subsequent appeasement, a term I do not care about. . . . The German demands which are increasing, have now behind them a very formidable armed force, and I am very anxious lest, by our conciliatory attitude and our desire to see justice done to Germany, all the German desires will take the form of grievances which, when the Germans are strong enough, they will seek

to enforce by force of arms. . . . I should like to see our Government undertaking a bold policy. . . . I feel that all our friendly approaches should be tempered in such a way as to show that . . . we want to know where Germany's aspirations are leading, and . . . I shall press for a categorical statement from Germany as to the limit of their desires, . . . unless something like this (is) forthcoming I shall have to come to the reluctant conclusion that the only thing we can do, and I certainly think it would be a powerful safeguard, is to go on arming ourselves so as to counter the German bid for hegemony, for that is what it really amounts to.[18]

Within the month, however, Mr. Chamberlain had taken another step toward appeasement by removing Sir Robert Vansittart as active head of the Foreign Office to a newly created post called "Chief Diplomatic Adviser." Ribbentrop thought at first that this was a real promotion because it seemed unlikely that Mr. Chamberlain would wish to eliminate one of his ablest civil officials from the handling of foreign affairs, but he soon perceived the truth. It is significant that the change was made during the Christmas recess when the House of Commons could not ask embarrassing questions.

Two weeks later, in mid-January, Mr. Chamberlain once more intervened to weaken the country's diplomatic position. According to Mr. Churchill, this was the incident which caused Anthony Eden to resign, though he had to wait for an occasion which could be discussed publicly in the House of Commons. The circumstances were as follows: on January 11, 1938, President Roosevelt, who was now convinced that Hitler intended war,[19] made an effort to close ranks. He sent a secret message to the British government proposing a meeting of representatives of certain governments in Washington to consider the underlying causes of the international tension. Without consulting Mr. Eden, who was in France, the Prime Minister gave instructions for a reply in which he suggested that the President should postpone the launching of his plan because it would cut athwart British efforts to secure agreements with Germany and Italy—particularly Italy, to whom the Prime Minister was prepared to offer *de jure* recognition of her Abyssinian conquest. Dismayed, the Foreign Office alerted Mr. Eden in Brussels. The Foreign Secretary returned in time to participate in a cabinet discussion of the American reply to Mr. Chamberlain. Mr. Roosevelt had expressed grave concern at the proposed recognition of Italy's position, as having a bad effect upon Japanese policy in the Far East and upon American public opinion. In the course of the cabinet discussion, Mr. Eden succeeded in modifying the draft of the second British reply, but he could not bring the cabinet to his view that it was better to offend the European dictators than to lose American good will.

Mr. Chamberlain, about this time, rebuffed several Soviet offers of co-operation similarly—partly, no doubt, because he distrusted them but chiefly, I believe, because he was desperately trying to prove to Hitler and Mussolini that they would find Great Britain a loyal member of a four-power pact. Mr. Churchill's summing-up of his behavior cannot be bettered:

> That Mr. Chamberlain, with his limited outlook and inexperience of the European scene, should have possessed the self-sufficiency to wave away the proffered hand stretched out across the Atlantic leaves one, even at this date, breathless with amazement. The lack of all sense of proportion, and even of self-preservation, which this episode reveals in an upright, competent, well-meaning man, charged with the destinies of our country and all who depended upon it is appalling. One can not today even reconstruct the state of mind which would render such gestures possible.
>
> I have yet to unfold the story of the treatment of the Russian offers of collaboration in the advent of Munich. If only the British people could have known and realised that, having neglected our defences and sought to diminish the defences of France, we were now disengaging ourselves from the two mighty nations whose extreme efforts were needed to save our lives and their own, history might have taken a different turn.[20]

Mr. Churchill here touches upon the heart of the problem of the part played by the House of Commons in 1938. The fact that the tenor of the Halifax interview at Berchtesgaden and its issue were never revealed officially to the House of Commons but merely disclosed gradually as they furnished the basis of the Prime Minister's actions is of very great importance in appraising the attitudes of various Members of the House during these critical months. Much of the truth was suspected, and in the case of certain Members it was actually known under pledges of confidence. The rights and wrongs of the policy to which the nation was committed could not, however, be debated publicly because it was not officially known. Indeed, there were repeated asseverations on the floor of the House that the policy of His Majesty's government had not changed. This is one of those little tricks in semantics which served Mr. Chamberlain frequently in justifying his acts and statements. If one said that the policy of His Majesty's government was to secure peace, no one could deny that it had not changed. Outside the House, the new policy was debated, but not so effectively as it should have been—partly because some of the most influential journals were under pressure by the government and partly because discussion of great public questions in Great Britain takes off, to a considerable extent, from official statements or replies to questions on the floor of the House of Commons. During the 1937–38 session, the policy of the government with respect to the House was one of extreme secrecy, and even irascibility, in the face of questions. As one examines the *Debates and Questions* and the section called "Business of the House" in the official reports, it is evident that a wholly unsatisfactory relationship developed between the government and the House during the parliamentary year.

THE HOUSE OF COMMONS AND BERCHTESGADEN, I
NOVEMBER 17, 1937

As with most analogies, the likeness of the House of Commons to a Greek chorus is not quite complete. By its very existence and by the force of its tradition and history, the House had to be something more than a purely passive element in the tragedy. The unhappy consequence was that the Prime Minister, in his work for appeasement, felt compelled to adopt one humiliating expedient after another, and, to make a bad matter worse, this was fully known to the dictators. This dangerous situation is seen with increasing distinctness as new official documents are published—particularly the third series of documents on British foreign policy which began to appear in 1948. Even without these documents, however, the debates, answers to questions, and the tactics resorted to by the government in the day-to-day conduct of parliamentary business, when integrated with subsequent events not known to the public at the time, are enough to reveal the tragic story to the imaginative reader.

From the first of the 1937–38 session, the Prime Minister is seen to be in the position of giving one impression to the House of Commons and a totally different one to Hitler and Mussolini.

When he had to choose between deceiving the one or the other, he chose to deceive the House. It might have been supposed that a Prime Minister controlling both his own party and the cabinet, as Mr. Chamberlain did after Mr. Eden's resignation in February, could thenceforward have gone his way without let or hindrance except on the part of France and, of course, Czechoslovakia. Not so, for we find that he relied upon evasion, leakages, and subterfuges right through the session until the final crisis. It almost seems that some of the enthusiasm with which the House greeted him on his return from Munich was due to its feeling that during those harrowing days he had laid aside evasion and subterfuge and stood before them honestly, telling them the truth as he saw it.

The 1937–38 session opened on October 26, after Lord Halifax' visit to Germany had been decided upon but more than three weeks before it took place and two weeks before the decision was generally known outside the government. The time sequence here, as in many of the critical situations during the session, was of psychological importance, for it enabled the government to clear the hurdle of the first great foreign-policy discussion without unduly offensive references to Hitler. Because of an attack of gout, the Prime Minister did not attend the opening, his place being taken by the Chancellor of the Exchequer, Sir John Simon. The burden of criticism was directed primarily against the government's policy toward Italy (including Franco Spain) and Japan. The reproach of a Conservative Member was not unmerited:

> The Opposition have a habit of talking a great deal about dictators. They denounce them quite gaily when it is a question of Italy or Japan, but like Agag [*sic*] they walk very delicately when it comes to the case of Germany. I should like to see a little more courage in the Opposition when they are facing Germany, for, after all, every other problem is small compared with the German problem. It is in South Eastern Europe that the real danger spots are to be found.[21]

This first debate of the parliamentary year is traditionally much more than a debate on foreign affairs, for it arises as a consequence of a Speech from the Throne which states the government's legislative aims and policies for the coming year. This is referred to variously as the "Speech from the Throne," the "King's Speech," or the "Speech." It is more succinct than the American State of the Union Message because the details are developed subsequently by the government's Ministers during the debate on the address. This debate, which runs for six or seven days, is initiated by a motion, moved and seconded by junior supporters of the government,[22] thanking His Majesty for the "Gracious Speech." The major Opposition parties are likely to offer amendments to the motion, which are, in fact, complete substitutions for the government's proposed reply. These amendments are never adopted, and sometimes are withdrawn "by leave" before the end of the debate, but they officially place on record the general objections of the Opposition to the policies enumerated in the King's Speech. Like the statements in the Speech itself, the details of the objections are developed in subsequent speeches—in this case by the Opposition front benches.

In Great Britain the slightest difference from King's Speeches of previous years is examined with great care, because both the pattern as a whole and much of the phraseology are established by custom. Consequently, deviations, especially from the Speech of the session just past, are likely to be highly significant.

Perhaps the most vital change in the 1937 Speech was the reduction in space allotted to external affairs, from about 45 per cent of the total to about 25 per cent. Doubtless, Mr. Chamberlain meant to give the House and the country a "lead" as he had in the sanctions controversy. This effort to curtail foreign policy debates in 1937 and 1938 would have been less ominous had the Prime Minister not at the same time tried to carry on foreign relations without the counsel of the Foreign Office experts. His chief mentor and close companion in this critical period was Sir Horace Wilson, an industrial adviser to the Treasury. Perhaps Mr. Chamberlain, himself an industrial executive, felt that the judgment of such a man would be more objective and less emotional than that of the Foreign Office officials. At any rate he installed Sir Horace in an office adjoining his own and walked alone with him in the park every day during a three-year period, in the course of which we are told by Lord Vansittart (then Sir Robert) that the Prime Minister spoke "a total of three times, and never alone" with his chief diplomatic adviser, Sir Robert himself.[23]

It was probably on Sir Horace's advice, or at least with his concurrence, that the Speech from the Throne, at the opening of a session which was to see Austria and much of Czechoslovakia fall to the Nazis, referred to Germany only obliquely—in the promise to bring in an Air Raids Precaution Bill. The Speech announced a policy of strict adherence to nonintervention in Spain, continued attempts to co-operate with other governments in bringing the conflict in the Far East to a close, and that was all.

The Opposition parties found this statement something less than satisfactory. Sir Archibald Sinclair sagely observed that the Speech was less remarkable for its content than for its omissions. There was a shrewd thrust at Sir Horace Wilson, the Prime Minister's intimate adviser, and one of the keenest appraisals of the speech by Mr. Maxton, the leader of the small Independent Labour party:

> I was asking an honourable Member who is more experienced in the service of the House than I am, who it is that actually writes this Speech. I do not know; I do not know whether anyone knows. Evidently he is a good stylist; he has a good command of English grammar; but how he collects the points that are ultimately put in, and whether or not he had a free hand in the matter, I do not know. I do not know whether the more obtrusive Ministers obtrude their ideas on his notice, and the more modest ones keep in the background. But certainly this King's Speech seems to me to fail in the comprehensive stating to the nation of the task and the responsibilities that this Government has to face in the near future, and it fails to recognize the urgent needs of a very large proportion of the people of this country and of its dependencies across the seas.
>
> In these days Members of the House and people throughout the country are worried, some about the rise of Fascist Powers like Germany and Italy, others about the increasing strength and power of the Soviet Republic in Russia. They are worried about these new phenomena, as they appear to be, and think they are very terrible. But one thing can be said about these countries, Fascists or workers' republics. They know what they want, they state it clearly and definitely and they go confidently forward. If a democracy of free peoples is to survive, it must be as clear and definite, and must have its objectives as clearly defined. Here in this document there is no clear definition of what Great Britain desires the future of its citizens to be; and, because there is neither a clear objective nor any stated ideals in the King's Speech, it fails to be the document that is required at this stage in the history of a nation with the history, the importance and the influence of this nation in the world's affairs.[24]

It was noted disapprovingly by several speakers that, for the first time since 1931, the King's Speech contained no pledge with respect to the League of Nations and that for the preceding three years the assurances had been progressively less positive.[25]

Mr. Mander, speaking for the Liberal party, declared:

The Government, with their present policy do not rely on the support of any of these countries. They cannot even rely upon the support of all the Members of the British Empire itself. The Government apparently are prepared to fight all right, but only for certain specified things. They will fight for Hong Kong, but not for Holland, they will fight for the Falkland Islands, but will not lift a hand to help Austria. They will fight for Tanganyika, but will not assist Czechoslovakia. If it is made clear that overwhelming might is to be brought against aggressors wherever they are, no war is ever likely to take place.[26]

In moving the Labour amendment,[27] Mr. Herbert Morrison also called for the mobilization of as many states as possible on the side of peace, the strengthening and stimulating of the moral authority of the League, and for speeches by ministers "in the Roosevelt spirit, calling the world to a great crusade for peace."

Mr. Roger Acland, a Liberal, complained of Conservative speeches which assumed that the whole situation was static:

The Opposition is well aware of the fact that on any particular day it is always more dangerous to do something for international justice than to do nothing, but I do beg . . . hon. Members opposite . . . to try to see the history of international affairs, not as a series of isolated incidents with no connnection but as a steadily developing, consequential story.

For six years we have seen the steady advance of the dictators by threat of force, by use of force. . . . Do hon. Members opposite assume that, at some stage, these dictators . . . will stop? If not, is it not certain that, sooner or later, in the course of this steady advance, these dictators will tread on a corn which will make even a Tory wince?[28]

On the fifth day of the debate on the address, Mr. Eden, as Foreign Secretary, threw up a few road blocks in an attempt to strengthen the government's foreign policy. He referred to the fact that "our former ally, Italy" had now championed Germany's claim to African colonies: "I must now declare plainly that we do not admit the right of any Government to call upon us for a contribution when there is no evidence to show that that Government are prepared to make any contribution on their own account."[29] His remarks concerning His Majesty's government's policy with respect to the League of Nations must have given the absent Prime Minister a jolt—it is small wonder that Mr. Chamberlain felt the necessity of explaining the British position to the Nazis through his press chief, Mr. Stewart.[30] Mr. Eden said plainly:

We shall not get an enduring peace . . . until all nations accept to be bound, as we accept to be bound, by international law, and until the force against any potential aggressor is overwhelming. Neither of these conditions exists to-day. . . . I deplore . . . the growing disrespect for Treaties, and we see only too clearly the ultimate consequences if that practice continues. . . . I have noted of late a tendency to use as part of the diplomatic machinery methods which are highly dangerous. There is an inclination to threaten, to issue orders from the housetops, to proclaim what is virtually an ultimatum and to call it peace. Such methods will never have any response here. Such orders will never be obeyed by the British public. We are ready enough . . . to discuss difficulties and issues with those concerned, but we are not prepared to stand and deliver at anyone's command. . . . While we recognize that the League of Nations is at present seriously handicapped by incomplete membership, we believe it still provides the best means for obtaining that result [the settlement of disputes by peaceful means].[31]

A Conservative back-bencher, Mr. Emrys-Evans, brought up the peculiar nature of the correspondence to which the *Times* had seen fit to open its columns:

We can not, of course, be bound, we never shall be bound in any automatic way, but we can not remain indifferent to the problems of South Eastern Europe; and these problems, as hon. Members will be aware who have been following the correspondence in the "Times," are very closely related to the question of the surrender of the ex-German colonies. In the course of that correspondence in the "Times" the drummers of retreat have been few, but they have been called up over and over again, and they have shown a tendency to support a policy which I might describe as a policy of fright. Many of them have recommended a speedy surrender. They now have the powerful support of Signor Mussolini.[32] Many of the arguments used in the course of this correspondence were no doubt used by the Anglo-Saxon Government of King Ethelred the Unready at the time when it was decided to buy off the aggressor.

This correspondence, however, is having a very bad effect in Europe to-day. A friend of mine who returned only recently from Central Europe says that we are looked upon there very much as Turkey used to be, in the old days, as the "sick man of Europe."

He was of the opinion that the Conservative party in the country was far ahead of the government, and he suggested that it was time for the government to make up their mind and to take a much firmer line than in the past:

The conduct of this discussion on the ex-German colonies has been carried on by a great, powerful journal. It seems to me that this is the place where this question should be raised. Would surrender indeed make for peace, which is our main object? That seems to me the real question we have to consider. Would it make the slightest difference to German aims or deflect German ambitions in Eastern and South Eastern Europe to which, as I have said, we can not remain indifferent? If we surrendered to threats they would surely be the starting off point for new demands.

The whole speech has an intriguing Churchillian air, particularly Mr. Emrys-Evans' final complaint about letters in the *Times* which charged His Majesty's government with refusal to negotiate with Germany:

This afternoon we had from the Secretary of State for Foreign Affairs a most striking speech. The hopes of the dictators that the Foreign Secretary will fall, will be belied, for he has established himself not only in the hearts of this House but of the whole people. I do not believe that there is any escape from the difficulties which surround us by a policy of flight, such as has been recommended in the powerful journal to which I have referred. You can not buy off an aggressor. I believe the only possible way of dealing with this problem is to push on steadily and as quickly as we can with our rearmament programme, and at the same time to show a steady, determined and, if need be, a conciliatory front to the dictator powers.[33]

The Liberal amendment to the address called for the prosecution of active measures in concert with the Dominions, the United States, and other countries and for the reduction of economic barriers; and it was noted by Mr. Owen Edwards that almost every subsequent speaker had welcomed the raising of the issue of collaboration with the United States. Mr. Chamberlain made several efforts to placate these Members during the next few weeks, perhaps as a means of counteracting unfavorable comments upon the Halifax trip. At the Guildhall Banquet on November 9, for example, he welcomed co-operation by the United States in the Far East but was careful to restrict it geographically. After the Halifax-Hitler conversation, however, he made fewer references to the United States.

The first great debate of the parliamentary year, the debate on the address, fairly represented the lines upon which the Opposition parties and the dissident Conservatives argued throughout the 1937–38 session. There was no great change in the fundamental ideas of these groups, such as could be observed in the 1935–36 session, with the gradual acceptance by both Opposition parties during that year of the belief that the risk of war must be run to stop aggression—a position which the controlling elements of the Conservative party did not accept until 1939.

By the fall of 1937, both the Opposition parties had dug themselves into their new positions. They forced debates at every turn. Not a move by the government but was explored at question time or brought up on motions for adjournment. Mr. Chamberlain heartily disliked this "waste of time," and with some justification, for a Prime Minister is always hard put to it to arrange adequate time for securing necessary legislation to implement government policy. Nevertheless, although Mr. Chamberlain's hold upon the operational processes of government was, by this time, fairly secure, his domination was, after all, of a temporary sort, and in this matter it broke against the rock of House of Commons procedure and tradition. A request for a motion for adjournment in order to discuss a subject of urgent public importance could rarely be denied, nor could questions remain wholly unanswered. "It would not be in the public interest" is in itself a kind of answer. Moreover, it is one which makes the government appear ridiculous if resorted to frequently.

One of the debates on an adjournment motion occurred on November 8, in connection with the government's decision to exchange missions with Franco, predicted by the *New York Times* as early as August, 1937, in a dispatch which was quoted in the House: "Salamanca believes that the British Government is more sympathetic towards Franco under Neville Chamberlain than under Stanley Baldwin."[34] It was asserted by the Opposition that France had been informed of the government's decision but not consulted. The striking thing about this debate is that it exhibits the Labour Opposition in the absurd role of defending the Conservative government's Foreign Secretary. Pointing out that the decision to exchange missions had been announced while Mr. Eden was attending the Brussels conference on China, Mr. Attlee asked whether the arrangement was concluded in the Foreign Secretary's absence or before he went away. If in his absence, it seemed a curious way of dealing with important matters. Mr.

Eden, in his reply, conspicuously failed to deny that the decision had been reached in his absence.

At this time Mr. Chamberlain was endeavoring to establish certain conditions which Hitler considered prerequisites for an Anglo-German understanding, conditions for which Mr. Eden saw less necessity. They had been explicitly laid down during Lord Halifax' interview at Berchtesgaden:

1. The Conservatives must accept the principle of colonial concessions.

2. The press must be induced to be more helpful, both positively and negatively.

3. Obstreperous minorities must not be allowed to interfere with *rapprochement,* or bind the government to the League of Nations or to collective security of any variety.

The first task was undertaken largely by word of mouth, but it was facilitated by the achievement of the second. The second, in turn, was facilitated by the universal respect felt in Great Britain for the character of Lord Halifax. He carried a conviction with leaders of the press which Mr. Chamberlain did not command. Mr. Geoffrey Dawson, a close friend of Lord Halifax, placed the editorial and correspondence columns of the *Times* at the disposal of the government. The *Observer,* a Sunday paper controlled by Viscount Astor, had always followed the Nazi line. Other reputable papers, like the *Manchester Guardian* and the *Yorkshire Post,* controlled by Mr. Eden's father-in-law, did not participate in a positive sense, but they were probably somewhat affected by Lord Halifax' appeal for restraint. The influence of the *Times* was the most baleful by far. In November and December, 1937, and at subsequent critical stages (especially in May, June, and September), certain of its editorials were unquestionably inspired by the government with the intention of hurting the position of the government of Czechoslovakia. One of the most mendacious lines followed was the effort to rouse British sympathy for the mistreated Sudeten German minority in Czechoslovakia. There were also charges that Czechoslovakia was unwilling to make peace. This implication is seen in an editorial quoted by Mr. Kuhn in a dispatch to the *New York Times* to remind American readers "of the forces working in and out of the British Cabinet to give Germany what she wants in Austria and Czechoslovakia." Among other things, the *Times* had said: "If there is to be peace there can be no exemption from contribution and concession—neither for Germans, nor for Czechs, nor for the British Empire," warning Czechoslovakia that anyone looking at the conformation of its boundaries inevitably saw that German good will was an essential element of its security: "It will be a safer policy to expect and allow for the expansion of German interests along lines it is patently destined to follow . . . than to oppose to a normal historic process an opposition which is both timorous and inefficient."[35] Mr. Kuhn reported that the government, nevertheless, did not win all along the line. A battle was raging in the press, which he thought at the moment (November, 1937) more significant than the attitude of the House of Commons: "It showed a clear-cut division between the few who want settlement with Germany at the expense of France and her Eastern allies, and the many who insist that Britain must not buy a settlement by sacrificing others."[36] There was a universal yearning for a settlement which would avert the danger of German bombers, but a difference of opinion as to method—basically the difference between the policy of appeasement and the policy of accumulating deterrents.

On November 29, 1937, on the eve of an Anglo-French conversation, Mr. Kuhn wired a dispatch which was referred to later in the House of Commons as the "coup" of the *New York Times*. He had, he said, received from an official source an outline of British policy which was the clearest given at Whitehall since Lord Halifax' trip to Germany earlier in the month:

The French will find tomorrow that British policy is moving slowly but unmistakably in the direction of German wishes. The British have no intention yet of giving the Nazi Reich a free hand in Central and Eastern Europe or returning all the former German colonies as the price of a few years' peace. But this does not preclude a discreet request to the French to urge concessions upon their Czech allies. Moreover, the British talked today officially of bringing the Berlin-Rome Axis and the London-Paris partnership closer together if it can be done without cost to the Czechs, the Austrians, or the others. . . .

Britain is also ready to consider colonial concessions to Germany, but only, according to an authoritative spokesman tonight, by the mandatory Powers.[37]

At this point, the *New York Times* entered the fray with a three-section editorial, which was soon famous, ending with the words:

> The *New York Times* believes that the American people can be wakened to the facts which menace this nation; and the world will learn that events are conceivable, that circumstances can arise, outside this hemisphere, which will undoubtedly range American public opinion behind an effective peace policy and make junk overnight of the so-called Neutrality Act.[38]

It was undoubtedly a feeler as well as a warning, but Neville Chamberlain's government did not wish to associate themselves with rabble rousers in the Western Hemisphere.

The practice, which Mr. Kuhn's outline of official British policy reveals, of stating government policy to the press of another nation before stating it on the floor of the House of Commons was deeply resented. Later in the 1937–38 session there was an instance in which Mr. Chamberlain's behavior to his fellow-Members was more heinous. It occurred about a week before the May crisis (when German troops were thought to have moved, and Czechoslovakia mobilized). On May 10, at a party given by Lady Astor for about a dozen journalists, the Prime Minister gave an unofficial interview to a representative of an American and a Canadian newspaper. The dispatch was cabled to America on May 14, at the time of a visit to London made by Konrad Henlein, the Sudeten leader. The reporter, Mr. Joseph Driscoll, stated in his dispatch that it shed "what can truly be called official light on the real British attitude towards Czechoslovakia" and upon certain other matters, among them Mr. Eden's resignation. When asked if France and Russia would fight for Czechoslovakia, Mr. Driscoll's informant had replied, "How can they fight?" It was made equally clear to Mr. Driscoll that Great Britain did not expect to fight either.

It was not until a month later that this incident reached the floor of the House, but then a painful scene ensued. Mr. Mander, a Liberal leader, questioned the Prime Minister, who at first tried to throw the blame on the irresponsibility of newsmen and later accused Mr. Mander of seeking information "to satisfy his restless and mischievous curiosity," adding that he proposed to let him guess as to the origin and truth of the story: "I am not going to satisfy the curiosity of the hon. Member. . . . That is my final word and I do not think there is more to be said."[39] Mr. Mander left the House to the accompaniment of jeers from the Prime Minister's supporters. This was an unprecedented way for a Prime Minister to behave toward a colleague in the House of Commons. The following day in Committee of Supply, during the debate on the Foreign Office vote, Sir Archibald Sinclair pointed out that the Prime Minister's attitude had insured wide publicity for Mr. Driscoll's dispatch, and he pressed for a denial by the Prime Minister on the ground that the part of the reported interview which dealt with the Czechs was an exceedingly dangerous statement of British policy. There was irony in his comment: "It has often seemed to me that one of the Prime Minister's weaknesses . . . in handling foreign affairs is that he does not seem able to foresee the effect of his words and actions."[40] Clearly, the giving of this unofficial interview at the very time when Henlein had come to London to obtain support for the Sudeten cause had been deliberate.

The incident shows that, in carrying out the third task set by Hitler, the restraining of Parliament, the Prime Minister had more to consider than divisions. The questions were often embarrassing, and a debate which made a dramatic appeal to an unprepared public could very well damage his foreign policy seriously, however the division went. The momentum of the tidal wave of public opinion which had swept Sir Samuel Hoare out of the cabinet in 1935 was not forgotten. Mr. Chamberlain, who was often very astute tactically, took care in 1937 and 1938 to allow such waves time to recede before they reached the House. A well-timed leak could be utilized to exhaust the force of public indignation, and it had the further advantage that the initial presentation could be one-sided. By the time the subject was brought to the attention of the House, the country was already either persuaded or its anger assuaged, so that the danger of building up dynamic pressure upon the government's supporters was avoided.

Mr. Chamberlain was also given to admonishing the Opposition in the press, creating a talking point against them which diverted attention from the issues being debated. Just before the Christmas recess, the *Times* argued editorially against the idea of an adjournment debate on foreign policy, implying irresponsibil-

ity on the part of the leaders of the Opposition parties in requesting it at so critical a time.[41] Again, much later in the session, the
country was told that the debates on the Sandys Privilege of the
House case were being unnecessarily drawn out and that it was a
boresome affair, better dropped. These public admonishments did
not improve the relations between the Prime Minister and the
House of Commons, but they were advantageous to him tactically
in counteracting somewhat the influence of the speeches made
during the debates.

Looking back, it seems that if there was ever a time when the
House of Commons could have stopped Neville Chamberlain, it
was before his policy really began to go into effect—not after Mr.
Eden's resignation, because by that time the Prime Minister had
got himself so deeply involved that no pressure could have made
him back down. If other factors had not been present, perhaps
the Prime Minister's mind might have been changed by a powerful demand by the House in December, 1937, just before the recess. Unfortunately, there were other factors. For example, the
Opposition could not exert the necessary influence upon him because he was in no danger of having to dissolve, in the absence of
pressure from the country, and because not enough of his own
supporters yet understood the dangerous path he was following
to be persuaded that a change of course was called for. Mr.
Churchill's speech on December 21 was able, profound, and
shrewd, but it fell on the ears of a House ready to slough off political burdens and to engage in holiday festivities and end-of-the-year
preoccupations. More important, it was read by a country which
had not yet fallen under Mr. Churchill's spell. Indeed, with all
his glory of heroic stature, he is not a great popular leader. He
has always been a great House of Commons man, but 1938 was a
year when the splendor of that concept was tarnished and not
evident to the British public. The strength and authority of the
House is not a stable asset but requires public confidence and admiration to give it reality.

Other psychological elements underlay the failure of either the
Opposition or Mr. Churchill's group of dissident Conservatives to
arouse any resistance to appeasement which was politically comparable to the anger over the Hoare-Laval agreement. This kind

of pressure upon government is almost invariably directed against a specific issue; whereas in 1935 there had actually been an agreement set down on paper and signed, this was not the case in November and December, 1937. At Berchtesgaden Lord Halifax had, in effect, made a far more important commitment than Sir Samuel had, but, during the Christmas recess debate and in reply to questions, the Prime Minister thought himself justified in making an explicit denial, and no responsible Members wished to contradict him. The abdication crisis—only a year past—undoubtedly played a part in making felt the need to stand by the Prime Minister. It would not do to allow his integrity to become a national issue. It was all very well to badger and bait him in the House, but the British Commonwealth and Empire was not, in December, 1937, psychologically prepared to go through another crisis of loss of confidence, however secondary. There was universal conviction that for the present the motto had to be "Steady does it."

The abdication crisis affected events in 1938 in yet another way. The Hoare-Laval reversal had been produced by a people who were then enjoying and had long enjoyed the utmost freedom of exchange of opinion in press and forum; they had not yet been subjected to an intense Nazi propaganda campaign. On the other hand, they had been indoctrinated thoroughly, at a high moral level and over a long period of years, with League of Nations propaganda, which, though it was intended to be honest, did actually obscure for many people the risk of war which it involved. When the protest of December, 1935, burst upon an astonished House of Commons, it carried weight because it was born of confidence and a conviction of right. Now, two years later, the intellectual and moral position of the people was wholly changed. The failure to make the protest stick (for Sir Samuel was soon aboard again, and Abyssinia was abandoned) had caused leaders in every community to lose confidence in their ability to bring effective pressure to bear on the government. This traumatic experience had soon been followed by the abdication crisis. It is true that this problem, unlike the sanctions issue, was settled by the government in a manner satisfactory to nearly everyone. Nevertheless, Britishers could not forget the fact (nor are they quite easy today over it) that, without notice and in peacetime, a complete censorship had been clamped upon the entire country. Moreover, it had been done not officially by the government but by voluntary conspiracy on the part of the press and the distributors of news publications. The consequences were disastrous. The government, whose powers of moral discrimination were already dull, learned to resort to manipulation of the press, and the press itself learned that it might actually serve the country by exercising increasing selectivity in the publication of news. Hitler, too, learned the lesson and made a veiled reference to it in his conversation with Sir Nevile Henderson on March 3, 1938.[42] Perhaps the worst result of all was that there developed in the mind and soul of the British people a nearly fatal cynicism of the sort we are familiar with in American isolationism.

Thus, at the time of the Christmas recess debate, which set the pattern of relations between the Prime Minister and the House of Commons during the year of Munich, the only political force which could have changed his course had already been dissipated.

The first thing in the relationship which strikes an outsider is the dislike for the Prime Minister exhibited by Opposition Members. Mr. Herbert Morrison frequently delivered himself of savage little word pictures of the Prime Minister's character which remind one of nothing so much as David Low's cartoons. These exhibitions of dislike are the more striking if one has read debates under Mr. Baldwin's leadership, when there was plenty of opposition but no dislike. Later in the 1937–38 session, dislike was reinforced by distrust; but in the beginning one feels that, although the Opposition disliked Mr. Chamberlain and found him difficult to deal with, perhaps too evasive, most of them still accepted what he told them in the House as truth.

Perhaps nothing in the Christmas recess debate reveals the relationship better than Sir Archibald Sinclair's rebuke: It was not, he thought, the Opposition which was doing harm in requesting the debate:

So far as harm goes, it struck me that a phrase at the beginning of the Prime Minister's speech might do a great deal more harm, when he turned to the benches opposite and accused honourable Members of wanting war . . . . It is a pity that the Prime Minister should use words which may give foreign countries the impression . . . and the country and the world the impression that the Labour party in this country . . . is a war-mongering party. I do not believe that is true, and I do not think it should be said. . . . If we are not to have this Debate, what would be the alternative? Would there be complete silence? Would nobody say anything at all? Would there not be speeches in the country? Would there not be inspired interviews, and articles in newspapers, and would not the impressions that those articles would make on public opinion be at least as detrimental to the public interest and the smooth running of international affairs as a Debate in this House? For my own part, I believe that the proper place to discuss these issues is the House of Commons. Obviously this country is not content to run the dangers inherent in the present international situation without having these discussions and obtaining information. . . . The Opposition have done a public service in asking for this Debate to-day.[43]

One feels the usual temptation to quote Mr. Churchill's speech *in extenso*. It was "deftly done, craftily contrived," and—though more humorous—his pronouncement upon the "educative effects" of such diplomatic visits as that of Lord Halifax to Berchtesgaden yields nothing to *The Prince* in clarity of exposition. He hoped that the cordiality shown recently to the French Ministers was an indication and reaffirmation of Anglo-French solidarity for mutual safety and for the discharge of their duties under the Covenant. He castigated the writer of a letter to the *Times:*

> But I read this letter, in which the gentleman showed that these ideas of preventing war by international courts and by reasonable discussions had been tried over and over again . . . and failed. If that is true it is a very melancholy fact, but what was astonishing was the crazy glee with which the writer hailed such lapses. I was told the other day, though I have not verified it, of a quotation from Carlyle in which he describes the laugh of the hyena on being assured that after all the world is only carrion.

He warned the House that small countries all over Europe were watching Great Britain:

> If it were thought that we were making terms for ourselves at the expense either of small nations or of large conceptions which are dear to millions of people in every nation, I think that a knell of despair would resound through many parts of Europe.[44]

This effort to stiffen the government's attitude through pressure in the House was worth a try, he probably thought, for Mr. Eden and Mr. Duff Cooper were still in the cabinet and hope never quite left him until, as he tells so movingly in *The Gathering Storm,* Mr. Eden resigned. He closed with a warning to the government's supporters on the back benches that nothing could be more improvident or more imprudent than for Great Britain to ignore the moral force involved in the public opinion of the world.

As between Mr. Churchill and Mr. Chamberlain, the latter felt sure he could, by his own efforts, stave off the war and probably avoid it altogether. He therefore undervalued national unity and international good will. (He often spoke of them as needed, but by "national unity" he meant doing things his way and by "international good will," doing things Hitler's way.) Mr. Churchill, because he knew war was not only inevitable but imminent, cared little for the effect of his speeches upon dictator sensibilities, but much for the approbation of potential allies and neutrals in a world war. Domestically, he recognized that life or death depended upon national unity and good morale. In this critical year, therefore, Mr. Churchill cast no insults at Members, abstained from cutting remarks, and tamed his thunderbolts. Toward Labour, Liberal, and Conservative, even toward the single Communist, Mr. William Gallacher, he was uniformly courteous and kindly. Whenever opportunity presented itself, he repaired the damage worked by the Prime Minister's disagreeable and exacerbating manner. Later he reaped his reward when the very same House of Commons supported him in a spirit it could never display toward Neville Chamberlain and when Mr. Chamberlain himself was willing to work under his erstwhile adversary with the utmost loyalty.

THE HOUSE OF COMMONS AND BERCHTESGADEN, II
FEBRUARY 12, 1938

It is never easy for a British Prime Minister whose Foreign Secretary and Foreign Office officials oppose him to launch a policy which he is unwilling to declare boldly and defend honestly on the floor of the House of Commons. A man whose warm personal charm had already endeared him to the House might achieve it —certainly not Neville Chamberlain. Or if, like Henry VIII, he had understood how to say:

We at no time stand so highly in our estate royal as in the time of Parliament, wherein we, as head and you as members are conjoined and knit together in one body politic so as whatsoever offence or injury during that time is offered to the meanest member of the House, is to be judged as done against our presence and the whole court of Parliament,[45]

his position vis-à-vis Hitler and Mussolini would have been materially strenghtened. Instead, he was driven into a strategy, compounded partly of necessity and partly of personal predilection, in which the timing of moves was very important. The twin policies of allowing Germany to expand into Austria and Czechoslovakia "by peaceful means" and of securing stability in Europe, by the creation of a four-power condominium headed by Germany and Great Britain, were at once too dangerous and too iniquitous to be disclosed to the House of Commons in December on the eve of the long Christmas recess.

A preparatory step had been taken in October, when the British Ambassador at Rome approached Ciano with regard to renewing the conversations interrupted by the Nyon Conference in September. It is now known that Mr. Chamberlain at that time designated an agent to serve as a "direct and secret link" between himself and Dino Grandi, the Italian Ambassador in London. After January 15 this agent saw and talked with the Ambassador almost daily up to the time of Mr. Eden's resignation on February 20. How much advice was given and received, one does not know.

When Parliament reconvened on February 1, it was evident that Germany was preparing to move in Austria. By February 11 His Majesty's government were informed by their representatives abroad that Dr. Schuschnigg had accepted an invitation to Berchtesgaden for the following day. Anschluss was on its way, and Mussolini ran for cover. On February 16, his Foreign Minister wrote to Grandi that it was "imperative to use the interval between the fourth and fifth acts of the Austrian affair" for negotiating with London:

Tomorrow, should the *Anschluss* be an accomplished fact, should Greater Germany by then press on our frontiers with the weight of its whole seventy million, then it would become increasingly difficult for us to reach an agreement or even talk with the English, since it would be impossible to prevent the entire world interpreting our policy of *rapprochement* with London as a journey to Canossa under German pressure.

It made no difference whether results of the *pourparlers* were positive or negative:

But there must be a conclusion—and that quickly. For should still further delays be caused by the Chinese wall of prejudices and conditions, should the Nazis' march into Austria in the meantime make its final advance and present us with a *fait accompli,* then there would exist no alternative and we would have to direct our policy in a spirit of sharp, open, immutable hostility towards the Western Powers. . . . I am certain that you will find a way of making the English understand.[46]

This quotation takes care nicely of the arguments in the House of Commons as to whether Mr. Eden and the late Under-Secretary Lord Cranborne, who resigned with him, were exaggerating when they spoke of threats, intimations of "now or never," and "surrender to blackmail." The Prime Minister thought they were, and he indignantly denied that pressure had been exerted by the Italians.

The incredible cloak-and-dagger atmosphere in which Mr. Eden came to resign through the connivance of the Prime Minister, his secret agent, and the Italian Ambassador is described in a letter from Grandi to Ciano, dated February 19, 1938:

Chamberlain, in fact, addressing his questions directly to me, expected from me—this was obvious—nothing more nor less than those details and definite answers which were useful to him as ammunition against Eden. This I at once realized and tried to supply . . . all the ammunition which I considered might be useful. . . . There is no doubt that in this connection the contacts previously established between myself and Chamberlain through his confidential agent proved to be very valuable. . . . Yesterday evening after the Downing Street meeting, Chamberlain secretly sent his agent to me (we made the appointment in an ordinary public taxi) to say that he "sent me cordial greetings, that he had appreciated my statements which had been very useful to him, and that he was confident that everything would go very well next day."[47]

It was clear in the debate that followed Mr. Eden's resignation on February 21 and Labour's motion of censure on February 22 that certain Members had some inkling of the secret agent and of some of the language used by Grandi. Mr. Lloyd George was able to trap Mr. Chamberlain into damaging admissions in his attempt, so to speak, to establish an alibi. The Prime Minister was forced to acknowledge that he had withheld the contents of an Italian document from the Foreign Secretary until after Mr. Eden's resignation was in his hands:

PM: The right hon. Gentleman is evidently trying to say that I have done something disgraceful.

LG: Yes.

PM: I want to be perfectly frank. I do not see that I have done anything of the kind.

LG: Why wasn't the document communicated until Monday after the Foreign Secretary had resigned?

PM: What is the implication against me?

LG: The document should have been received and turned over to the Foreign Secretary before his resignation.

PM: Is that the disgraceful thing I did?

LG: Yes, certainly when such great issues are involved.[48]

Some severe strictures have been passed upon the House of Commons for its failures in 1938, but it must be confessed that it is hard to see where the British parliamentary system provides checks against such behavior on the part of a Prime Minister. The House assumes, and must assume, that it is dealing with a Prime Minister whose personal honor is above reproach. It has not the equipment for dealing with a man who carries on conspiratorial relations with a foreign power.

It is clear, too, from the debates that Mr. Chamberlain, like his father, was a mean fighter in a tight spot. On these occasions a wave of nostalgia for Mr. Baldwin usually swept the House. On the first day of the February debates centering about Mr. Eden's resignation of February 20, the Prime Minister exercised considerable restraint, but the second day's debate took place as a result of a Labour motion censuring the government for the circumstances under which the resignation had taken place, and on motions of censure Mr. Chamberlain was likely to throw virtue to the winds. He had already permitted his anti-Eden clique to start a rumor, brought into the House the first day of debate by Mr. Lennox-Boyd, that the late Foreign Secretary had collapsed physically and mentally under the strain of office. There were traces of this idea in the Prime Minister's speech on the second day, but, what was worse, there was an implication of some lack of integrity in Mr. Eden. At this point a Labour party back-bencher, thoroughly disgusted, shouted: "In boxing you'd be disqualified." In the division, for reasons already discussed in connection with the relations of the parties, the government won almost their normal majority.

Between February 22 and March 24, when the Prime Minister made the formal restatement of policy necessitated by Anschluss, all groups who opposed appeasement worked to modify or reverse the government's policy toward Czechoslovakia. Labour wanted a general election, but would not accept a popular front. The dissident Conservatives tried to weaken Mr. Chamberlain's position within the party by convincing Members of the necessity of collective security and the danger of bilateral arrangements with the dictators. Mr. Kuhn of the *New York Times,* however, estimated that not more than 80 out of 429 government supporters, and probably only 50, would have supported Mr. Churchill in a policy of military commitments in Europe. Someone remarked that the dissidents were stronger in quality than in numbers.

Between the factual statement on the Nazi march into Austria on March 14 and the restatement of foreign policy necessitated by this coup, the Prime Minister allowed ten days to elapse, though he was pressed strongly by Labour and Liberal Members. The statement as finally made was strong enough to give hope to friends of Czechoslovakia, but not strong enough to anger or alarm Hitler. It included the sentences to which Mr. Newton, the British Minister at Prague, referred in his letter of April 12:[49]

> So far as Czechoslovakia is concerned, it seems to His Majesty's Government that now is the time when all the resources of diplomacy should be enlisted in the cause of peace. . . . For their part His Majesty's Government will at all times be ready to render any help in their power, by whatever means might seem most appropriate, towards the solution of questions likely to cause difficulties between the German and the Czechoslovakian Governments.[50]

For purely technical reasons the Labour party did not demand a division, but the press made an effort to create the impression that there was no real opposition in Great Britain to the government's foreign policy—an idea that was scotched ten days later by a Labour motion of censure:

> That, as the foreign policy of His Majesty's Government can not arrest the dangerous drift toward war, and is inconsistent with their electoral pledges, this House is of the opinion that the issue should be submitted to the country without delay.[51]

Since, on the occasion of the ensuing debate, the Prime Minister was wholly unable to answer the questions directed to him in such a way as to controvert the terms of the motion, he neglected them completely and chose instead to treat the entire debate as a party contest. Sir Archibald Sinclair, though out of sympathy with the demand for a general election under the existing critical circumstances, nevertheless dealt the Prime Minister some hard blows. He rebuked him for flippant references to Russia and, in effect, accused him of lying during the February debates. Several other Members spoke with distaste of the Prime Minister's remarks and of his failure to answer questions. Mr. Alexander, in closing for Labour, criticized the government for engaging in a whole network of secret diplomacy:

> The Prime Minister's statement of February 22 with regard to its being wrong to delude weak and small nations that the Covenant of the League protected them, in my view sealed the fate of Austria. He has now been sealing the fate of Spain. If he does he may also seal the fate of France.[52]

What emerges from the debates of the session taken as a whole is that all sides of the House soon detected new turns and twists of Mr. Chamberlain's tactics but that the attempts of various groups to block or divert him never had more than nuisance value. In fact, they had the effect of driving him to use more and more questionable methods. Lord Halifax' appointment in February to succeed Mr. Eden transferred the Foreign Secretary from the House of Commons to the House of Lords and thereafter the Prime Minister himself had to bear the brunt of foreign-policy debates and questions. On March 2, with full knowledge of what had actually happened between Hitler and Dr. Schuschnigg at Berchtesgaden, he told the House that there appeared to be no juridical violation of treaties regarding Austrian independence "if two statesmen have agreed to certain conditions to improve relations." This reply may not have hoodwinked his interrogator, but it served as an assurance to Hitler that Great Britain would not interfere with Anschluss, however brutally it might be carried out. Thus one of the very preventives available to the House, question time, was perverted and pressed into the service of appeasement.

THE DEMOCRATIC PROCESS AND BERCHTESGADEN, III
SEPTEMBER 29, 1938

The Prime Minister's policy statement subsequent to the invasion of Austria marked the actual turning point of the struggle

with his opponents in the House of Commons. Labour's motion
of censure on April 4 was only a rear-guard battle. Austria, nevertheless, had changed the course of Conservative thinking, and one
result was that within two months the Prime Minister was dealt
his first defeat—not in foreign policy to be sure, but in the matter
of air defenses.

This came about in an interesting way. In the balloting early in
the session, Mr. Perkins, a private Member, won the right to introduce a bill, and the bill he introduced called for an investigation of air navigation. A committee was actually appointed by
the Prime Minister from men whom he thought completely safe
politically, but when its chairman, Lord Cadmon, submitted his
report to the government a few months later, it proved to contain
severe criticisms. There was a debate in Commons on May 12, in
which Lord Winterton, speaking for his chief in the Air Ministry,
who was a peer, was completely unable to satisfy his critics. This
was followed by three demands for independent inquiries, one by
Labour, one by the Liberal party, and one by disgruntled Conservatives. Now a request for an inquiry need not have been interpreted as a vote of censure, but the Prime Minister chose so to
treat Labour's request; a "three-line Whip was put on, supplemented by what the *Times* referred to as "a moral appeal for support from Members." This maneuver left in an equivocal position those government supporters who had sought an inquiry.
Most of them withdrew their names. At first it seemed as though
the old pattern was holding, but there was a significant difference.
Dr. Dalton described it in his speech moving the Labour motion:

> What happened next? The Prime Minister made a clean sweep of all
> politicians to whom he had hitherto given responsibility for air defence. . . .
> The three principal politicians have been removed. Do these changes of per-
> sonnel weaken the case for an inquiry? On the contrary they strengthen it.
> . . . The case for inquiry is even stronger now than it was a fortnight
> ago.[53]

True, the House did not get its inquiry, but it did force the Prime
Minister to do something he had not wished to do—he had had
to make a change in his cabinet under pressure from Commons.

No comparable change of course can be seen in the field of foreign affairs until after Munich and the end of the 1937–38 session.

But there was a change in the climate of opinion in House and country similar to that revealed by Lord Londonderry's letter of December 6, 1937.[54] After the far-reaching ramifications of Anschluss began to be understood, government propaganda about the miserable Czechs was of no avail. The Nazis were seen for what they were, and appeasement henceforth had no basis in German gievances—only in British expediency. "Expediency" is not a word wholly anathema in Great Britain. For seven hundred years democracy had climbed from freedom to freedom on its shoulders, and it was not until after the Prime Minister's visit to Berchtesgaden in September, 1938, that the demands which may be made in the name of expediency began to revolt the British people. That, however, takes us into the 1938–39 session of Parliament.

What goes before indicates pretty well how Berchtesgaden III came to be possible and suggests some issues of importance in the functioning of democratic processes, especially in Great Britain. From the standpoint of the British government, there are three ways of bringing about a change in the nation's foreign policy:

1. To tell the country frankly what change is contemplated and why, using parliamentary debate and free newspaper discussion to obtain the nation's approval.
2. To make a change and try to carry it out without telling the country at all until the aim has been achieved.
3. To tell the country part of the change contemplated, but not all, relying upon secret diplomacy and chicanery to bring the new policy into effect.

The choice of the third method by the Chamberlain government created a difficult situation. In the first place, Labour, the Liberals, and the dissident Conservatives were opposed to the part of the Prime Minister's program which was announced and were even more bitterly opposed to the part which they felt to be beneath the surface, not to be reached effectively in debate. On the other hand, a sufficiently large number of the Conservative supporters of the government were in sympathy with the announced policy and blind to the criminal, unannounced policy, so that no vote against the government was ever possible. The Dominions, who had always to be considered, were not seriously at odds with the announced policy, partly because they were never fully alive to the dangers into which the government were heading, and this in turn was partly owing to the fact that there was a good deal of censorship and even management of the British press during the late 1930's. This management was exerted chiefly with respect to the *Times,* the very journal which is relatively more influential in the Dominions than in the United Kingdom. Consequently, little opposition to appeasement was voiced in the Dominions at first. Finally, the opposition of the dictators to the government's policy as announced in the House of Commons and the courage and determination of the Czechs in face of the unannounced policy united to force the Chamberlain government into the machinations that culminated in Munich. Through the elimination of the House of Commons from effective participation in foreign policy, especially after March, 1938, Mr. Chamberlain faced Hitler and Mussolini at Munich without the powerful moral support of the elected representatives of the British people. The two dictators took advantage of his exposed position to make of him an unwilling tool for the destruction of Czechoslovakia, the weakening of France, and the isolation of Russia.

Here we have a fundamental factor in the execution of foreign policy which Mr. Chamberlain was completely unable to appraise, and it is this inability that, in my opinion, made him a far more dangerous premier than Mr. Baldwin. When a government, especially in a democratic nation, long pursues a policy which, if revealed fully in all its aspects, would contravene the nation's common sense of morality and human values, the government will be forced to act in secretive and devious ways. Secrecy and deviousness in diplomacy need not be fatal, provided that later, when the whole story can be known, the general conscience of the nation will be satisfied that the aim was correct. This was the case with President Roosevelt's prewar policy. It is, however, fatal to the effectiveness of the government's policy if all the world perceives that the course pursued is at odds with the nation's conscience.

Is it unfair to say that Hitler was so strikingly successful in his international policies partly because the world felt that he was *not* out on a limb—it was felt that his actions in the field of foreign policy were *not* at odds with the deeper feelings of the German people? On the other hand, the weakness of Neville Chamberlain's policy lay just here. The world did not understand what was going wrong in England, but no one trusted in Neville Chamberlain's ability "to deliver the goods," because it was felt that he did not carry with him the English conscience. He could never be friends with Hitler and Mussolini, and they knew it. He failed not only because he chose the wrong policies and because no one was able to stop him from pursuing them; but, over and above this, he failed because, in the 1930's, the policies he pursued, even if they had been shrewd, were not really open to a British government functioning democratically.

One can see this more clearly by comparing Mr. Chamberlain with Mr. Churchill. Winston Churchill surely was not naturally a League of Nations man. He was a patriot in the good, old-fashioned sense, and, I think, a really strong system of alliances would have been good enough for him; but in March, 1936, he addressed the Conservative Members' Committee on Foreign Affairs in words which Mr. Chamberlain would have done well to ponder. After a magnificent panorama of British foreign policy in the past, Mr. Churchill concluded:

The League of Nations is, in a practical sense, a British conception and it harmonizes perfectly with all our past methods and actions. Moreover, it harmonizes with those broad ideas of right and wrong which we have always followed. We wish for the reign of law and freedom among nations and within nations, and it was for that, and nothing less than that, that those bygone architects of our repute, magnitude, and civilisation fought, and won. The dreams of a reign of international law and of the settlement of disputes by patient discussion, but still in accordance with what is lawful and just, is very clear to the British people. You must not underrate the force which these ideals exert upon the modern British democracy. One does not know how these seeds are planted by the winds of centuries in the hearts of the working people. They are there, and just as strong as their love of liberty. We should not neglect them, because they are the essence of the genius of this island. Therefore, we believe that in the fostering and fortifying of the League of Nations will be found the best means of defending our island security, as well as maintaining grand universal causes with which we have very often found our own interests in natural accord.[55]

Why, though, if the policy of the Chamberlain government was at odds with the nation's moral character, could it not have been altered by the determined opposition of the better elements in a great democracy? The answer yielded by this analysis seems to be that Great Britain in 1938 was, for all practical purposes of foreign policy, not a democracy but an oligarchy, in which Mr. Chamberlain functioned almost dictatorially. The period from early 1936, when Sir Samuel Hoare was brought back into the cabinet, to February 21, 1938, when Mr. Eden made his personal statement to the House of Commons on resigning from the cabinet, was marked by a succession of steps which amounted to a seizure of power by Mr. Chamberlain and his immediate supporters. During the remainder of 1938 Great Britain's foreign policy and, one is tempted to add, that of France as well were completely controlled by a small inner cabinet group, and these men themselves apparently were entirely submissive to Neville Chamberlain.

This raises another question. How came it that a seizure of power could occur in one of the world's greatest democracies? At least one explanation seems to fit the circumstances.

In Great Britain the single-member constituency is likely to (and between the wars did) operate to give the government a decisive majority in the House of Commons. Under the strict party discipline which is exercised there, this is not the source of embarrassment that a large majority may be to an American administration. It does not become unwieldy and tend to get out of control. Under all but the most unusual circumstances the government in Great Britain can count on carrying through all their important policies, foreign and domestic, without a successful vote of no confidence. It is easily possible under the British system to run the country dictatorially for five years at least.

Normally, there are several checks on any tendency to govern dictatorially. One of these is applicable to all parties; this general restraint is effected by the solid belief of the British people in democracy. A Prime Minister who wishes to stay in power another five years must curb his natural tendencies toward authoritarianism. But this was not the case in the 1937–38 session. Mr. Chamberlain was older than Lord Baldwin, who had already retired. His ambitions were less to stay in office after the next general election than to lead his country to safety and to establish her on the road to prosperity within the years of his present government. This could be achieved, he knew, only if peace could be preserved. To achieve peace, it seemed to him justifiable to ignore and defy, openly and by subterfuge, the principles which are necessary if parliamentary government is to function democratically.

A second important check or safeguard of democracy may lie in a democratic organization of the parties. If the parties themselves are run on democratic lines, it is less dangerous than at first appears that the British system frowns on dissent from party policy on the floor of the House. The safeguard of a democratic party organization is the one upon which the Labour party in particular is inclined to pride itself.

A third safeguard is expressed in the phrase "he is a good House of Commons man." Its meaning is fairly obvious—it involves loyalty to House of Commons history and traditions, a certain decent respect for your opponent, a willingness to accept honest criticism and to deliver it without venom and with absolute honesty on the floor. Its full flavor and all its gallantry can be appreciated only after hours spent reading the *Journals* and learning to understand the significance of a host of little incidents. One of the most endearing traits of the House is its habit of picking up a phrase from a speech and keeping it at hand for use again and again, so that on each occasion of reuse it comes to have new connotations. At the opening of the new Parliament in 1935, a new speaker had to be chosen. In his acceptance he, of course, referred to his own inadequacy, but he also expressed the hope that under his speakership there would be more of the "cut-and-thrust" of debate. This delighted the House, and one runs across it throughout the subsequent reports. In this community Neville Chamberlain was not at home, despite his facility in parliamentary technicalities. He was not at heart "a good House of Commons man." To the Conservative, Winston Churchill, as to the Communist, William Gallacher, no worse could be said of a colleague. This third safeguard of British democracy is a very powerful one on which all parties pride themselves.

A fourth safeguard is closely related to this feeling for the spirit of the House of Commons, and it is the one upon which the Conservative party chiefly relied. This is a high standard of personal integrity. In other words, the party placed its honor in the hands of the leader, who in the 1930's was the Prime Minister as well. Under such circumstances the kind of integrity required to serve as a safeguard of democracy is not the day-to-day kind that serves most of us well enough. If the Prime Minister is a good House of Commons man, the traditions of the House automatically protect him against himself; but if he is not and has to rely upon his own ethics alone to keep him from self-deception and from betraying his party's trust, then his critical sense must be delicately poised and sensitive to the slightest deviations in his own conduct.

Unfortunately, Neville Chamberlain lacked the two safeguards upon which his party depended most heavily. He was never at heart a good House of Commons man, and he was somewhat obtuse with respect to the fine distinctions which must be drawn by a man who accepts for himself the total responsibility for making the moral decisions of a nation. When democratic principles most needed courageous expression, not only did he fail to supply it, but he even connived at their destruction. And for what? "Peace in our time." After Munich one Member of the House bitterly remarked that the Prime Minister was an old man: "It might be peace in his time, but it certainly would not be for the rest of us." This remark in itself is not in the House of Commons spirit, and it is one of many which reveal the deterioration of the manners of the House under Mr. Chamberlain's leadership.

It must be concluded that the House of Commons was excluded from positive participation in foreign policy during 1938 by deliberate intention of the Prime Minister, but its indirect influence was inevitably significant for the future. Innumerable questions and frequent debates revealed more and more clearly to the world, and to the British people themselves, that the Prime Minister's policy was dangerous and at odds with the basic tenets of British society; this, in turn, made it impossible for Mr. Chamberlain to collaborate with the dictators as an equal; it encouraged Americans who believed in Great Britain to organize public opinion in the United States against the isolationists; and perhaps it was this which at a later date facilitated co-operation between Mr. Churchill's coalition government and Soviet Russia in the defeat of Hitler.

SOME ASPECTS OF LONDON MERCANTILE ACTIVITY DURING THE REIGN OF QUEEN ELIZABETH

By J. R. JONES

Moravian College

> I would have men of such constancy put to sea, that their business might be everything and their intent everywhere; for that's it that always makes a good voyage of nothing.
>
> SHAKESPEARE, *Twelfth Night* (Act II, scene 4)

SO SHAKESPEARE described the merchants of his day. Men made up of a curious blend of caution and daring, whose cupidity was so great that they scoured the known and the unknown in search of wealth—at the same time carefully working out methods that would allow them to gain security for the wealth that they had already garnered. Yet these men who founded the lines of trade that were to make England the wealthiest nation of the world in the eighteenth and nineteenth centuries and to insure her position among the powerful nations of the twentieth have been forgotten. Their techniques are still used, but their inventors are unknown; the outposts that they established and made permanent still are great marts of trade for English commodities, but the men who established them are forgotten, unless they were sailors who dramatically sailed the seven seas, preying, with spectacular success, upon the ships of the king of Spain. Nevertheless, the men who demonstrated the practical uses for trade of the new discoveries were men who risked their lives and their fortunes during the sixteenth century to bring English commodities to strange ports and return with strange goods to introduce them to Englishmen.

To study the work of these men; to get the day-by-day record of their painful and sometimes disastrous struggle to build up England's trade, one must turn to that vast repository of trade mi-

186

nutiae known as the "Port Books." If the student should quail at the endless vista of trade detail, whose only order is chronological, let him be of good faith, for from those fragments the pictures of men will arise that have been long forgotten but which are the faithful images of those that laid the foundation for the England that the modern world has known.

To give some idea of those merchants and their activity during the reign of Elizabeth, one of the Port Books has been selected. This book is listed in the Public Record Office as E. 190, bundle 7, book 8; and it covers the period from the feast of St. Michael the Archangel, or Michaelmas, 1587, to the following Easter, in the twenty-ninth year of Elizabeth, 1588. It is the report of the collector of the tax called "subsidy and poundage," from imports on all items brought into the port of London, except the taxes collected on wine.[1] This book contains seventy-eight complete folios.

Upon opening the book to examine the pages, it will be noted that each page is divided into four columns. The first column is reserved for the number of the entry that is to be made. This is followed by the name of the vessel, its port of registry, its tonnage, the name of the master, and the port whence it came. This last bit of information is sometimes conveyed by the term *ab ibidem* when the shipment is coming from the same port as that from which the vessel is registered. Likewise, the term *ut predictus* is used if the vessel, which is always named, discharged goods that were noted in entries subsequent to the initial one. The line containing all the information pertaining to the ship extends across the second and largest column but will, occasionally, extend into the third column. The second line is always restricted to the middle column and commences with information concerning the merchant. Apparently most of the merchants carried on their importing business as individuals; but, when two of them joined forces to import goods from a particular port, both names were mentioned; when, presumably, more than two merchants were so engaged, the notations *et alias, et sociis,* or even "& company," were used, following the name of one of the merchants. After the name of the merchant was given, the name of the London livery company was given, if he belonged to one. If he did not, the term "indigenous" was given, if a resident of London. If the merchant was a citizen of another English town, the name of that town was given; if he was an alien, it was so stated.

Immediately following the information concerning the merchants, and still within the second column, came the names of the containers of the goods and their contents, together with their weights or measures. In the third column was placed the combined value of the articles named in the second column, according to the official rates. In the fourth column was placed the subsidy of tonnage and poundage as charged against the value totaled in the third column. This subsidy amounted to a tax of 1*s.* on the pound. At the foot of this column the charges for the subsidy are totaled. These figures are then added up in a grand total expressed at the end of the book, which, for the period between September 30, 1587, and April 7, 1588, amounted to £9,425 18*s.* 1½*d.* A careful examination of the page totals will uncover some discrepancies, but the modern researcher will forgive the customer for his errors, as Roman numerals were used to keep these accounts.

As an example of the kind of information to be provided by the Port Books, let us take the scope of the foreign trade that found its way to London in the fall and winter of 1587–88. There were fifty-eight different ports recorded as being the source of the goods contained in the 2,195 entries reported. Of the fifty-eight ports, only nineteen were credited with 10 or more entries. This can be taken to indicate that the ports with less than 10 entries for the six and one-half months that this record runs, had only a casual trade with London and that the bulk of the trade was carried on with the ports that were credited with the greater number of entries. On the other hand, little is served by reducing the classification to narrower limits on the basis of the number of entries, for the reason that this method does not consider the value or size of the entries for the particular ports. For example, the 31 entries from the Russian Company's port of St. Nicholas in Russia were more valuable, according to the official rate, than were the whole of the 307 entries from Rouen. However, our classification of the nineteen ports that have the largest number of entries can be relied upon to have included the most important sources of goods for the London market. The list, arranged according to the number of entries from each port, is shown in the accompanying tabulation.

Stade	513	Rochelle	37
Middleborough	458	Dorte	34
Rouen	307	St. Nicholas	31
Barbary	116	Ancusen (Enkhuisen)	30
Hamburg	116	Bordeaux	27
Elbing	103	Rotterdam	23
Amsterdam	64	Calais	20
St. Juan de Luce	63	Dieppe	16
Flushing	48	St. Lucas (St. Lucar)	15
Embden	41		

The scope of London's active trade with other countries in 1587–88, stretched from the Arctic Sea to the Mediterranean. This active trade amounts to more than 94 per cent of the entire foreign trade. But over 74 per cent of that trade, as represented by the nineteen ports with the most entries, occurred between Stade and Hamburg in western Germany and Rouen in northern France.[2] Thus the bulk of London's trade was centered upon the area that was, principally, the monopoly of the Merchant Adventurers.

The homelands of the aliens who brought goods to London also corroborate the evidence of the entries that London's trade was principally with those countries bordering the North Sea and the English Channel. Of the forty-five aliens listed as importing merchants for the period covered, twenty-nine were identified as captains of vessels, all of which were registered in Dutch ports excepting two from Kircaldy, Scotland. These Dutch masters were credited with only thirty-seven entries. From the rest of the alien entries, six were classified as merchants of the Hansa, credited with 37 entries, and five of the ten aliens whose country was not mentioned may be identified with reasonable assurance as merchants of Dutch towns, bringing the total of Dutch importers up to forty out of the total of forty-five aliens bringing goods to London during this period. More important, the total number of entries credited to aliens amounted to only 80, in contrast to the 2,195 entries for the entire book. This is eloquent and persuasive evidence that London's merchants dominated the trade that London carried on with countries across the seas.

The observation that English trade was principally centered between Rouen and Hamburg certainly cannot be classified as a contribution to the knowledge of England's sixteenth-century trade, although the precise ratio of London's trade that came from that area may have some interest. For many years that area had been the scene of great activity in trade, as carried on by the Merchant Adventurers and the Merchant Staplers. By Elizabeth's day, however, the Merchant Staplers had ceased to be a great factor in English trade, first, because of the attacks from the Merchant Adventurers, who wanted to force them to come under the regulation of the Merchant Adventurers and be members of it when they sold cloth; second, because of the loss of their staple town at Calais during the reign of Queen Mary; and, finally, because of the general advance of English weaving[3] that had taken place during the second half of the century.[4] But the evidence considered here has to do with the imports that were brought to London by the merchants of that famous company.

The importance of the Merchant Adventurers to the city that was designated as their staple town is demonstrated by a comparison of the entries listed for Stade and Embden. At this time, 1587, Stade was substituted for the unfavorably located Embden as the headquarters of the company.[5] The effect of this transfer seems to have been immediate, for Stade leads all other ports in the number of entries recorded, with 513, all entries being recorded between November 28 and December 5; and Embden drops to 41 entries, which gained tenth place for her on the comparative list of entries. Middleburg in Zeeland was made the staple town of the Merchant Adventurers in 1586 for the Low Countries, and here, too, we find the favorable effect that the Merchant Adventurers had upon the trade of the cities that gave them trading opportunities, for Middleburg ranks second in number of entries, with 458. Hamburg, with 116 entries, is tied for fourth place with the Barbary Coast, but the important point here is its comparison with Stade. Hamburg in 1576[6] had refused to renew the privileges to the Merchant Adventurers that she had granted in 1567.[7] Thus from 1578 to 1611 Hamburg was not a staple of the company, and, in 1587 at least, she had the bitter experience of seeing the neighboring city of Stade[8] get the lion's share of London's trade.

These figures indicate the great importance of the Merchant Adventurers to the import trade of England. Just under 60 per cent of all the entries in this book came from the area that was their monopoly. This result is based on figures that do not attempt to discriminate between interlopers and Merchant Adventurers; but it is safe to say that the greatest share was brought in by members of the company, and this seems to establish the commanding position that the Merchant Adventurers held in the development of the London market in the sixteenth century.

The network of trade that the merchants of London were weaving over northern Europe was not restricted to the North Sea area of the Low Countries and the western Hanseatic towns. The Eastland merchants established a flourishing outpost in Elbing about 1580,[9] in order to secure supplies of wax, pitch, lumber, grain, and hemp at its source in the Baltic. Such supplies were not available in sufficient quantities at Stade and Hamburg[10] for London's demand, and Elbing, in the heart of the Baltic area, had large supplies of such commodities. The Russian Company was at this time bringing in competing supplies; nevertheless, the demand in London was so active that London merchants brought in sufficient quantities of goods from Elbing to give her sixth place among the towns exporting to London, contained in 103 entries. Elbing is likewise the third of the Hanseatic towns among the first six towns that were the principal exporters to London, whereas the Low Countries have only one town that ranked in that list.

The evidence presented here leaves no doubt that the English were actively engaged in exploiting the trading possibilities of the Hanseatic area. This area was easily accessible by sea, but a more important consideration is the fact that the area was the regional center of a large trade that had been laboriously built up by the merchants of the Hanseatic cities. By Elizabeth's time, as the Port Book for 1587–88 shows, the merchants of London were making a determined effort to capture that trade—at least that part of it going to London. The effort that the Elizabethan merchants were making to capture this northern European trade was the principal attempt to expand the trade of England. The advantages which the area offered included well-established trade centers, where the modes and techniques of trade were understood by all, where the area was in need of English wool and had the commodities that were essential to English welfare. In short, they complemented one another. When such situations exist, the trade will always be greater than to areas where trade is poorly established, although greater profits might be offered for greater risks.[11]

This generality is borne out by the trade of 1587–88 with the Hanseatic and Low Country cities. The entries show that the Merchant Adventurers were as interested in tapping the trade built up in those regions as they were in disposing of English cloths. Just as the Merchant Adventurers of the Russian Company were intent upon trying to tap the Eastern and Indian trade centered in Persia[12] by way of Russia, so the Merchant Adventurers were interested in trying to reach the northern and middle European trade centered in the Hanseatic cities and the Low Countries. This conception of English trading expansion might go far in explaining the reasons for the difficulties of the Merchant Adventurers in finding a satisfactory staple town after they had to leave Antwerp in 1567.[13] The trade routes for which Antwerp was the terminus had spread their tentacles throughout the interior of Europe—a terminus that could no longer be used after the Spanish capture of the city in 1585 and the subsequent blockade imposed by the Dutch. This was a tragedy that one is reminded of when the Port Book for 1587–88 fails to record a single entry from that greatest of all ports of the sixteenth century.

Although the London merchant prudently centered his activity in the well-established areas across the Channel and the North Sea, he was by no means averse to experimenting with other trading areas. The Russian Company, established in 1555, the French Company in 1577, the Turkey Company in 1581, the Venetian Company in 1582, and the Barbary Company in 1585 testify, through their membership lists, to the willingness of the London merchant to venture to unknown shores in search of new trading opportunities. The names of these companies indicate the scope of their bounding ambitions, and the Port Book for 1587–88 shows that these ambitions were not doomed to remain as paper plans but were exploited with energy.

The Russian Company seems to have been quite active in 1587, although there are only 13 entries credited to Robert Wake, mercer, agent for the company.[14] The total value, according to the official rate book, amounted to £12,560 brought in between the second of October and the ninth of November. This sum, which was far below the market value of the goods, was in itself double the original capitalization of the company.[15] Conseqently, the Russian Company must have been carrying on a fair amount of business with Russia. Also, since the principal commodities brought in were tallow, wax, flax, cordage, train oil, seal skins, and various types of hides, it would appear that the grandiose schemes that stemmed from the trips of Chancellor and Jenkinson to Persia through Russia to exploit the trade in that direction[16] had not been realized. Since the commodities that were brought from Russia were the same as those brought from Elbing, it suggests a very good reason for the difficulties that the Russian Company was to have later on in the sixteenth century and the first part of the seventeenth.[17] It is obvious that, if the same commodities could be obtained from Elbing, of comparable quality, that port would be the more desirable source because of its proximity to England, as compared to the far-northern journey to St. Nicholas or Archangel. In fact, the only conceivable way that the Russian trade could be kept alive under such circumstances would be by way of the relatively high prices that English cloths could fetch in Russia, as compared to the commodities purchased for export. But the danger would always exist that competition in one form or another would drive down the price of English cloths in Russian commodities, and the trade would have to cease until the price ratio, necessary for its existence, was re-established.[18]

The Russian Company entries provide information in quite another direction, as well as the character of the trade that they pursued. Following the first 6 entries devoted to the Russian Company's goods on Octobr 2, 1587, there are 6 more entries registering goods brought to London from Russia by Sir Francis Walsingham and his brother-in-law by his first wife, Sir George Barnes, haberdasher, alderman, and Lord Mayor of London in 1586.[19] Although Lady Walsingham died in 1564, this evidence seems to indicate that the family attachment, so formed, had been strong and lasting. The goods brought in by the two men amounted to £606 13s. 4d., all of it invested in 27,000 pounds of flax. This information throws some light upon Sir Francis Walsingham's interest in Russian trade. Since the vessels that brought the knightly partners' goods to London were the same vessels that were laden with the Russian Company's goods, it can at least be said that they were associated with the Russian Company in 1587.[20] However, the records do not make it clear that either of them was a member of the company, although it seems hard to believe that the company would have permitted nonmembers to trade within their monopoly and use their own ships to convey the goods.

The practice of private trade to Russia was not confined to Sir Francis Walsingham and Sir George Barnes. Francis Cherrie, vintner; William Wilkes, indigenous; Stephan Hosier and John Spencer, a partnership of indigenous merchants; Thomas Bassard, master of the "George Noble" of London, and his company; and Zacharie May, purser of the "Mary Roase" of London also brought in goods from Russia in Russian Company ships. The imports of Thomas Bassard and his company and the imports of the purser, Zacharie May, might be explained on the ground that they were brought in under the ancient privilege of portage that was granted to mariners. But the rest of the importers were not mariners. Francis Cherrie, whose imports were evalued at £173 11*s.* 8*d.,* had been and continued to be a very active importer in London for many years. It would seem incredible that these men could bring goods to London in Russian Company ships, and from the same Russian ports, unless they were members of the company. Any other explanation would imply that they were interlopers and acting in direct violation of the company's monopolistic charter. The facts do not warrant that assumption. Consequently, there must have been some method whereby the members of the company could take part in the Russian trade as private traders, while the company continued to do business as a joint-stock company. There can be no doubt but that the Russian Company was still acting as a joint-stock company, for all the entries are headed "Roberto Wake agent for Company in Russia,"[21] or some variation of that phrase. Thus it seems plain that Roberto Wake was an agent and his principal was the Russian Company, operating with a general fund contributed by members of that company.

Some clarification of the situation is presented by two incidents that directly concerned the principals mentioned here. In 1581 Sir Jerome Horsey had suggested to Sir Francis Walsingham that they undertake private trading to Russia.[22] Again, in 1605, Sir Francis

Cherrie, the same Francis Cherrie, vintner, who has already been noted as trading privately with Russia in 1587, had difficulty with the company over the amount of money that he owed to the corporation as a result of his activities as governor.[23] A part of the difference of opinion was due to the bill that the company entered against his account for "private trade."[24] Thus it seems reasonable to infer that Horsey suggested a legitimate procedure to Walsingham that apparently has been acted upon. This is made clear by the fact that the company recognized such an arrangement when it presented a bill for such private trading to Sir Francis Cherrie.

The fact that some private trading was done, and that very likely done under the provisions of the charter, suggests that the joint-stock feature of the company was adopted to meet the circumstances surrounding the trade to Russia rather than through a desire to create a new business technique. The long and dangerous voyage to Russia did not enhance the attractiveness of the Russian trade to the merchants. The large expenditures required to provide ships large and sturdy enough to sail the turbulent northern waters, as well as the additional expenditures for ship's supplies and wages resulting from such a long voyage, increased the speculative character of the trade. These factors, plus the initially unknown character of the trade, might have induced the sponsors to try to raise funds from merchants who might take a "flyer" to the amount of £25, rather than risk the larger sums necessary to make such a voyage pay a reasonable profit.

Later experience disclosed the fact that it was almost impossible for the company to control their factors[25] and insure honest dealing in Russia. This situation, coupled with large returns in certain years,[26] apparently induced adventurers with larger capital resources to try a larger gamble by trading privately. This would permit them to exercise more adequate control over the factors and receive better returns if fortune favored them. The charter apparently did not interpose a bar to this action, for it was "not explicit on the specifically joint-stock character of the concern."[27] According to this reading of the evidence, it was a matter for the company to settle in its "comonalty": the details for the arrangements of carrying goods in the ships of the company that were returning with Russian goods to London and the charges to be made for such privileges, as well as any additional charges for the privilege of private trade. Certainly, it cannot be denied that some merchants were ready to forego the advantages of the joint-stock company device in favor of the older, established form of private trading under a regulated company.

The Barbary Company, formed in 1585, seems to have done a rather thriving trade in 1587. The entries for this company are simply listed as coming from "Barbary," no mention being made of any particular ports on the Barbary Coast. The 116 entries from Barbary give that trade fourth place, a tie with the city of Hamburg. The principal items of trade were sugar, pannulles, anneill, wax, suckett, almonds, silk nubbes, and even marmalade (fol. 75r), probably thrown in to sweeten the trade.

The trade from Spain likewise continues, despite the fact that the English and Spanish governments were only a few months away from the battle of the narrow seas, where the Armada was defeated. Although the Spanish Company had apparently abandoned their control of the trade,[28] private traders continued to take their chances that the uneasy peace would prevail long enough for them to complete their personal ventures. St. Lucas (or St. Lucar) was the recorded port for 15 entries, and Cadiz for 4. Six entries were merely listed as coming from the coast of Spain. It is interesting to note that all these entries came in during the months of December, January, February, and March, 1587–88, and that they were brought in by English merchants in English vessels, as well as by alien merchants and vessels. Apparently, the ill feeling between the monarchs was not shared by the merchants to the extent that they would cease to trade when it was possible. Furthermore, the reports are by no means complete for the Spanish trade, as the unreported wine trade was probably of far greater importance than the articles listed here.[29]

Thus far this study has surveyed areas of trade that were or had been under the monopoly of one of the great mercantile companies that were principally centered in London. The only region reported in this book that had not been granted to such a company at one time or another in Elizabeth's reign was France. It is interesting to contrast the trade that London carried on with France in 1587–88 with that of the other areas already discussed, using the number of entries as our guide.

Of the nineteen towns listed as having 15 or more entries to their credit, six of them are French towns: Rouen, 307; St. Juan de Luce, 63; Rochelle, 37; Bordeaux, 27; Calais, 20; Dieppe, 16. The total number of entries amount to 472, or 22.8 per cent of all the entries credited to the entire nineteen. Since these nineteen ports accounted for 94.1 per cent of the entries listed in the entire book, we are safe in taking 22 per cent as our figure for the percentage of trade carried on between London and the French ports during the period under discussion.[30] Roughly one-fifth of London's trade was with French ports. Since these figures do not include wine entries, it is justifiable to believe that London's trade with France would actually reach a much higher figure than is indicated.

It is interesting to note the regional differences within France and the regional similarities that ignore the conventional political boundaries. For example, the trade of Rouen, aside from its emphasis on canvas and glass, is hardly to be distinguished from that of Middleburgh. Both export a large quantity of manufactured goods, and both export a smaller amount of spices, sugar, and fruits that are obviously re-exported and prove that both ports have an extensive market that brings goods from all parts of the then known world. The same is true, in lesser degree, of Calais and Dieppe. Rochelle and Bordeaux form a second regional trade area that emphasizes those products that are generally regarded as specifically French in character—such products as salt, wood, feathers, and fruits. These products are typical of the area and, while they might be found in other parts of the world, are more characteristic of their origin than the textiles and metal manufactures of the Rouen area. St. Juan de Luce, at the extreme southern border of France, constitutes a third area, for here Spanish iron, Spanish wool, Seville oil, and other Spanish products were exported to London. The character of the exports from this region had a strongly Spanish flavor throughout. It would make an interesting study to compare prices in separate centers of each of these French regions and the prices of the same articles in London. The findings of this study could then be compared with the price differential existing for London's commodities in the same centers. Such a study would add much to the understanding of the part played by transportation in the structure of prices and would give some inkling of the other factors that likewise influenced prices. This would be especially valuable if the Franco-London trade material was used, because there were no restrictions placed upon individuals who wished to take part in this trade by the government of either France or England during the Elizabethan reign.

The Port Books also yield considerable information about the breadth of the activities of particular merchants during this period. Sir George Barnes has already been mentioned with respect to the Russian trade that he carried on. In addition to his Russian trade, Sir George imported goods amounting to £115 0s. 0d. from Barbary. Whether Sir George was a member of the Barbary Company or not is not stated. Another merchant of interest was Richard Stapers, clothworker. This merchant, whose monument lays claim to the title "the greates merchant in his tyme and the chiefest actor in discovere of the trades of Turkey and East India,"[31] was, with Sir Edward Osborne, the motivating force in exploring the possibilities of the Turkey trade in 1575, which resulted in the letters patent which granted them the monopoly of that trade in 1581.[32] But Stapers' trade was far greater than the Turkey trade in 1587–88. In fact, it is not at all clear that either Stapers or Osborne brought in goods from Turkey during the period covered in this book. The only possibility of such trade is in connection with the trade carried on by Stapers and Osborne with "Petrassa," a port otherwise unidentified. Since the goods that the partners brought in were raw silk, currants, and aniseed (and they were the only merchants who are credited with receiving shipments from this port), it seems likely that the port was either in Barbary or in Turkey. This trade amounted to the large sum of £6,453 6s. 8d.[33] The partners likewise brought in £175 6s. 8d. worth of goods from Amsterdam.[34] Stapers, on his own account, brought in £849 10s. 0d. from Malaga;[35] £73 6s. 8d. from Eymonty;[36] £306 13s. 4d. from Cadiz;[37] £36 13s. 4d. from Hamburg;[38] £210 0s. 0d. from Rouen.[39] Richard Stapers and Company brought in £72 10s. 0d. worth of goods from Rouen;[40] with Alexander Aevnow as partner, Stapers brought in goods valued at £479 10s. 0d. from Barbary[41] and £354 10s. 0d. from the same place, again on his own account.[42] The combined total of the trade that Stapers engaged in, individually and with partners, amounts to £9,099 6s. 8d. This trade ranged from Germany and Holland through France and Spain, into the Mediterranean to the Barbary Coast, and possibly as far as Turkey. Certainly, a tremendous range and activity for a merchant.

It must be pointed out that Stapers, in common with others who depended on foreign trade for their fortunes, did not specialize as does the modern trader. His goods were brought with an eye to the London market, no doubt, but they were the general goods of the territories where he traded. He might have specialized in textiles when exporting from London, but he did not specialize when he returned with goods for London. In this he was very like the Yankee skipper who scoured the seven seas for trade in the early nineteenth century, taking in any kind of goods for which he saw a likelihood for sale when he returned home. Certainly, he was one of those that would have "men of such constancy put to sea, that their business might be everything and their intent everywhere; for that's it that make a good voyage of nothing."

THE GENESIS OF INDUSTRIALISM AND OF MODERN SCIENCE (1560–1640)

By JOHN U. NEF

University of Chicago

I. THE COINCIDENCE OF THE EARLY INDUSTRIAL WITH THE SCIENTIFIC REVOLUTION

BOTH industrialism and the spirit of natural science are novel in history. No earlier civilization than that which emerged in modern Europe was dominated by power-driven machinery and by large-scale enterprise in industry and communications. Never before has this planet been so thickly populated, never has it been so urbanized, with a million or more inhabitants in dozens of cities. Never before have any large proportion of the people gained their livelihood in mechanized occupations, away from the soil and from handicrafts; never before have their leisure hours been filled by mechanized entertainment. In no earlier civilization have learned men looked at nature and at man himself mainly through the eyes of the natural scientist. Alfred North Whitehead, whose philosophical inquiries opened a fresh historical interest in the subject, called the rise of modern science "the most intimate change in outlook which the human race has yet encountered. . . . The quiet growth of science has practically recoloured our mentality so that modes of thought which in former times were exceptional are now broadly spread through the educated world."[1]

It is a commonplace that the coming of industrialism and of modern science are connected. A better understanding of the nature of the connections might help to clarify the changes in human outlook and purpose which have resulted from the combined triumph of industrialism and modern science. A better understanding of the connections might also contribute to knowledge concerning a fundamental issue for philosophy and theology: How far have economic institutions determined thought? How far has the mind itself determined the nature and history of economic institutions?

200

While it is taken for granted that industrialism and modern science are interrelated, it is not realized how closely their beginnings are identified. The conventional view of the industrial revolution has led the learned man and the public alike, in western Europe and the United States, to relate the origins of industrial civilization to the reign of the English King George III, which began in 1760. Every schoolboy is told about Arkwright's water frame, Watt's new steam engine, and many other mechanical inventions of the late eighteenth century. These inventions are represented as transferring English industry from the home to the factory in the period covered by the widely read books of J. L. and Barbara Hammond. The schoolboy takes it as axiomatic that "the rise of modern industry" occurred between 1760 and 1832.

The same schoolboy is taught to relate the rise of modern science to an earlier period. It is hardly necessary to emphasize the spectacular nature of the discovery associated with the Polish astronomer Copernicus (1473–1543), that the earth is not flat and fixed as the center of the universe; that it is instead a revolving sphere moving through space along with a myriad of other spheres. Such a change in man's view of the physical world today catches the imagination of all but the dullest in the industrialized countries, for there almost every child has been impressed with modern scientific knowledge and has had his thinking colored by the scientific outlook. So it is not difficult to make the early history of modern science popular. The teacher can explain that, as a result, above all, of the work of Galileo (1564–1642), Kepler (1571–1630), and Newton (1642–1727), what were to be long regarded as the correct views of the motion of the spheres and the correct laws of all motion superseded older, incorrect, and, as it has been made to seem, childish views which possessed the learned men of antiquity and the Middle Ages.

Newton died a generation before the time when, as we were taught, the industrial revolution began. His major scientific work was done a generation before his death, and so before the end of the seventeenth century. In point of time, therefore, the scientific revolution appears separate from the industrial revolution.

During the last fifty years, much that is new has been learned about economic history and the history of ideas. The view of both which prevailed in the late nineteenth century has been altered. One consequence is to bring the origins of industrialism and of modern science closer together.

According to the new view, what was the course of European economic history during the two hundred years or so that followed the childhood of Copernicus, the period which was marked by the birth of modern science? In 1453 the Hundred Years' War ended with the expulsion of the English from most of the possessions on the Continent which their kings had held. For a hundred years following that protracted conflict between France and England, economic expansion was characteristic of most of Continental Europe. All the way from Poland and the Balkans to the toe of Italy and the Portuguese coast of the Spanish peninsula, there were remarkable increases between 1460 and 1540 in the yield of the soil and the subsoil—more grains and ores of every kind, more sheep and goats and other cattle—remarkable increases in the volume of industrial products—more metal, more cloth, more books and paper, more guns—and remarkable increases in the commercial prosperity from which many shopkeepers and traders, and also merchants in a considerable way of business, reaped profits. When this period of nearly a hundred years drew to a close about the middle of the sixteenth century, Europe had split for the first time in its Christian history over the appropriate forms of religious worship.

During the next hundred years or so, during the century that followed the Reformation, the prosperity characteristic of Continental Europe in the late fifteenth and early sixteenth centuries was on the wane. The wars of religion from 1562 to 1648 were in many countries a period of industrial retrogression, brought about partly by the fighting. In the mid-sixteenth century, Spain, Belgium, Germany, Bohemia, and much of Austria—all at least nominally under the rule of Charles V (who combined the thrones of Spain and the Holy Roman Empire)—were in the vanguard of a remarkable industrial expansion. A century later, when the Thirty Years' War ended with the collapse of the Empire, all these countries had been reduced in population and industrial productivity, until they had hardly as many inhabitants or as large an output of ores, metals, and most manufactured goods as two centuries before, when the Hundred Years' War ended. The rest of Continental Europe fared better than Spain and the Empire from 1562 to 1648. In point of population and production, Italy and Switzerland more than held their own, and so perhaps did France, in spite of the religious disputes and the wars which set neighbor against neighbor during the second half of the sixteenth century.

A different kind of industrial development began in the sixteenth century as the first movement played itself out. The new development occurred mainly in the north of Europe, in countries which had not shared fully in the industrial prosperity of the late fifteenth and early sixteenth centuries, in countries which broke most decisively in the sixteenth century with the authority of the church of Rome: in Sweden, Denmark, Holland, Scotland, and Wales, and, above all, in England, where striking industrial expansion continued with few interruptions for a hundred years, from the dissolution of the English monasteries in 1536 and 1539 to the outbreak of the Civil War in 1642. Copper exports from Sweden increased twenty-five fold from 1548 to 1650.[2] In Holland, as in England, the expansion was most rapid during the last two decades of the sixteenth century and the first two decades of the seventeenth, a great era in Dutch painting and in English literature. The cloth production of Leiden, for example, increased more than fourfold in thirty-five years, from 26,620 pieces in 1584 to 109,560 pieces in 1619, when the ten-year-old Rembrandt left this town of his birth for Amsterdam.[3] Shipments of coal from Newcastle-upon-Tyne grew nearly fourteen times over in a span of seventy years, from 32,952 tons in 1564 to 452,625 tons in 1634.[4] Describing the condition of the English people before the "great rebellion," as he called the Civil War, the Earl of Clarendon wrote that they had "enjoyed . . . the fullest measure of felicity, that any people, in any age, for so long time together, have been blessed with."[5]

What was no less singular than the length of this "felicity" was its character. In ancient China, in Roman Britain, and in medieval Europe, at places where coal seams outcropped, some use had been made of these black stones as fuel, especially by lime-burners and by smiths in rough ironwork, such as the forging of anchors or horseshoes. But it was not until the seventeenth century that the economy of any nation was built on coal. In Great Britain on the eve of the Civil War coal was becoming the prevailing fuel for heating rooms, for cooking, and for laundry work. Coal was beginning to be widely used in industry—not only at limekilns and at a few of the forges where iron was made into the crudest ironwares such as horseshoes, but at saltworks, alumworks, in soap boiling, in making saltpeter and gunpowder, in brewing beer, in baking bricks, tiles, and tobacco pipes, and in making glass and steel.

Among our European ancestors, as among other civilized peoples, gathering firewood, kindling, peat, and turf had been the ordinary means of obtaining fuel. These occupations had rarely lent themselves to a capitalist organization of labor, and the making of charcoal, which alone among them required heat, had been largely annexed to the metallurgical industries, the principal consumers of charred wood. With the rise of coal mining in Great Britain, the provision of fuel changed its nature. It became necessary often to dig deep for supplies; shafts of thirty or forty fathoms became common. The capital required for starting and maintaining a colliery, already of some consequence in the chief coal-mining districts during the later Middle Ages, multiplied many fold.

Coal played an even more important part in the genesis of industrial civilization by its influence upon the industries it was coming to serve. The composition of most coals made their fires more harmful than the fires of firewood or charcoal to most of the industrial materials touched by the flames and fumes. That is one reason why, during the Middle Ages and the Renaissance, coal fuel was used only in making crude products. But coal was more plentiful than either firewood or turf; once coal began to be seriously exploited, its very abundance stimulated a desire to multiply the output of manufactures. With the rise of the British coal industry, a source of heat was opened below the earth's surface capable of supplying manufacturers on a scale without precedent, a source of heat destined to discourage production for quality but to encourage production for quantity.

In earlier civilizations than that of western Europe iron had been almost always obtained directly from its ore, in the form of a pasty mass, in a forge with a charcoal fire. To rid the metal of its impurities, this pasty mass was subjected to repeated heatings and hammerings on the anvil. Small-scale operations alone were possible, and much of the iron present in the ore was lost as slag and scale. A strong heat had, on occasion, reduced iron ore to liquid. But nothing intensive had been done to exploit the discovery that iron ore would melt, any more than to exploit the discovery that the earth contained stones that would burn.

In the Middle Ages, certainly before the end of the fourteenth century and possibly earlier, a primitive form of blast furnace was introduced in northeastern France, the Rhineland, and northern Italy. The greater heat obtained at these furnaces, by means of more powerful bellows and a taller structure, reduced the ore to liquid iron. The carbon was absorbed by the reduced iron, forming, when it cooled, an alloy, cast iron or pig iron, of much lower melting point than the pure metal.

The consequences of this change in the method of making iron were eventually no less revolutionary and no less fundamental to the triumph of modern industrial civilization than the consequences of substituting coal for wood, charcoal, turf, and other fuels derived from surface vegetation rather than from the bowels of the earth. Industrialism is linked historically to cheap metal as well as to cheap fuel, and the introduction of cast iron paved the way for a phenomenal growth in the output of metal, once means were devised for using coal in place of charcoal in smelting. But cast iron did not become suddenly the principal product derived from iron ore. In spite of the introduction of blast furnaces in the fourteenth and fifteenth centuries, older methods of producing iron had a tenacious hold on the Europeans. Even after the considerable growth of industrial output in the era preceding the Reformation, very little of the iron ore, which was being dug in hundreds of districts in Europe, was melted at blast furnaces. Central Europe—Austria, Hungary, western Poland, Bohemia, and Saxony—provided the scene for a spectacular development of mining and metallurgy from about 1460 to 1540, which attracted the attention of miners and craftsmen in metal all over Europe. The

development was marked by the spread of several new metallurgical processes, among them an important new method of sepa-
rating silver from argentiferous copper ore with the help of lead
—an innovation which helped to increase notably the output of
copper as well as of silver. But modern industrial civilization is
not founded on silver or even on copper to the extent that it is
founded on iron, and, as late as the mid-sixteenth century, the
blast furnace for making iron was apparently unknown east of the
Rhine. The most comprehensive and systematic early treatise on
mining and metallurgy, *De re metallica,* which was written between 1529 and 1550, is innocent of a reference to such a furnace.
The author, Georgius Agricola, was a learned physician with a profound knowledge of conditions in the leading metallurgical districts of central Europe, at the very time when the prosperity of
the copper and silver industries reached a height in the German-
speaking countries that was not equaled before the late nineteenth
century. Cast iron played no significant role, any more than coal,
in the industrial growth of the late fifteenth and early sixteenth
centuries.[6]

A decisive change in the methods of making iron first came in
the hundred years following the Reformation, and then only in the
north of Europe—above all, in the Principality of Liége and in
Great Britain. In the 1630's, on the eve of the English Civil War,
there were probably between 100 and 150 blast furnaces in operation in England and Wales.[7] For the first time in history the major
portion of all the iron produced in a great country either passed
through the pig-iron stage or was used in the form of cast iron.

As a result of the adoption of the blast furnace, the metallic ore
was purged of impurities which persisted in the pasty masses of
wrought iron obtained at the older types of forge or furnace. Consequently, the adoption of the new method of smelting reduced
the quantity of iron lost as slag and scale. It became feasible to
exploit less pure ores than in the past. This, combined with the
reduction in the costs of production, encouraged the manufacture
of larger quantities of iron products.

In Great Britain, in Sweden, and in Holland—the chief scenes
of industrial expansion during the late sixteenth and early seventeenth centuries—cast iron itself was used for a wide range of

products, among them cannon and firebacks. But a larger quantity of the iron ore melted in the blast furnaces was cast into pig shapes to be treated usually at two forges—the "finery" and the "chafery." There the pig iron was reheated under oxidizing conditions and hammered into bars. Certain types of bar iron were then carried to slitting mills to be rolled and cut into rods. The new forges and slitting mills, like the new blast furnaces, had to be equipped with machinery and supplied with water power to drive it. Each new forge and slitting mill, like each new blast furnace, required more capital and a larger labor force than had been commonly needed at the old forges, where wrought iron was extracted gradually but directly from the ore. The making of iron for the metalfinishing trades, which had been in earlier times an operation requiring only one principal establishment, and that frequently a small one, came to be carried on in three and sometimes four stages. Thus the spread of the roundabout method of iron manufacturing, like the general adoption of coal as fuel, marked an important step in the direction of large-scale capitalist industry.

The bars and rods derived from pig iron by the new methods of treatment provided an equivalent for the older wrought iron, which proved superior for the purposes of modern industry and eventually of mass production. While it was not until the end of the eighteenth century, when coal was first widely substituted for charcoal in iron metallurgy, that the new kinds of iron were made available in much larger quantities, we can trace to the late sixteenth and early seventeenth centuries in Great Britain the beginning of a historical process which was to turn the emphasis in connection with industrial work from the goals of quality and beauty to the goals of quantity and lower costs of production. Already in the times of Elizabeth I and the first two Stuarts, the fashioning of objects beautiful to contemplate—such as windows of stained or painted glass and elegantly designed and decorated suits of plate armor—was giving way to the manufacture of substantial comforts, such as plain glass windows to keep out the cold and let in the light, and iron grates (with firebacks and andirons) to hold the new coal fires which warmed the rooms.

The twentieth-century observer almost invariably looks back at the Elizabethan period with a mentality that the triumph of industrialism and of modern science has created. For him, *invention* relates to technical discoveries which reduce the death rate or the labor costs of production and so make it possible to prolong life and to multiply output tremendously. This very outlook prevents him from recognizing the full significance of industrial history in the late sixteenth and early seventeenth centuries.

Notable reductions were actually made at that time in the north of Europe in labor costs of production, and not only in the manufacture of iron. In glass- and steelmaking a new kind of furnace was devised in which the materials were separated in closed pots from the flames. This enabled the workmen to replace dear wood and charcoal by cheaper coal. The spread of coal and cast iron also provided many other industries with cheaper fuel and cheaper metal than would otherwise have been available. Further reductions in costs of transportation and production were effected by the introduction of railed ways with horse-driven wagons; of ships with more hold space; of boring rods for testing the underground strata before sinking shafts; of coke for drying malt to be used in brewing; of more mechanical looms for weaving stockings, ribbons, and various small wares. Horsepower and water power were coming to be more extensively used for driving machinery, and this also tended to cheapen production.

Yet, when all is said—and more might be said—the saving of labor effected in the north of Europe during the lives of Shakespeare and Rembrandt was not spectacular if it is judged by the statistical mind of the twentieth century, proud of the fact that "steel is now cheaper than dirt," as the head of the United States Steel Corporation remarked recently in a speech. Furthermore, the saving of labor resulted less from new inventive ideas than from the exploitation of old ones; if cast iron and coal had an earlier history, a considerable use of crude water-driven machinery can be traced back in Europe to at least the eleventh century.

The important matter which the twentieth-century mind misses is that neither the magnitude of the changes nor the originality of the inventive ideas is decisive in estimating the significance of this period for modern industrialism. What is decisive is that, especially in the north of Europe and, above all, in Great Britain, men came to attach a *value* that was novel to inventive ideas whose only purpose was to reduce labor costs and to multiply production.

The novel emphasis in the time of Shakespeare and Francis Bacon on quantity as the purpose of industrial effort provides a striking analogy to developments which were taking place at much the same time in the realm of scientific speculation. Science, like industry, was beginning to emancipate itself from a dependence on the experiences of the artist and the craftsman who worked with matter. Science, like industry, was beginning to be concerned with quantities more and with qualities less than in the earlier centuries of Western civilization. A kinship exists between the spirit of industrial change and the spirit of scientific change manifested in Europe during the age of Elizabeth I and the first two Stuarts. But were the changes in industrial outlook sufficiently widespread during this period to be compared to the changes in scientific outlook?

Even in the England of Charles I the industrial world—the world of coal mining, of metallurgy, and of other rising heavy industries, such as salt, alum, sugar, and soap manufacturing—was a small world. The numbers employed in these industries ran into some tens of thousands, but the English people numbered, in all probability, between five and six million. The country was still primarily agricultural,[8] though less predominantly so than a hundred years before, when Henry VIII had broken with Rome. Anything approaching an "early industrial revolution"—involving decisive changes in economic purpose—was confined, moreover, to Great Britain, to the United Provinces, and to Sweden.

Central Europe was apparently as innocent of blast furnaces for ironmaking in 1640 as in 1540. There is little evidence of a growing use of coal, except in Holland, which got coal increasingly from England and Scotland. In the Principality of Liége, where coal mining had been more important during the Middle Ages than in any part of Great Britain,[9] the output of the local mines stopped increasing after the middle of the sixteenth century.[10] The output of iron grew little, if at all, from 1550 to 1650 in Belgium. In Spain, where the ironmakers were apparently as slow in adopting the roundabout process as in central Europe, the output of iron almost certainly diminished during the first half of the seventeenth century.

France, Italy, and Switzerland (countries which suffered much less economically from 1550 to 1650 than did Spain and the Empire) were moving industrially in directions different from those characteristic of the north of Europe. After the worst phases of the French religious wars had ended in 1589, the art of statesmanship was practiced with greater success in France than in any other European country. During the Thirty Years' War, Cardinal Richelieu established French political hegemony in Europe. There is a story that he was once asked what was his principal passion and that, instead of answering as his interlocutor had expected—the welfare of the French people—he said: "Writing verses." However that may be (he was certainly not a good poet), his predilections were for art. What pleased him most in connection with the products of manufactures, as well as with the products of craftsmen's workshops and artists' studios (which the French were incorporating in their "manufactures"), was the delight that the objects gave rather than reductions in the costs of making them.[11]

In this outlook Richelieu reflected the predilections of the most influential of his countrymen. He carried out an economic policy which he inherited from Sully, the remarkably gifted chief minister of Henry IV. The records of the Conseil d'État for Henry IV's reign suggest that the French government was less interested in encouraging inventions which aimed at abridging labor than in encouraging others which promised novelty in the service of beauty. The treatment accorded Claude Dangon, a craftsman of Lyons, is characteristic. In 1606 Dangon claimed to have invented a loom which could weave more beautiful silks. Royal officials encouraged him to make three trips to Paris to demonstrate before the Conseil d'État. He was then granted a substantial subvention by the crown to help him in spreading his loom among the craftsmen of Lyons, the chief center of the French silk manufacture.

The silk-making industry, the weaving of tapestries, the making of fine glass and pottery, and similar artistic manufactures were the main concern of the French state, at the time when the state in France was greatly increasing its power over economic life. In all the arts and crafts, as in the arts of painting, music, and architecture, France owed much to Italian models and to the revival of the interest manifested especially in Italy during the fourteenth and fifteenth centuries in the models provided by classical Greece and Rome. Under French leadership the traditional values of beauty, splendor, and elegance were renewed and given fresh life, at a time when French ways of craftsmanship, like French manners, were influencing the economic development of Continental Europe more than the new industrial outlook exemplified by the English. In the industrial life of most of Europe, considerations of quality retained their ascendancy.

We must not be misled by the persistence among the Europeans of older values, which provided scope for a different kind of progress, into minimizing the significance of the new industrial outlook—the emphasis on quantity—which was manifested especially in Great Britain. That was as revolutionary in its way as the new scientific outlook. It is a part of our purpose in this essay to try to discover how and to what extent the two changes in outlook were related, how far the early industrial revolution contributed to the scientific revolution and how far it was brought about by the scientific revolution. Between them, these two revolutions made almost inevitable the eventual triumph of industrialism. After the middle of the seventeenth century, when the religious wars ended, the new industrial economy, which had evolved mainly in England, gradually attracted the Continental countries. After about 1740–50 its attractions became irresistible. But during the hundred years from 1540 to 1640, the century preceding the English Civil War, the industrial changes which prepared the ground for the triumph of industrialism were confined mainly to the northern countries and especially to Great Britain. The scene, therefore, is the same as that which has attracted Professor Read in his principal historical studies.

Fundamental changes in human outlook are written large only by the later generations, whose state of mind is derived from the ideas of earlier innovators. The new emphasis which, as we shall see, distinguished the science of early modern Europe from earlier science was confined to a very few. The scientific revolution was even less a mass movement than the "early industrial revolution." Most sixteenth- and seventeenth-century Europeans were not innovators in their thought. The intellectual changes which now seem, and which were, in fact, momentous were at the time inconspicuous. In writing of the scientific revolution, Whitehead remarks: "Since a babe was born in a manger, it may be doubted whether so great a thing has happened with so little stir."

It may be granted, then, that the changes in emphasis before the

English Civil War in connection with industrial values were comparable in magnitude to the changes in emphasis in connection with scientific values and procedures. The general reader is likely to say, however, that the scientific revolution came first. He thinks of the scientific revolution as occurring in the time of Copernicus. And Copernicus' life was contemporary with an earlier movement of industrial development which was less "revolutionary" in its implications for industrial values than the "early English industrial revolution," because the earlier movement brought no decisive break from an emphasis on quality to an emphasis on quantity.

Must we not also distinguish the scientific outlook and the scientific results of Copernicus' time, however, from the outlook and results of the late sixteenth and early seventeenth centuries, the time of Galileo, Kepler, and Harvey? Ought we not to regard the later period as revolutionary for science, as well as for industry, in a sense that the earlier period was not?

The recent work of Sir Charles Sherrington and Professor Herbert Butterfield indicates that there were two periods in the history of science, as in the history of industry, during the two centuries which began, roughly speaking, with the birth of Leonardo da Vinci in 1452 and ended with the death of Galileo in 1642. Each of the periods occupied approximately a hundred years. The first lasted from the mid-fifteenth to the mid-sixteenth century, included the great epoch in painting associated with Botticelli, Titian, Giorgione, Raphael, Michelangelo, Leonardo, Dürer, Cranach, Grünewald, and Fouquet; included also the discovery of America, the conquests of Mexico and Peru, and the Reformation; and so was contemporaneous with the industrial expansion of the Renaissance. The second period lasted from the mid-sixteenth to the mid-seventeenth century; included the wars of religion, the art of El Greco, Shakespeare, Cervantes, Rubens, Poussin, Velasquez, Hals, and Rembrandt, the settlement in North America of the Atlantic seaboard; and so was contemporaneous with the "early industrial revolution."

Among the major figures in the history of science during the earlier period were Leonardo (1452–1519); Copernicus (1473–1543); Vesalius (1514–64), the celebrated Italian professor of anatomy; Jean Fernel (1497–1558), the French doctor and physiologist; and Paracelsus (1493–1541), the Swiss physician. Let us examine the nature of their achievements and the sources of these achievements in order to compare their work with that of the greatest scientists of the late sixteenth and early seventeenth centuries.

The inventiveness of the scientific mind in the earlier period— the period of the Renaissance—was more closely related to the inventiveness of the artist than in the period of the religious wars and the early industrial revolution. What the artist seeks to achieve is works which will endure because of the impression of beauty and truth concerning every side of man's experience which they convey to human beings of his own and future generations. What the modern natural scientist seeks to achieve is knowledge, and ever more knowledge, concerning the nature of the physical world and of all kinds of matter. The part played by direct meaning in determining the value of a work of art varies from a prose essay, where what is actually expressed in words is of the first importance, to a piano concerto, where an interpretation of the meaning in words is likely to dim the beauty. Yet form and content are inseparable in all works of art; the success of every artist's effort depends in no small measure upon an approach to perfect unity between the two. Form is not irrelevant to the success of the works of the scientist, but the decisive question is whether the results obtained are in accord with tangible evidence relating to a precise problem, evidence which other scientists can verify beyond peradventure by repeating the observations or the experiments.

Works of art have to be verified in a different way, because authentic results depend upon a successful unification of far more complicated subject matter, in which intangibles always play some part and frequently the dominant part. That is why Marcel Proust speaks of this artistic verification as "la rencontre fortuite avec un grand esprit"[12]—the accidental meeting which a serious reader, or observer, or listener has with a book, a painting, or a symphony, a meeting in which his assent is enlisted with abiding enthusiasm. This kind of assent by many other minds besides the mind of the author is what establishes a work of art. Artistic verification is a compound of a far greater variety of elements than are involved in scientific verification, including the humanity of the artist and that of his audience. There can be no objective test of the verification; instructed artists may and often do make grievous mistakes in judging the merits of their own works or those of others, mistakes which are less likely to occur when a leading scientist judges his own work or that of another scientist. This is not because science is superior to art; it is because the natural scientist deals with far more limited categories than the artist, because questions of human nature and destiny hardly enter into his judgments, and because, until very recently, he dealt only with phenomena which could be directly observed.

The emergence of this special world of science, where men have detached certain categories of material problems for examination, especially for quantitative examination, and have brought the entire arsenal of human genius to bear upon their solution, is a novel achievement of the modern mind. To it men owe their great new powers of construction, of survival, and of destruction.

During the late fifteenth and the early sixteenth centuries, the search for scientific knowledge remained a by-product of the vision of the artist and the philosopher or a by-product of the experience of the mine, of the workshop, and of the practice of some traditional profession like that of the physician. If we examine the careers of Leonardo, Copernicus, Vesalius, Fernel, and Paracelsus, I think we shall conclude that none of them made the decisive break away from tradition that characterized the scientific revolution. Science did not occupy a special world of its own in the mid-sixteenth century such as it occupied a hundred years afterward.

Leonardo's notebooks show us a self-educated natural scientist, whose adventures in the world of matter and space were a part of his efforts to use the experience of his senses in fresh ways in the service of drawing and painting. Under the influence of the ancients, Archimedes in particular, he began to ask questions about the first principles of dynamics, about motion in itself; and he then went on to ask questions which seem never to have been asked before concerning winds, clouds, the age of the earth, generation, and the nature of the human heart. Of his contributions to the work of later scientists there can be no doubt. But what were most important were the questions he asked, not the results he achieved. One of the leading art critics of our age, Sir Kenneth Clark, has suggested that the burden Leonardo assumed of trying to be at the same time a universal artist and a universal scientist proved too heavy for him to carry. The weight of this burden partly explains the small quantity of Leonardo's artistic output and its fragmentary character.[13]

The experiences of the artist, which Leonardo employed in scientific speculation, were making possible new visions for future ages to explore and verify, but the conversion of the visions into accepted realities, into new systems of scientific truth, was not accomplished by the Renaissance mind. We think of Copernicus as a supreme innovator concerning the structure of the physical universe, and so he was. But the establishment of his innovation as positively true demanded a different kind of investigation from his. The new system of the movement of the heavenly bodies, which Copernicus invented, was not derived from "a rational dynamical explanation of those movements." It was derived from art and theology, from the classical aesthetic concept that "the most perfect curve . . . is the circle," and from the religious concept that in God's universe heavenly bodies must move in the most perfect ways. Therefore, Copernicus believed erroneously that "heavenly bodies can move only in perfect [circles]."[14]

In his recent book, *The Origins of Modern Science,* Professor Butterfield suggests that during the late fifteenth and early sixteenth centuries the chief factor in the progress of anatomical knowledge "was the actual development of the visual arts and the sharpening kind of observation which the eye of the artist was able to achieve." Art was the principal source of Vesalius' contributions to anatomy,[15] and of all the men of the age that was closing, he contributed most, through *De fabrica,* which was published in 1543, to a correct understanding of the structure of the human body.

The work of the two physicians, Fernel and Paracelsus, shows how it was possible to derive in Europe at the time of the Reformation new views concerning the functions of human organisms (as distinguished from their structure) and the nature and treatment of disease, from the practice of medicine and from the industrial experience of the mines and workshops. Fernel has been called the greatest French doctor of his time. It was the knowledge he acquired in the sickrooms of Paris, especially his observations of patients who died before his eyes, which led him to issue in 1542 his book *The Natural Part of Medicine*. Later he changed its name to *Physiology*. After more than thirteen centuries it supplanted Galen's treatise on the subject.[16]

Paracelsus' adventures in medicine are inseparable from his many travels among the developing mines and metallurgical works of central Europe and his participation in some of these enterprises. As a young man he was employed for five years in the smelting plants at Schwaz, in the valley of the Inn, one of the most productive centers of the age for copper and silver, whose ores are much scarcer than iron ore and therefore much less susceptible to treatment in the interest of abundance. Later Paracelsus spent some time at another leading metallurgical plant, the one at Villach in Carinthia, which was operated under the direction of the celebrated German merchant family, the Fuggers of Augsburg. It seems to be agreed that Paracelsus' monograph, *On the Miners' Sickness and Other Miners' Diseases,* grew out of these experiences. He studied the poisonous effects of metals and the morbid conditions of mercury poisoning. Paracelsus' works cannot be understood completely without his Galenic background—his familiarity with the medical writings which had survived classical antiquity—plus a strong dose of mysticism. But his extensive practical knowledge of mining and metallurgy was of immediate importance to him in the composition of all his treatises, including the one which dealt with mental diseases.[17]

It is not difficult to understand why historical students have been frequently led to treat the period of the late fifteenth and the early sixteenth centuries as the true starting point of modern science. Not only were the minds of the age attracted by their great classical predecessors, especially the Greeks and Romans, they were also looking on nature and the human body afresh. With the development of perspective and of painting in oils since the fourteenth century, artists acquired a new curiosity concerning the physical structure and functions of men, animals, plants, mountains, forests, and the heavens. Their curiosity led them to see and record phenomena which had escaped their ancestors. The medieval mind had been more concerned with the abstract world that it could create by means of its inner resources, with what the greatest English theologian of Queen Elizabeth's reign, Richard Hooker, called "things that are and are not sensible,"[18] with the Christian's vision of man's nature and destiny. That destiny transcended the world of matter, space, and time and so led men to look within themselves beyond all these tangibles. During the fifteenth and early sixteenth centuries, they looked more directly at the material world than their ancestors had looked from the tenth through the thirteenth century. A new interest, derived from art, arose "in natural objects and in natural occurrences, for their own sakes."[19] This helped Vesalius to see more exactly the actual structure of the bodies of men and animals as he dissected; it helped Leonardo to examine more exactly the nature of a bloody battle between two armies; it helped Copernicus to see the heavens anew and Fernel to look on his patients with more attention than his medieval predecessors to the actual physical circumstances of disease and death.

This disposition to look at man, the earth, and the rest of the visible universe with fresh eyes, to tune all the senses more to the tangible nature of things, was the main source of Renaissance visions of reality. The novelty of those visions was partly a product of the industrial development which accompanied the Renaissance, because this industrial development increased the scope of observation. It drew men to work in new surroundings in Europe, at the very time when explorers were sailing to new islands and continents. Men in search of a livelihood went deeper into the earth, farther among the mountains. They were introduced to natural substances and to natural phenomena that had been little observed before. Mineral resources were tapped which had hardly been touched during the Middle Ages, for example, cinnabar, the ore of mercury, and calamine, the ore of zinc. The discovery during the fifteenth century of abundant supplies of calamine in the Tyrol and Carinthia and especially at Moresnet, near Aachen, made possible the extensive manufacture of brass, an alloy produced by heating prepared calamine with copper in a charcoal fire.

Thus the picture of the material world opened by men of the Renaissance differed from that which their medieval ancestors had seen. It also differed from that which the classical Greeks and Romans had seen, although the Renaissance has been persuasively described and explained as mainly "a classical revival." However we describe or explain the Renaissance in the time of Copernicus (it is well known that this "renaissance" began before his birth and that there had been still earlier renaissances), it is important for the historian to recognize that this was not the first time that civilized men had looked at nature more directly than had their ancestors of immediately preceding generations.

An experience with groups of statues from the Parthenon, as these are preserved in London in the British Museum, shows that Attic art presented the human body with a reality, as well as a splendor, which has never been excelled and which was not approached among the Mediterranean or the European peoples for a millennium after Christ. An experience with the scenes portrayed in stone in the cathedrals of western Europe from the early twelfth through the thirteenth century suggests that the artists of that age were looking at animals, landscapes, and human features much more closely than the artists of the tenth and early eleventh centuries had. Yet, in spite of the fresh outlook of the artists and craftsmen, neither the great age of Greek, nor the great age of Gothic, art led directly to the scientific revolution.

What distinguishes modern science from all science of the past is not the observation of nature but a peculiar purpose and method in the examination of nature. What distinguishes modern science is, first, the persistent use of the experiment or of controlled observation as the final arbiter in reaching any result and, second, the employment of quantitative methods as the major means of achieving the results which are subject to the control of positive evidence.

The eye of the artist can discover an immense amount about nature and about the behavior of the human body. What the artist's eyes and other senses seek, above all, are not precise measurements but the entire atmosphere surrounding the things observed and the transfiguration of these things into enduring forms by means of the inner life vouchsafed the human being. In the interest of truth and delight the artist seeks, not quantities or precise space relationships, but qualities which transcend analysis and measurement. The exact dimensions of Chartres Cathedral and the surrounding landscape were not the concern of Corot when he painted the version of the scene which now hangs in the Petit Palais in Paris, and the mind accustomed to precise measurements will be startled by Corot's picture.

The discoveries of a mind that is primarily artistic in outlook are not irrelevant to modern knowledge of the physical and the biological world. No modern has perhaps excelled the great Greek physician, Hippocrates, in the acuteness of his observations of the behavior of the body during illness, observations carried out nearly twenty-five hundred years ago. It would seem that these observations of the human being in a morbid state were similar in their nature to the observations which guided Phidias in his portrayal of the human being in a state of health. We may speak of Hippocrates as a great artist. But I do not think we can speak as legitimately of Lister or of Claude Bernard as great artists, though neither lacked those imaginative faculties without which no important work of the mind is possible. It is not the experience of the artist but a use of the mind and senses in some ways antipathetic to art which characterizes modern science. The Renaissance delight "in natural objects and natural occurrences for their own sakes" was insufficient to bring about the scientific revolution. That earlier delight had to be supplemented and to some extent supplanted by what Sherrington describes as "new-found delight in natural observation for its own sake"[20] and by observation for the sake of quantities and precise space relationships, even at the expense of a knowledge of qualities. What was needed for the birth of modern science was less art than a breaking away from art. Fancy, mystery, and the disciplined imagination with which the artist draws on both, had to be brought under the rigid control of tangible, positively demonstrable facts and logically demonstrable mathematical propositions.

The leading scientists of the late fifteenth and early sixteenth centuries by no means made such a break away from art or from the sources of artistic imagination. They hardly seem to have been interested in precise quantitative statements concerning biological or physical phenomena. Paracelsus' last treatise was devoted to nymphs, sylphs, pygmies, and salamanders, which he conceived of as the makers and guardians of the treasures in the mines. Much as Grünewald in some of his paintings, now in Colmar, by a return to medieval abstraction, combined the more direct art of the Renaissance with an abstract art which almost suggests twentieth-century cubism, Paracelsus combined his new medicine with medieval folklore and mysticism.[21] For all his insight, Copernicus studied within the framework of an ancient set of ideas. While his world system differed from the world systems of Aristotle and Ptolemy, it was mystical like theirs, with its insistence that the heavenly bodies move in perfect circles. Vesalius deliberately accommodated his anatomical results to the teachings of Galen, and he failed to realize the need for a new account of the movements of the heart and blood.[22] Working at the functions, rather than the structure, of the body, Fernel was as far as Vesalius from establishing a firm basis for the modern biological sciences. Sherrington has written of Fernel, "he and the Renaissance, with all their zest for doing and for progress, were still in reality little forwarder than were the Middle Ages. . . . Far more were wanted than comment, conciliation and mere systematization," the achievements which made it possible for Fernel's physiological treatise to supplant Galen's. "There had to be re-foundation."[23]

Re-foundation involved a use of the intellect that is novel because of a twofold *emphasis,* which it is perhaps desirable to repeat. There is, first, the emphasis upon the systematic pursuit of experiments and observations (which are not a by-product of the artist's interest in objects and occurrences for their own sakes and which have no immediate practical purpose, whether it be the purpose of the artist or the modern engineer), for the sake of discovering physical and biological laws. There is, second, the emphasis upon the quantitative method of treating all phenomena, in the interest of these laws. The quantitative method, which extends the range of *scientific* certainty, brings with it ever more precise and ever more ingenious scientific statements with the progress of the mathematical knowledge which such emphasis helps to inspire. These crucial changes in emphasis, which were to lead eventually to the triumph of the scientific outlook, came in the late sixteenth and early seventeenth centuries, in the age of the "early industrial revolution."

The contrasts between the industrial experience of different European countries during that period help to bring the English industrial revolution into relief.[24] It is natural, therefore, to compare the development of science in different parts of Europe during the same period, both as a means of understanding the nature of the scientific revolution and as a means of inquiry into the genesis of industrialism.

Lack of historical knowledge has obliged me to concern myself mainly with the contrasts between Great Britain and France. This historical limitation is unfortunate. Yet, in view of the course taken by European history down to the mid-nineteenth century, there is some justification in concentrating, if one has to concentrate, upon England and France. All the great European countries had a share in producing the unique civilization of modern times. But, at least until after 1850, the strongest elements in the compound were British and French.

II. THE STUDY OF THE BODY

In the biological sciences the re-foundation of which Sherrington spoke was provided by William Harvey. He carried out, in the early seventeenth century, fundamental work concerning the movements of the heart and blood, and he managed to discover what is still regarded as the correct explanation of these movements. In the older physiology of Fernel and Galen, the heart was a kind of "hearth supporting a vital fire." Harvey showed it to be "a little hydraulic power-plant,"[25] and, by so doing, he "released physiology for a new start in the study of living creatures."[26] From the appearance, in 1628, of his Latin treatise, *Exercitatio anatomica de mortu cordis et sanguinis in animalibus,* "we may date the beginning of experimental medicine."[27]

How did Harvey's approach to physiology differ from the approaches of his predecessors? Experimenting in itself was no great novelty. It was the persistent use of experiment that distinguished Harvey's work from that of the scientists of the Renaissance, as well as of the Middle Ages and antiquity. He cut the arteries and veins of living things, from large animals to tiny insects, observing and recording with unending care and patience the flow of the blood and the motion of the heart. He had recourse to the new magnifying glass, produced by progressive glassmakers, to observe wasps, hornets, and flies. [28]

Like Fernel, Harvey was a physician. This makes the contrasts in the methods of the two the more striking. There is no evidence that Fernel experimented at all; his knowledge of physiology was gained mainly from his practice. But Harvey derived little or no data from his practice. Almost all of them came from planned experiments, carried out with extraordinary persistence over a period of more than two decades.

With Harvey, experiment became the arbiter in reaching every conclusion. Old experiences were abandoned as a basis for knowledge, in favor of new ones. These new experiences were not the product of any traditional intellectual discipline, of any craft, or even of any new industry. The entire inquiry was devised without practical purpose, solely for the sake of solving specific problems in the biological sciences. As the English poet, Abraham Cowley, wrote in an ode composed on the occasion of Harvey's death:

> . . . Harvey sought for Truth in Truth's own Book,
> The Creatures, which by God himself was writ,
>   And wisely thought 'twas fit
> Not to read Comments only upon it,
> But on th' Original it self to look.[29]

Such energy and assiduity in vivisection, as a means of reaching generalizations concerning the physical nature of life, had never before been equaled. While Galen had made some experiments on living animals,[30] in Greco-Roman times and in the Middle Ages the learned men of the Mediterranean countries and of Europe apparently felt that it was illegitimate and repulsive to penetrate the living body as an experiment, an analogue perhaps to the notion prevalent among the Romans in the time of Pliny the Elder that it was thievish and sacrilegious to take ores or other minerals in large quantities from the subsoil. The first restraint stood in the way of modern biology. The second stood in the way of industrialism, for the rise of industrialism depended upon new economic values which would make a virtue of more production for its own sake, as well as for the sake of the consumer, even if more production made it necessary to ransack ruthlessly the resources of the earth.

In recent times it has become usual to regard these restraints as prejudices. (Although antivivisection societies have been organized in the nineteenth and twentieth centuries, they are not taken seriously in respectable intellectual circles.) History shows that the accepted procedures of one age sometimes seem only prejudices to another, and the methods and values associated with modern science and modern economics may not prove to be immortal. It is possible that the scientific and industrial outlook of our times, which puts experiment, quantitative statement, and material productivity almost beyond criticism as values in science and industry, which makes these methods and values touchstones by which all other methods and values are judged, may seem prejudiced in future times. However that may be, the astounding progress of experimental science and heavy industry in the modern world depended partly on a collapse of the restraints, now widely treated as prejudices, which once stood in the way both of planned experiments and of the exploitation of the natural resources of the earth. Like the increased emphasis placed on *quantity* in production, the increased emphasis placed by Harvey on vivisection was indicative of the revolutionary character of changes in modes of thought in the late sixteenth and early seventeenth centuries.

No fundamental changes are brought about easily in the conventional ways in which men regard life and the universe and use their minds trying to understand them. At the time of the Renaissance, with the revival of learning and the introduction and spread of printing, the scientific knowledge possessed by the famous men of antiquity gained a new prestige. One effect was to give the learning of the past even greater authority than it had possessed among the Europeans of the twelfth and thirteenth centuries. As we shall try to show later in this essay, the scientific revolution derived a stimulus from the Renaissance as a classical revival, especially from the new interest which arose in geometry as a result of the increase in the knowledge of Plato and Archimedes. Yet there were other aspects of the classical revival which were more of a handicap than a help to the scientific revolution. The Renaissance gave an increasing prestige to the actual scientific theories of antiquity, many of which were to appear misguided or definitely false to the modern scientist. Thus the classical revival often intrenched the mind in erroneous views concerning the nature of material phenomena. The old ideas of Galen concerning the circulation of the blood gained new adherents in the fifteenth and sixteenth centuries and pervaded the minds of even the most advanced students of physiology.

Harvey learned much from past knowledge in biology. He was familiar with the great classical authorities, especially Hippocrates, Aristotle, and Galen. As a young man studying in Italy at the close of the sixteenth century, he was introduced to the works of Vesalius. From these and from the lips of Fabricius, Vesalius' successor in the famous chair of anatomy at the University of Padua, Harvey became familiar with the additions recently made to anatomical knowledge. But Harvey's discovery depended on a break with the teachings of his masters as well as with earlier authorities, and not simply a break of the kind that men of genius always make, whether in science, art, or philosophy, but a break into a new mode of procedure in seeking results.

The systematic attack on living creatures in search of evidence, which Harvey conducted after he returned to England at the age of twenty-four in 1602, involved special difficulties on account of its novelty. These difficulties, which confronted all the natural scientists of Harvey's time, did not arise mainly from the danger that, in a period of religious controversy and war, the church might take sanctions against learned persons who employed the new experimental method to obtain unorthodox results. That danger existed, but there has been a tendency to exaggerate it, because of the just horror felt by our immediate ancestors for religious persecution. In any event, this particular danger was hardly present in seventeenth-century England, to which Harvey returned to live the rest of his long life. The difficulties that are of greater moment in connection with intellectual history arose because it was necessary for the experimenter to proceed as none of his predecessors had done, without any guidance or ready recognition from his contemporaries, from past knowledge, or from Faith, to proceed more and more as experimental evidence dictated and to put his final faith in experimental evidence. It was not until 1616, at least fourteen years after he began his experiments, that Harvey's labors bore fruit in his lectures to students of the Royal College of Physicians in London. It was another twelve years before he published any of his results. By that time King James I was dead, so that Harvey's researches concerning the motion of the heart and blood, begun under Elizabeth, stretched into a third reign. During the whole time, Harvey was ceaselessly moving along untrodden ways.

Today these ways seem to most men the only rational roads for the mind to follow. But we must remember that, in Harvey's time, what most men regarded as rational was different. According to Hooker, who was much older than Harvey, reason is the means by which "man attaineth a knowledge of things that are and are not sensible." It has now become the custom to think of sensible verification as the only guaranty of reason, but in Harvey's time that was a revolutionary idea. The methods adopted by Harvey subjected him, therefore, to an agonizing intellectual ordeal. He tells us so himself:

> When I first gave my mind to vivisections as a means of discovering the motions and uses of the heart, and sought to discover these from actual inspection, and not from the writings of others, I found the task so truly arduous, so full of difficulties, that I was almost tempted to think with Fracastorius [an Italian physician, contemporary of Fernel and Paracelsus], that the motion of the heart was only to be comprehended by God.

This reference to the intellectual capitulation of Fracastoro (1483–1553), the first Western writer on syphilis,[31] suggests both how arduous were the problems confronting the earliest experimenters and how much more difficult it was for the generation of Fernel than for the generation of Harvey to surmount them. Harvey proceeds:

> At length, and by using greater and daily diligence, having frequent recourse to vivisections, employing a variety of animals for the purpose, and collating numerous observations, I thought that I had attained to the truth, that I should extricate myself from this labyrinth, and that I had discovered what I so much desired, both the motion and the use of the heart and arteries.[32]

From the success of his long labors, Harvey drew a general conclusion about the value of the new method he had been employing. He observed:

> True philosophers . . . never regard themselves as already so thoroughly informed, but that they welcome further information from whomsoever and

from whencesoever it may come; nor are they so narrow-minded as to imagine any of the arts or sciences transmitted to us by the ancients, in such a state of forwardness or completeness, that nothing is left for the ingenuity and industry of others; very many, on the contrary, maintain that all we know is still infinitely less than still remains to be known.[33]

Harvey's enthusiasm for observation and experiment hardly flagged until after he was sixty. In 1636, on a visit to Germany, accompanied by the English ambassador, he caused his companions much anxiety by wandering alone into the woods to observe strange trees, plants, soils, etc. Sometimes he was "like to be lost," reported the artist Hollar, who was of the party, "so that my lord and ambassador would be really angry with him, for there was not only danger of wild beasts, but of thieves."[34] The quest, once begun, is not easily forsaken. As physician to Charles I, Harvey visited the royal deer parks and accompanied the king on stag hunts. He took advantage of the opportunity to cut up the doe at different stages in gestation, in an endeavor to understand the process as accurately as he understood the circulation of the blood.

These experiments led him to write his *Anatomical Exercises on the Generation of Animals.* This book was published late in his life, in 1651, when he was seventy-three, and, according to one account, without his permission. The new treatise marked no such sharp break with the past as had his book on the heart and blood. As Harvey grew old, he seems to have fallen back upon the training he had received in the schools and universities, to have returned to the habits of the generations of learned men who had preceded him. While vivisection and observation enabled him to correct a number of errors in the views of ancient authorities concerning generation, he depended much more than in his earlier treatise upon old scholastic views and methods. After the age of sixty or sixty-five most men find nature compelling them to follow well-beaten paths. In embryology, as well as in physiology, Harvey had shown that the new road of observation and experiment was the only one likely to lead to satisfactory results, if men were to correct the views of ancient authority concerning the real nature and functions of the body.[35] With the heavy weight of tradition still bred into the learned during the sixteenth century, more of a break with traditional methods of scientific procedure could hardly be expected from one man.

Such a successful expedition into the unknown as Harvey conducted depended, it may be suggested, both upon his natural genius
and upon the attitude of his colleagues and countrymen to a novel
emphasis on experiment. It seems that the kind of researches conducted by Harvey would have been more difficult for a contemporary Frenchman.

Support for this hypothesis comes from two lines of historical
inquiry. First, the reception accorded Harvey's discovery in France
suggests that, during the late sixteenth and early seventeenth centuries, French minds moved less readily toward the intelligent use
of the experimental method in biology than did English or Dutch
minds. Secondly, the somewhat earlier career of the great French
surgeon, Ambroise Paré (*ca.* 1510–*ca.* 1590), who died when Harvey was twelve, suggests that conditions in France made it more
natural than in England for the mind to depend for scientific
knowledge mainly upon older, more traditional ways of following occupations or of observing the experiences of practical life.

These differences in conditions persisted during the whole of
Harvey's lifetime. No man of that time in any country broke more
sharply away from the prejudices of ancient authorities in the
domain of *ideas* than did Descartes. Unlike other Frenchmen
touched by genius who were his contemporaries—among them
Mersenne, Poussin, Claude Lorrain—Descartes was not drawn to
Italy; the only foreign countries besides Holland that tempted
him as a place of residence were England and later Sweden. His
choice of Holland as a congenial setting for his mature thought is
indicative of the ardent desire that he had to free himself from all
past misconceptions and to found the true philosophy; for in Descartes's time (1596–1650) the United Provinces, after Great Britain,
provided the most revolutionary intellectual atmosphere in the
world. Yet even Descartes, who was in so many ways independent
of his native France, was unable to liberate himself, with Harvey,
from a priori deductions in the domain of *facts*.[36] He lacked genius
for observation and experiment, and this was partly a result of his
nationality. It appears that the France of his time was a less congenial country than England for the systematic development of
the experimental method.

At the very time when Harvey published his first treatise in
1628, the parlement of Paris issued an edict forbidding all instruc-

tors in France to teach anything concerning the circulation of the blood contrary to the accepted doctrines of classical and medieval authority.[37] It is not surprising that the first printed attack on Harvey's new theory of the motion of the heart and blood should come from France. This was written by a pupil of Joannes Riolanus, professor of anatomy in the University of Paris, and it appeared in 1630. So far as evidence was concerned, Riolanus' pupil thought it sufficient to set against Harvey's new explanation of the circulation of the blood the ancient theory of Galen, according to which the blood passed from the right to the left ventricle through the septum. Before the time of Harvey, Galen's view had already been questioned in some particulars by Vesalius, Fabricius, and others, but their criticisms had apparently made little impression in the lecture-rooms of Paris. Two decades passed before any university lecturer in France expressed open agreement with Harvey. The first to do so was a professor of medicine in the University of Montpellier. When he defended and taught Harvey's physiology, he created such a scandal that his colleagues called on him to resign his chair.[38] It was not until several decades later that the new description and explanation of the circulation of the blood won general acceptance in France. It was not until the last half of the eighteenth century, when learned Frenchmen began to give the new scientific methods pre-eminence among rational procedures and when France rivaled England in the progress of machines and heavy industry,[39] that Harvey's achievement was enthusiastically received, for example by writers on economic subjects such as Turgot and Quesnay. They compared the circulation of wealth through the nation to the circulation of blood through the body.[40] By this time, enlightened opinion in France would have fully indorsed the lines which Cowley had penned a hundred years before.

In most European countries the university faculties were hardly less backward than in France about accepting the validity of Harvey's methods and the accuracy of his results. The notable exceptions were England itself and, after England, Holland, economically the two most prosperous states of Europe during Harvey's lifetime and those which had moved farthest in the direction of modern industrial values. Harvey met with no serious opposition at home. It is true that some rival medical practitioners, jealous more of his success as a physician than as a scientist, took advantage of the appearance of his unorthodox treatise to spread a rumor that he was crackbrained. This seems to have cost him some patients, for the income from his practice apparently fell off. But his associates in the College of Physicians and his scientific contemporaries in England generally sided with him. His methods and his results were immediately taken up by contemporary philosophers, for example by Hobbes, and by contemporary men of letters, for example by Dryden.

Descartes was hardly less enthusiastic about the new explanation of the circulation of the blood than was Hobbes. In the Holland of his adoption, Descartes wrote and published in 1637 his agreement with the main conclusions of Harvey's treatise.[41] Two years after that, in 1639, a young Englishman, Roger Drake, successfully maintained before the faculty of the new University of Leiden a thesis in support of the fresh explanation of the circulation of the blood.[42]

The revolutionary methods of supporting rational arguments and reaching new explanations of physical phenomena by means of the experimental method evidently received a more sympathetic hearing in England than in France. Support for this view comes from the history of other sciences besides physiology. At the end of the sixteenth century the resistance to the Copernican hypothesis concerning the movement of the heavenly bodies appears to have been less strong in England than in most other countries.[43] It was in England, too, that the first steps were taken toward making a science of chemistry, which even before modern times was, in a crude and mystical sense, "experimental" among the alchemists. The establishment of chemistry as a science is usually regarded as primarily the work of Robert Boyle (1627–91). Of all European countries, England seems to have provided the most favorable intellectual, economic, social, and political conditions during the late sixteenth and seventeenth centuries for the systematic application of the experimental method, purged, in so far as the actual results are concerned, of mystical and superstitious elements.

It is true that Boyle and Newton, as well as Kepler, had a side that strikes the modern scientist as hardly less mystical and superstitious than the writings of Paracelsus.[44] The important difference is that the scientific principles stated by the great seventeenth-century scientists, unlike the theories of Paracelsus, were independent, in so far as proof is concerned, of these expeditions into the supernatural.

When we consider the contributions made in France to knowledge of the human body, we find that they came less from any revolution in the emphasis of the mind itself than from the pursuit of knowledge by old traditional methods, which were extended into new spheres as a consequence of economic and technical developments. The French may be said to have prolonged the ancient methods of assembling scientific data. In the biological sciences there was no such sharp break with the Renaissance as occurred in England. During the hundred years from 1540 to 1640 France had no physiologist or embryologist fit to rank with Harvey as an innovator. Great achievements like his were dependent partly upon the collapse of the prejudice against combining creative learning with manual work. This prejudice, which may have arisen partly out of the ancient association of manual labor with slavery, was prolonged after slavery had almost disappeared in western Europe by the medieval distinction (to which the scholastic philosophers of the twelfth and thirteenth centuries contributed) between the "liberal" and the "servile" arts, between work done with the mind alone and work which involved a change in matter.[45] Like the work of poets, logicians, or mathematicians, the work of the physician produced no such change. It was therefore "liberal." Like the work of sculptors, glaziers, or ironworkers, the work of the surgeon produced a change in matter. It was therefore "servile."

During the sixteenth and early seventeenth centuries this distinction seems to have possessed greater strength in France than in England. It was generally a handicap to the progress of the experimental method, because that involved a combination of intellectual with manual work for no more practical purpose than speculative inquiry, a combination for which no support existed in the medieval learned tradition of Europe.

There was one side of inquiry into the condition of the body, nevertheless, in which the French surpassed the English, partly because the very separation of manual from purely intellectual work reflected a greater concern with excellence in craftsmanship, at a time when much manual work was artistic and involved, consequently, subtle and tasteful decisions of the mind controlling the hands. Trained not in the schools and universities but as craftsmen in their gilds, the barber-surgeons were not restrained, as French physicians and learned scientists were, from working with matter, from manipulating and operating upon living human beings. Barber-surgeons, who wore short robes as a sign of social inferiority, were not accorded the same positions in society as were members of the medical faculties in the universities or surgeons of the long robe. But the barber-surgeons had the advantage of expert manual training in an age when the manual dexterity of the workshop carried more esteem than it does today and when the standards of craftsmanship were higher. Because the surgeons of the long robe would not condescend to operate and incur the loss of prestige involved, the barber-surgeons took over practically all the increasing surgical practice of an age of war, such as the sixteenth century proved to be for Continental Europe.[46] It was an age in which England had less war than France, as well as less craftsmanship.

French surgery was more skilful than English during the sixteenth and early seventeenth centuries. England had no surgeon whose advances in his art could equal those made by Ambroise Paré.[47] During the period from 1560 to 1640 no one in France made more important contributions to our knowledge of bodily processes than he. So it is not capricious to select Paré for comparison with Harvey. In doing this, however, it is necessary to remember that Paré was some sixty years Harvey's senior and that the European world in which he worked was different from the world in which Harvey worked. The time of Paré's mature life, the fifty years from about 1540 to 1590, should be regarded as a period of transition from the older science of the age of Fernel and Copernicus to the new science of the age of Harvey and Galileo. To a considerable extent Paré was working in the older tradition. In the fifty years following his death, 1590–1640, the time of Harvey, the French mind developed scientifically in novel ways which, as we shall see, helped, through mathematics, to make possible a revolution in scientific methods. But this development of mathematics in France seems to have had little or no influence on the study of the body until after the mid-seventeenth century. That is why it is perhaps legitimate to select Paré as the leading French figure in the development of the biological sciences in the period of the scientific revolution.

As a barber-surgeon, Paré was not a learned man. But he had behind him the medieval craft tradition; he cut the body with a skill equal to that exercised by the greatest French sculptors of his time, when they cut stone to fashion, for example, the cloisters which surround the choir of Chartres Cathedral. During Paré's early years, before he was admitted in 1541 to mastership in the Paris gild of barber-surgeons, cannon, culverins, arquebuses, muskets, and pistols were coming into widespread use for the first time, in the battles between the armies of the French King Francis I and the Emperor Charles V. The balls, bullets, and shot sprayed from these firearms tore new kinds of wounds in human flesh, of which neither Hippocrates nor Galen had had any knowledge. By virtue of his craft, the barber-surgeon was confronted with novel problems which called imperatively for a solution. Unlike the founders of the experimental method, he did not have to construct the problems in order to answer questions which had no immediate practical purpose. In caring for the wounded in the campaigns of the French army in Italy, Paré's skill and genius in the surgeon's craft were demonstrated with remarkable effect by his exercise of what seems little more than good sense. The accepted method of treating gunshot wounds was to pour on hot oil. In one of the battles in which Paré was engaged as army surgeon, the wounds came so fast that he was left without this "remedy." Next morning, when he examined the wounded, he found the men he had been unable to treat for want of supplies more comfortable and farther on the road to recovery than those he had subjected to the prescribed treatment.[48] So he abandoned hot oil.

His work with the army soon attracted the attention of Francis I, who made him his own surgeon, and he served as royal surgeon to five successive French sovereigns, the last of whom was Henry III. This position gave him special advantages in instruments and in conditions for making discoveries. He observed the harm done after amputations by applying hot irons to wounds to staunch the blood. He established the use of the ligature for the control of hemorrhages. He invented artificial limbs. Having found on the field of battle, in connection with novel problems of surgery, that accepted methods of treatment could be improved upon, he proceeded to try, as part of his craft, new methods in connection with perennial problems. In obstetrics he showed the advantages of inducing artificial labor by manipulations, when the natural process of birth was so delayed as to endanger the mother's life.[49]

Latin was still the preferred language of the learned, and Harvey wrote his celebrated treatise on the circulation of the blood in this ancient tongue. As a barber-surgeon, Paré had no knowledge of Latin. So he began to publish in French the results derived from his practice. This made his conclusions doubly offensive to a learned French audience. They challenged accepted knowledge, and they challenged it in uncouth language. On both counts, Paré's daring outraged the French faculties no less than had Harvey's unorthodox methods and results.

For a long time learned circles refused to adopt Paré's methods or accept his results. The appearance in 1575 of the first collected edition of his works drew a warning from the School of Medicine of the University of Paris that the writings of this "imprudent man, without any learning," should not be put on sale until they had been submitted to the medical faculty for approval.[50] Five years afterward the dean of the School of Medicine, Étienne Gourmelen, attacked Paré's work. Gourmelen found it enough to show that no ancient medical and surgical writers had used the ligature in place of hot irons in amputations or had employed any other of the tender methods introduced by Paré in treatment of wounds.[51] Against Paré's methods, Gourmelen had nothing to say which seems at all convincing to our age, because frequent innovations in matters of technique are now expected. In every realm the authority of past experience has lost the prestige it once possessed as a guide in dealing with problems of the present.

Gourmelen's comments were characteristic of learned authority on the Continent. When Athanasius Kircher (1601–80), the German philosopher and mathematician, tried to get a Jesuit professor to look through a telescope at the newly discovered sunspots, the professor brushed him aside with the remark, "It is useless, my son. I have read Aristotle through twice and have not found anything about spots on the sun in him. There are no spots on the sun. They arise either from the imperfections of your telescope or from the defects of your own eyes."[52]

It was easier to challenge ancient authority by the exercise of the surgeon's craft than by the establishment of new speculative sciences, such as biology or astronomy. This was partly because the eventual practical significance of discoveries in those sciences was apparent only to a rare genius like Descartes, who drew attention in his *Discours de la méthode* to the possibility that the new scientific methods might eventually prolong life, multiply commodities, and reduce the burden of manual labor.[53] What made the criticism of Paré's work ineffective was the immediate demonstrable effectiveness of his novel treatments among his patients. These included some of the most powerful members of the royal family. Paré retained his ascendancy at court, notwithstanding the attacks made on him by the faculties and notwithstanding the suspicion that he was a Huguenot, at a time when religious hatred and violence reached their peak in France. Catherine de Medici and Charles IX apparently intervened to save him from being massacred in Paris, along with other Protestants, on St. Bartholomew's Day. French royalty was not so stupid as to throw away, in its fit of zeal for religious orthodoxy, a man with unique gifts for relieving their physical sufferings. Paré had obtained solid results in the realm of surgery, which were destined to be valuable to medicine, once medicine adopted the experimental method. But his methods represented no such break with the past as did Harvey's. He was working in the Renaissance craft tradition.

While English conditions were more favorable than French to the progress of experimental science, they were less favorable to such scientific progress as was exemplified by the work of Paré. During the Middle Ages and still more during the hundred years following the Reformation, the French surpassed the English in the visual arts. Painting can serve as an example. In spite of Leonardo's claim that it was a "liberal" and not a "servile" art, painting, as carried on in early modern times, required exceptional manual dexterity and skill in mixing and manipulating materials. Where are the English painters to rival the French before the eighteenth century, before the time of Hogarth and Gainsborough? There are no English equivalents for Fouquet, Clouet, Le Nain, Georges de La Tour, Poussin, Philippe de Champagne, or Claude Lorrain. The miniature portraits of Nicholas Hilliard (1537–1619) are memorable for the famous men who provided the subjects: Sir Francis Drake or Sir Walter Raleigh, for example. As works of art they are insignificant beside the paintings of any one of fifty of Hilliard's great Continental contemporaries. Down well into the sixteenth century in France, art was inseparable from the ancient crafts; during the hundred years that followed, the artist became a species of supercraftsman, often under the patronage of the French court. Surveys preserved in documents of the Châtelet in the Archives Nationales suggest that in many quarters of Paris the proportion, among the gainfully employed, of artist-craftsmen—sculptors, painters, silk-workers, tapestry-makers, etc.—was remarkably large, at least until after the middle of the seventeenth century. The strength of tradition in France combined with the absence of an early industrial revolution, with its emphasis on quantity production, to make it more natural for Frenchmen than for Englishmen to excel in craftsmanship. Barber-surgeons were craftsmen. Consequently, it was more natural for the French than for the English to make contributions to surgery which were of scientific importance.

III. THE STUDY OF THE PHYSICAL WORLD

The contrasts between England and France in the physical sciences seem, at first sight, almost as striking as the contrasts between the two countries in the biological sciences. It is frequently forgotten that the first modern man to found a science on the experimental method was probably William Gilbert of Colchester. As Gilbert was born in 1544, he was a generation older than Harvey. He was also much the elder of both Galileo and Kepler, and his discoveries, which had an influence on them, preceded their more momentous discoveries.

Gilbert showed that the behavior of the compass, which had come to be used extensively by seamen from Colchester and other ports, is explained by the fact that the earth is itself a great magnet. Before Gilbert's time it had been supposed that amber alone could be excited by friction to attract other bodies, but Gilbert showed that many commonplace substances, such as glass, sulphur, and resin, had the same properties of attraction. While he found that virtually all bodies could be made electric, he discovered that only bodies containing iron could be made magnetic. Thus he founded the sciences of magnetism and electricity. Before his work no accurate knowledge existed concerning these subjects, and it is perhaps justifiable to follow a recent scientist in calling Gilbert "a prodigy of originality."[54]

Gilbert's manner of obtaining his results has been described by one of his followers, Sir Kenelm Digby, the author, diplomatist, and naval commander, who was born in 1603, the year that Gilbert died. According to Digby, Gilbert's curiosity led him to form "a little load-stone into the shape of the earth. By which means he compassed a wonderful designe, which was, to make the whole globe of the earth maniable; for he found the properties of the whole earth in that little body; which he therefore called a terrella, or little earth; and which he could manage and try his experiences upon at his will."[55] Here was an almost perfect setting for his persistent application of the experimental method.

Gilbert was conscious of the revolutionary nature of his procedure—in putting exclusive faith in the experimental method—and he was confident of its superiority to the procedures hitherto in use for understanding natural phenomena. "We have no hesitation," he wrote in *De magnete,* a Latin treatise published in 1600, "in setting forth in hypotheses that are provable, the things that we have through a long experience discovered." He denounced with assurance and considerable contempt the common practice of depending on written authority for knowledge of natural phenomena, at a time when books were becoming more abundant than ever before and when most writers simply repeated the views found in ancient authorities, particularly those in the surviving works of Aristotle. He asked:

Why should I, in so vast an ocean of books whereby the minds of the studious are bemuddled and vexed; of books of the more stupid sort whereby the common herd and fellows without a spark of talent are made intoxicated, crazy, puffed up; are led to write numerous books and to profess themselves philosophers, physicians, mathematicians, and astrologers . . . why . . . should I submit this noble and (as comparing many things before unheard of) this new and inadmissible philosophy to the judgment of men who have taken oath to follow the opinions of others, to the most senseless corrupters of the arts, to lettered clowns, grammatists, sophists, spouters, and the wrong-headed rable, to be denounced, torn to tatters and heaped with contumely? To you alone, true philosophers . . . who not only in books but in things themselves look for knowledge, have I dedicated these foundations of magnetic science—a new style of philosophizing.[56]

Gilbert advised those who pretend to inform and instruct others to give up dialectics and betake themselves immediately to this "new style of philosophizing," to betake themselves to the experimental method.

On the Continent in Gilbert's time such diatribes as he (and, soon after him, Bacon) directed at the neoscholastic philosophers were hardly possible. Paré, for example, never thought of meeting head-on the attacks made upon him by the faculty of the University of Paris. He was satisfied to pull the dean's leg, by describing what Gourmelen regarded as his objectionable manner of amputating a gentleman's limb without the use of a hot iron: "I dressed him, and God cured him. I sent him to his house, merry, with a wooden leg, and he was content, saying that he had got off cheap, not to have been miserably burned to stop the blood, as you write in your book, *mon petit maistre.*"[57]

The "wrong-headed rable," who attacked the new scientific discoveries, seem to have been at the time less numerous and less articulate in England than in other European countries. If a Frenchman had felt the inclination and found the courage to write against dialectics as vigorously as Gilbert wrote, he would not have been rewarded. He would have been attacked in the universities and perhaps even at court, where he might have been welcomed as a physician, but hardly as a physical scientist. Gilbert was treated handsomely. Queen Elizabeth saw to it that he got a pension to provide him with the leisure he needed for his researches.[58] Like the treatises of Harvey, *De magnete* made a strong impression

among a wide circle of learned Englishmen. Its influence extended
to the mercantile class and the gentry, for many rising merchants
and squires were coming to be interested as amateurs in scientific
progress.

The favorable treatment accorded Gilbert by the English Crown
provides further evidence that the new methods of observation and
experiment were becoming congenial to the English scene. Dryden
celebrated Gilbert's achievements, along with Bacon's, Harvey's,
and Boyle's, as enthusiastically as Cowley celebrated the achievements of Harvey or as Pope was to celebrate the still greater
achievements of Newton. Dryden spoke against the tyranny of the
ancient Aristotelian philosophy with as much vigor as Macaulay
two centuries later:

> The longest tyranny that ever sway'd,
> Was that wherein our ancestors betray'd
> Their free-born reason to the Stagyrite,
> And made his torch their universal light.
> So truth, while only one supply'd the state,
> Grew scarce, and dear, and yet sophisticate.
> Still it was bought, like emp'ric wares, or charmes,
> Hard words deal'd up with Aristotle's arms.
>
> . . . .
>
>   Among th' asserters of free reason's claim,
> Our nation's not the least in worth or fame.
>
> . . . .
>
> Gilbert shall live, till loadstones cease to draw,
> Or British fleets the boundless ocean awe.[62]

For Dryden the word "reason," which to Hooker and his predecessors was the instrument for achieving agreement in matters
that "are not sensible," has come to be identified with experiences
which are subject to sensible verification. The mind has turned
full circle in its concept of the nature of firm truth. At the very
time when Hooker lived, "reason" in its older sense was beginning
to be undermined. The work of Gilbert bore a share of the responsibility.

Such disparagement of the Aristotelian "tyranny" as Dryden's
lines express and such enthusiasm for the experimental method
would have been impossible for a French poet of Dryden's time. It
was not until the age of Voltaire, nearly a century after Dryden,

that French poets or men of letters began to identify reason as definitely as Dryden had identified it with the new work of the natural scientist, in which proof by tangible demonstration in terms accessible to sensory verification becomes the final arbiter. In the age of Louis XIV "reason" still meant to the French mind much the same as it had meant to the Greek. It was common sense raised to an art. As Pascal explains in one of the most celebrated passages of *Les Pensées,* an approach to perfection in reason enlists not only the mathematical mind, the *esprit de géométrie,* which proceeds logically from principles artificially created, but also the *esprit de finesse,* the nimbly discerning mind, which enables one at "a single bound" to grasp intuitively something of the infinitely complicated and delicate world in which human beings move by virtue of their inner selves, the world of common experience which confronts us all.

The French mind was not emphasizing the experimental method or any form of inductive reasoning to the same extent as was the English mind. Nevertheless, the French made valuable direct contributions to knowledge of the physical world during the period from 1560 to 1640. It is interesting to find that these contributions resulted from the same kinds of inquiry which brought French contributions to knowledge of the body. The contrasts between the methods of Harvey and Paré are of much the same kind as the contrasts between the methods of Gilbert and a French contemporary of Paré—Bernard Palissy, who was the greatest French naturalist born between 1500 and 1615. Everybody called him "Maître Bernard." His life, like that of Paré, stretched clear across the sixteenth century. Both men were born between 1510 and 1520, and both died in 1589 or 1590. Most of those who think of Palissy today (and their number outside France is not large) think of him as the rediscoverer of enamel and the father of the French art of pottery. We are filled with delight by the color and charm of his works, as they are displayed for us in Paris in the Musée de Cluny and in provincial museums, notably at Dijon and Agen. There are his graciously proportioned pitchers and his great plates, filled with fantastic scenes in many colors, always conceived in the Italian manner, like most French art of the time. Rather overloaded with animal figures, his pitchers and plates nevertheless leave an impression of much beauty, enhanced by the clear luster of the enamel. They reveal in their author a life full of taste, imagination, and extraordinary vigor.

Conditions for work with matter were changing rapidly in Palissy's time, and circumstances combined with his remarkable energy and long life to carry him into many kinds of labor. He served his apprenticeship as a glazier. As the demand for beautiful painted glass windows died out in France after 1540, he turned to other occupations. When he was about thirty, he was shown an enamel cup which had been made in Italy, and he set himself the task of experimenting with materials in order to find out how this glassy composition could be produced and embodied in pottery. After years of labor he began to get the results for which he remains renowned.[63] He was called on by the royal officials in his native province of Saintonge, north of Bordeaux, to make plans for new salt marshes along the Bay of Biscay at Brouage, Marennes, and Soubise, wanted by the government at the time of the reorganization of the *gabelle,* which was to increase notably the financial resources of the crown.[64] His skill in making plans of this kind became so great that his help was sought in planning fortresses, at a time when fortress building was still mainly an art.[65] He planned the beautiful gardens of Chenonceaux, one of the finest French châteaux, and thus became a predecessor of Le Nôtre, the most renowned of all landscape architects.

Palissy was no more a doctor of philosophy than was Paré. There was nothing in his schooling, as there was in that of learned Frenchmen like Descartes, to keep him from handling matter and acquiring manual dexterity; all his schooling as a craftsman was designed to help him in such tasks. In his extraordinarily resourceful work as a glazier and potter, he obtained an insight into the nature and properties of many mineral and vegetable substances. In his hardly less skilful work in laying out salt marshes, gardens, and fortresses, he obtained much knowledge of the behavior of water. He incorporated this learning in his published writings and probably in the public lectures which he inaugurated in the open air near the Louvre. His treatises show that he obtained an understanding of the behavior of matter novel in many respects. He seems to have worked out the law that water will always seek its own level. He commented upon the force of steam. He attacked some of the chemical theories of the alchemists. In geology he gave an explanation of petrified wood, fossil fuel, and mollusks that proved correct.[66] The cabinet of natural history that he collected was perhaps the first of its kind.

The difference between the scientific work of Palissy and that of Gilbert was fundamental, because it was a difference of aim as well as of emphasis. Palissy's work represents no such break with Renaissance science as does Gilbert's work or Harvey's. Palissy was not concerned, as Gilbert was, with bringing about a change in the basic principles of knowledge as these were taught in the schools and universities. He did not set out, as Harvey did, to devise experiments for the sake of discovering general laws to supplant the generalizations of medieval and classical authorities. The scientific discoveries of Palissy, like those of Leonardo, were a by-product of his career as an artistic craftsman. What he said that has scientific value was not said with the mathematical precision that in modern times has come to entitle a man to a place in the highest rank of scientists.

Although Palissy was much less revolutionary as a scientist than Gilbert, the scientific implications of his work provoked a storm among learned Frenchmen. During the religious wars Palissy's open-air lectures in Paris drew a distinguished audience. Paré came, and with him other surgeons and a sprinkling of doctors and apothecaries. There were also some representatives of the gentry and of the reformed church, to which Palissy belonged, like many of the innovators in modern science. Unlike the merchants, the men of letters, and the rising squirearchy in England, who applauded the discoveries of Gilbert and Harvey, the band who listened to Palissy was not in a position to influence learning, in the face of the tough prejudices that prevailed in France against the notion that the schools of liberal arts could learn from craftsmen anything that would be of value to knowledge. Palissy spoke outside the university only because its portals were closed to him, untrained as he was in the liberal arts. Although the comment of Michelet on these lectures is not sufficiently laudatory to suit Palissy's biographers, it is close to the truth. Michelet speaks of this "good potter" who "teaches with so little emphasis, so humbly, in so low a voice, that he is scarcely heard." Beside the self-confidence of Harvey and the strident assertiveness of Gilbert, the tone of Palissy's writings is almost one of self-abnegation. Palissy begged his readers to examine his work "without regard to the weak, abject condition of the author, and the rustic, unadorned character of his language." The knowledge he expounded did not involve any attempt to bring the material world within the focus of the experimental mentality. He obtained novel results because his work as an artist-craftsman brought him novel experiences.

Palissy's work, like that of Paré, was pleasing to the royal family. He helped to lay out gardens for Catherine de Medici. But Palissy was less essential to the health of sovereigns and other princes than Paré, and he seems to have been less wary about concealing his religion. What most learned and powerful Frenchmen of the age heard or read of his scientific views was not to their taste, because some of his views ran counter to the teaching of the schools. He was eventually arrested and imprisoned in the Bastille. In spite of his advanced age, Palissy was apparently kept a prisoner until he died of want and ill-treatment.

It will have been noted that Dryden, in his poem, applauded Gilbert for having broken away from the tyranny of Aristotelian thought. But, in France, one learned Protestant was ordered to be cut in pieces in the massacre of St. Bartholomew because he had spoken ill of Aristotle. After 1589, with the end of the worst phases of the religious wars, violence diminished in France, but the attitude of the Sorbonne and even of the courts of justice toward natural science changed slowly. The older ways of looking at the material universe persisted not only in the sixteenth century but during much of the seventeenth. The past of Western civilization (including the Renaissance) was prolonged into modern times more in France than in England.

Was this prolongation of the past an insuperable barrier to new scientific methods and discoveries, such as were exemplified by the work of Gilbert and Harvey? The contrasts which the French scene presented to the English in the late sixteenth and early seventeenth centuries were characteristic of most of Continental Europe. Yet anyone acquainted with the history of science will realize that the methods and discoveries which are properly associated with the beginnings of modern science were no monopoly of Great Britain or of the group of countries in the north of Europe which moved in new industrial directions after about 1580 and which included the United Provinces, Sweden, and perhaps Denmark, as well as England and Scotland. The re-foundation of man's knowledge of the physical world before the advent of Newton has been represented correctly as the achievement, above all, of two great scientists, neither of whom belonged to the industrially progressive countries: the German Kepler, who spent some of his most productive years at the imperial court in Vienna, and the Italian Galileo, whose adventures in an atmosphere hostile to his researches provide one of the most widely read chapters in scientific history. The sympathetic reception that England accorded "the new philosophy" was evidently not indispensable for those revolutionary intellectual innovations which, as Donne wrote in one of his most famous poems, "called all in doubt."

It was in the time of Donne, between about 1580 and 1630, that the new views of the architecture of the physical universe actually replaced the Ptolemaic and Aristotelian views. Unlike the concepts of Copernicus, who made few fresh observations and who based his factual knowledge mainly upon old observed data hitherto differently interpreted, Kepler's laws of planetary motion were based on new observations obtained with the help of better instruments. The data were gathered chiefly from 1573 to 1595, above all by the Danish astronomer Tycho Brahe (1546–1601), who was an almost exact contemporary of Gilbert. Like Gilbert, but unlike Palissy and De Caus, Brahe secured government support for his researches. He was lavishly subsidized by King Frederick II of Denmark, who provided him with an island in the Danish Sound for his observatory, together with a handsome income to meet all his scientific and personal needs. The fame of Brahe's observations rapidly spread, and the Scottish king, who later reigned as James I in England and who was always anxious to appear as a prince remarkable for his learning, paid a visit to the observatory in 1590. It was only after Frederick's death, when the major work had been done, that Brahe, faced by the withdrawal of Danish royal support, left for Bohemia and was installed by the

Emperor Rudolph II in a castle near Prague, where the young Kepler joined him in 1600, on the eve of Brahe's death.

Gilbert's role in the foundation of astrophysics has received much less attention than Brahe's, perhaps less attention than it merits. Gilbert's experiments with magnetism led him to conclude that gravity is a form of magnetic attraction and that the movements of the planets, which Copernicus had described, could be accounted for on the principles of the magnet, of which Gilbert had made himself the master. This view became the basis for a doctrine of almost universal gravitation and an integral part of the system of the heavenly bodies, as that system was expounded by Kepler.[67]

It appears, therefore, that the voluminous data on which Kepler founded his laws were gathered partly by observers and experimenters from those countries where conditions seem to have been most favorable to the establishment of the experimental method as the arbiter in scientific knowledge. On the basis of tangible evidence, Kepler sacrificed the Copernican view that the motion of the planets is in perfect curves, becoming for the Christian mind of medieval times to an orderly universe designed by the Heavenly Father. Kepler substituted the view of a general movement of the planets along an elliptical orbit.[68] His greatest innovation consisted, not in assembling new data, but in the mathematical treatment of data. As Professor E. A. Burtt wrote some years ago, "The exactness or rigour with which the causal harmony must be verified in phenomena is the new and important feature in Kepler."[69] It was a combination of systematic observations and experiments with the concepts of measurement and periodicity, encouraged by the progress of mathematical theory, that made Kepler the founder of modern astronomy.

At much the same time Galileo was working out, in Italy, the laws of gravity and inertia and was laying the foundations of mechanics. Galileo has been frequently called "the real father of the experimental method in physics." But Professor Butterfield has called our attention to the fact that, "in one of the dialogues of Galileo, it is Simplicius, the spokesman of the Aristotelians— the butt of the whole piece, who defends the experimental method of Aristotle against what is described as the mathematical method of Galileo."[70] Whether or not, as Professor Alexandre Koyré has recently suggested, Galileo made a determined attempt to apply the principles of mathematical philosophy to physics,[71] it seems to be agreed that it was by submitting to mathematical treatment the tangible observations he made in his experiments that he reached his epoch-making conclusions. It was Galileo's use of mathematics, even more than his observations and experiments, that made him the founder of modern physics.

The work of Kepler and Galileo brings out the two-sided nature of the "scientific revolution." Without the rigor and exactness in connection with observations, without the quantitative concepts encouraged by the development of mathematical thought, especially the application of algebraic methods to geometry, the necessary mathematical approach to astrophysics, astronomy, and physics in the modern world would hardly have been possible.[72] This mathematical approach was essential to establish the ascendancy and prestige of experiment, of materially verifiable results. By means of the mathematical ideas of recurrence, of precise repetition, of geometrical similitude, it became possible to apply simple materially demonstrable propositions to the entire physical universe and to inflate man's knowledge of the very small until it seemed almost to explain the infinite.

IV. THE STUDY OF MATHEMATICS

Revolutionary advances in mathematical knowledge were hardly less essential, then, to the scientific revolution than were the revolutionary advances in the biological and the physical sciences which have already engaged our attention. But the revolution in the mathematical sciences which took place in the early seventeenth century depended mainly on different procedures. Little equipment was required beyond the brain of man and the materials for sketching and writing. It was not necessary to dissect animals and insects, to form a loadstone into the shape of the earth, or to drop objects from a height (as Galileo did). The processes of reasoning depended very little upon the exact observation of phenomena of the external world, for the essential problems were formulated artificially in the mind, with the help of a knowledge of what earlier mathematicians had done.

Before the usefulness in technology of the new theoretical mathematics of the seventeenth century began to be seriously exploited (which is to say before the mid-eighteenth century), these mathematical speculations were in a class of activities which is widely treated today (partly through the influence of "economic science"), as "futile," as unproductive. Yet in the traditional thought of Europe—derived from the Greeks, from Plato and his followers and also from Archimedes—the very "futility" of the creative work of the mind gave it a special dignity, and lifted it above the work of the craftsman, even above the work of those artists whose callings obliged them to labor with matter. Plutarch wrote that for Plato it was "utterly corrupt" to make "Geometry . . . discende from things not comprehensible, and without body, unto things sencible and materiall, and to bring it to a palpable substance, where the vile and base handie work of man is to be employed."[73]

Among our medieval ancestors there was a recognized and dignified place for mathematics among the "liberal arts," because the mathematician had no need, any more than the poet, to manipulate matter in order to achieve his results. Mathematics derived its most compelling problems from what were regarded as pure, "uncorrupt" speculations of the mind, until Thomas Hobbes, in the mid-seventeenth century, argued that the motions of the mind itself were nothing more than the products of sense-impressions.

Possibly the eight men born between 1500 and 1615 who made the most important contributions to mathematical knowledge were Cardan, Tartaglia, Rhetius, Vietà, Napier, Desargues, Descartes, and Fermat. Among them Napier, the Scot, was the only representative of Great Britain. Four of the other seven were French. Francis Vietà (1540–1603), who started life as a lawyer and became a privy counselor under Henry IV, denoted general quantities in algebra by letters of the alphabet, solved equations of the third and fourth degree, and applied algebraic transformations to trigonometry. Gérard Desargues (1593–1662), an engineer and architect of Lyons, laid the foundations of projective geometry at about the time that Descartes (1596–1650) laid the foundations of analytical geometry. Pierre de Fermat (1601–65), another lawyer and government official, who served in the provincial parlement at Toulouse, expounded many of the laws of numbers and founded the calculus of probabilities. During the early English industrial revolution, France established a leadership in the mathematical sciences that she was far from possessing in the biological or the physical sciences. France contributed more than any other nation to the theoretical progress which made possible later, in the times of Newton and Leibnitz and afterward, a more comprehensive and refined mathematical treatment of natural phenomena than could be achieved when Kepler and Galileo worked.

A historian concerned with the meaning of history is led, not unnaturally, to inquire whether the pursuit of mathematical speculations was particularly congenial to the French mind, especially in the early seventeenth century, and, if that was so, why it should have been so. It is perhaps significant that Pascal (1623–62), whose mathematical genius declared itself at a surprisingly early age and whose short life coincided with the ascendancy in France of a great mathematical school full of fresh ideas, should have said nothing in his celebrated passage on the rational processes about the experimental method or the direct observation of natural phenomena. For him scientific reasoning seems to have been mainly identified with mathematical reasoning, and he spoke of the conclusions reached by such reasoning as "palpable." If we consider closely the sense of this passage of Pascal's, we find that he seems to have thought of mathematics almost entirely as geometry. The late H. F. Stewart, who devoted most of his life to the study of Pascal, recently published a most carefully considered translation of *Les Pensées*. As a consequence, this work can be read in English for the first time with confidence. It is not accidental that Stewart translates Pascal's famous phrase, *l'esprit de géométrie,* as "the mathematical mind," for this conveys a true impression that for Pascal, as for the Greeks, the realm of mathematics was largely occupied by geometry.

When we consider the character of the revolutionary mathematical discoveries of the French school, which reached its full maturity in Pascal's time, we find that they were based mainly on geometrical concepts and on geometrical reasoning and that in France mathematicians seem at this time to have laid greater stress on geometry than they did in the sixteenth century. For example,

Vietà, the oldest of the group of four great French mathematicians of the period, whose work began at least as early as 1580, seems to have been more interested than the others in the algebraic side of mathematics. But his results were obtained primarily by the application of geometry to algebraic problems. In working under the influence of Italian mathematicians, the greatest European mathematicians of the early sixteenth century, Vietà seems to have stressed the qualitative sides of the subject, and he advanced on his Italian predecessors mainly by the greater generality of his algebraic speculations. The most important contributions of both Descartes and Desargues were to geometry; Descartes searched "for geometrical constructions of classical problems" and managed to solve many questions left unanswered by the ancients, particularly by the Greeks. Fermat, perhaps the greatest mathematical genius of the four, is most famous for his anticipation of the differential calculus, which we associate with Isaac Newton. This work of Fermat's represents an application of analytical geometry that was beyond the powers of Descartes. It was Fermat's method of tangents, which he discussed at length in his correspondence with Descartes, that gave Newton his idea for the development of the calculus.[74]

The influence of the great Greeks—Apollonius, Diophantus of Alexandria, and especially Archimedes—is apparent in many stages of the work of this French school. Its members were attracted by geometry and geometrical reasoning in no small measure because of the purity and sublimity of the subject matter and the methods of thought to which the Platonic philosophy gave such great prestige. The attraction for these Frenchmen of unsolved problems left by the Greeks seems to have been at the root of the revolution in mathematics, which was to prove so fruitful for the development of modern science.

As the words we have quoted from Plutarch suggest, the peculiar attraction of geometry lies in the purity of the ideas, their abstract character, their freedom from contamination with all that has body, all that is material substance. No question of personal interest or practical purpose can impede the search for truth. We have seen how much stronger than in England the traditional separation between the liberal (the nonmaterial) and the servile arts remained in France during the hundred years or so from the mid-sixteenth to the mid-seventeenth century. This separation gave French science advantages when it came to progress through the intellect alone, as in geometry. The leading French mathematicians were not craftsmen like Paré or Palissy. They were all the sons of men of higher social rank. In the schools and universities they were trained in the principles of knowledge inherited from the Gothic age and from classical antiquity. Their education was that of a small number of Frenchmen who were not brought up in the crafts or on the land but who were admitted to the liberal arts.

The French mathematicians seem to have set about consciously, especially from about 1619 or 1620 (when the classical and mainly geometrical rules of art were also being formulated in France), to take full advantage of the opportunities opened to them by the Greek and the medieval learned traditions, with their veneration for pure speculation. Descartes, the greatest philosopher of the age, became almost a disembodied mind. Together with the other leading French mathematicians, he held the view that, among his French predecessors, mathematics had fallen too much into the hands of craftsmen and had been debased by its association with manual labor and mechanics.

In this connection it is instructive to examine the work of one of these predecessors, an obscure Frenchman named Jacques Besson, professor of mathematics at Orléans in the mid-sixteenth century. Besson was much interested in the practical applications of his subject. He left behind a treatise, which must have aroused considerable interest, for it was reprinted several times. In it are many drawings of machines. These machines are not of the kind which came into more widespread use in England during the seventy years following Besson's death in *ca.* 1569. Besson was not trying to substitute horsepower and water power for manual labor, one of the principal objects of technicians in Great Britain. Almost all his machinery was designed to be operated by the hands and feet. In several cases his designs called for a substitution of manpower for water power or horsepower. He depended for his results upon a skilful transmission of muscle, by the multiplication of gears and pulleys and the use of better geometrical principles of balancing.[75]

Descartes and the other extraordinary French mathematicians

of his age looked upon work of that kind as beneath their dignity. It was part of Descartes's purpose to lift mathematics out of the slough to which it had descended as a mere craft at the service of mechanics. He reacted against the instruction he had received in his youth from a Jesuit teacher in mathematics at the college of La Flèche, a certain Father François, who talked, as Besson wrote, in terms of applied mathematics about land surveying, topography, hydrography, and hydrology. For Descartes the proper application of mathematics, which captivated him by what he called "the certainty of its demonstrations and the evidence of its reasoning," was not to mechanics but to philosophy.[76] Thus he and his French contemporaries in the science of mathematics were undertaking speculative inquiries which, like the inquiries of the founders of the modern experimental method, served no practical purpose.

The mathematicians built on the learned tradition of the past more directly than did the great innovators who were their contemporaries in the biological and even in the physical sciences. But they worked in a similar spirit, in the sense that they were no less confident than were Gilbert, Harvey, or Galileo of their power to achieve a certainty which they felt that all earlier scientists and philosophers, including the greatest Greeks, had failed to reach. Descartes built up his philosophy by means of mathematical reasoning. He confidently expected that his new method, which he set forth in 1637 in his celebrated *Discours de la méthode,* would enable men for the first time to obtain a clear and distinct view of the nature of the physical universe and even of its metaphysical foundations. The new mathematical relationships, which he and his contemporaries discovered, were no less demonstrable by the appeal to mathematical proof than Harvey's new explanation of the circulation of the blood was demonstrable by the appeal to experimental proof. All trained mathematicians who agreed on their premises were bound to reach identical conclusions. A way seemed to be opening to the intellect, unaided by revelation or even by grace, to reach the truth, a way that the medieval Christian thinkers had neglected. Plato and Archimedes had been on the right track in their insistence upon the priority of mathematical reasoning to the more common-sense reasoning of Aristotle, who had been hitherto the preponderant influence in European philosophy, but they had not gone far enough. Now the fresh mathematical discoveries made it possible to push beyond the conclusions of the wisest Greeks.[77] As Professor Gilson has written, Descartes's purpose was not to revise Aristotle but to replace him.

Apart from the emphasis on rigorous mathematical proof, what distinguished the abstract mind of most of the new mathematicians from the abstract mind of most of the scholastic philosophers of the twelfth and thirteenth centuries was this: The mathematicians treated the abstractions of the mind as both their starting point and their end rather than linking their powers of abstraction to God's grace. In retaining God, as nearly all of them did, they came perilously near to making Him a mathematician whose secrets they could discover, and so they came perilously near to identifying their own powers as mathematicians with ultimate Truth.

It is curious to observe the eventual consequences of the new mathematical knowledge in the realm of technology. The very desire to keep the mind free from materialism (which was characteristic of French learning) contributed no less to the genesis of modern science, by its effects on the study of mathematics, than the same desire hindered the genesis of modern science, by its effects in discouraging the learned man from experimenting. One of the eventual consequences of the scientific revolution was to produce a no less complete revolution in the very mechanical pursuits—in the handling of matter—from which the French mathematicians of the early seventeenth century sought to free the study of mathematics. Machinery has now replaced most manual labor in industry, in transport, and even to some extent in agriculture; and, contrary to the tendencies exemplified in the work of Jacques Besson, artificial power of various kinds has now replaced manual force in setting the machinery agoing.

Whether the prospect of such developments would have disturbed Descartes is doubtful. There is a celebrated passage in the *Discourse on Method,* where he wrote: "It is possible to acquire knowledge most useful for life . . . [by means of which] we can make ourselves lords and possessors of nature."[78] Such a statement is not in the least Platonic.

There was obviously a conflict between the social aspirations of

Descartes, as expressed in this passage, and the abstract and impractical nature of the speculations in the realm of mathematics, which he encouraged and in which he participated. While the mathematical discoveries of the French school in the early seventeenth century were essential to modern science, in order to use these discoveries for the ends which Descartes foresaw and welcomed, it was necessary in connection with science itself to stress the quantitative sides of mathematical inquiry. Professor Koyré has suggested that Kepler was prevented from formulating, as Newton was later able to formulate, the law of universal gravitation because of the persistence in his mind "of a *qualitative* conception of the universe."[79] The British mathematicians of the late sixteenth and early seventeenth centuries were far from equal to the French in the fundamental realm of mathematical theory, but the British seem to have been more interested than the French in algebra, in numbers, in precise numerical calculations, and in the invention of tangible mathematical instruments which could be employed practically in the scientific and even the economic life of the age.

The contrast between the British and the French outlook on mathematical studies, until the influence of the new French mathematics became strong in England, is brought out in a remark that an Englishman, John Wallis (1616–1703), made shortly before the mid-seventeenth century, in 1635. "Mathematics were scarce looked upon as Academic studies," he wrote, "but rather Mechanical."[80] It would almost appear that in Great Britain, during the first half of the seventeenth century, mathematicians stressed the very sides of mathematical inquiry which their contemporaries in France eschewed as unworthy of the dignity of the science. There is a danger undoubtedly of making this juxtaposition between the leading mathematicians of the two countries too sharp. Yet there can be no question that, in Great Britain (and perhaps also in Holland) at the juncture of the sixteenth and seventeenth centuries, the leading mathematical minds looked on the study of mathematics from a more practical standpoint than did the French geometers. This was true of Henry Briggs (1561–1630), of William Oughtred (1575–1660). It was also true of Adrian Vlacq (1600[?]–1667), a Dutchman. These men were all interested in facilitating numerical computations.

The difference in mathematical emphasis stands out in the mathematical work of John Napier (1550–1617), who, with the possible exception of the much less-well-known Thomas Hariot (1560–1621), was the leading mathematician of the period from 1540 to 1640 in Great Britain. Napier had a decidedly practical bent in the direction of modern machinery, which was not equaled by any French mathematician of the early seventeenth century. He designed an armored car, or tank, which was apparently in advance of most of the numerous engines of this kind which had been designed during the two centuries following the Hundred Years' War. He also wrote of an extraordinary explosive, of which he had the secret, capable of clearing the earth of life in an area some four miles in circumference. He devised an engine, driven by horsepower or water power, for draining coal pits.

A modern authority, W. R. MacDonald, has remarked that "towards the end of the sixteenth century, the further progress of science was greatly impeded by the continually increasing complexity and labor of numerical calculation."[81] He suggests that Napier's discovery of logarithms in the early years of the seventeenth century was made, at least partly, to get around that difficulty. That the discovery of logarithms contributed, at the same time, to quicker practical mathematical calculations is a fact too obvious to require emphasis. Napier's discovery was useful alike to students of the heavenly bodies and to merchants in keeping their accounts. Napier's practical bent in mathematics is brought out also by an invention less stressed by historians than his logarithms, by a device which came to be known as "Napier's bones." This was a group of rods upon which the multiplication table was placed. Of their immediate practical usefulness we have evidence in Napier's own little *Rabdologia,* first published in 1617. In it the rods are described, and Napier tells his readers that the "bones" were already in common use. This book of Napier's was reprinted in Latin in England; it was translated into Italian (1623), Dutch (1626), and German (1623 and 1630); so it is safe to assume that the "bones" were soon known throughout Europe. They retained a place even after Pascal and Leibnitz had introduced new adding and calculating machines later in the seventeenth century.[82]

This difference of emphasis in mathematical inquiry between France and England has persisted. France has generally excelled in "pure" mathematics, England in the "applied" variety. As Western civilization became more utilitarian at the end of the eighteenth century and during the nineteenth, French mathematicians were sometimes drawn into practical paths—as Gaspard Monge and Lazare Carnot were drawn into the trade of destruction at the time of the French Revolution.[83] Yet the distinction between the work of the two countries, which was manifested in the early seventeenth century, was deeply ingrained, as is shown by a comparison of the mathematical work of A. L. Cauchy (1789–1857) in France with that of G. G. Stokes (1819–1903) in England.[84] It is shown also by the stress laid on general culture in the curriculum of the École Polytechnique, the great French school of advanced mathematical study, founded by Monge. General culture can be less easily dispensed with in theoretical than in applied mathematics.

For the triumph of modern industrial civilization, both the geometrical and theoretical and the more practical and mechanical sides of mathematics were indispensable. The forms of mathematical speculation and reasoning in which the French excelled in the early seventeenth century provided fundamental ideas which have been of great use to scientists and even to inventors ever since. For the full exploitation of these fundamental ideas in science, and especially for their relentless practical application in finance, commerce, industry, agriculture, transport (in short, in every side of mechanical technology), there was a need for a greater emphasis on algebra and numerical calculation than was characteristic of the French school in the early seventeenth century. There was a need for the more quantitative approach to mathematics and the unyielding concern with material results and with the multiplication of results, exemplified by the English school.

Whatever Descartes's scientific mistakes may have been, whatever were the practical limitations of French mathematics in his time, Cartesian modes of thought were of predominant interest in seventeenth-century France and throughout much of Europe. Every cultivated person had to take account of Descartes; it was possible to take issue with him, but it was not possible to be ignorant of his views and methods. In the custody of most seventeenth-century Cartesians, mathematics was nonutilitarian in its objectives. There was no desire to overturn the old hierarchy of workmanship; as we have seen, the great French geometers were anxious to maintain the superiority of pure speculation to work with matter; consequently, they encouraged the ancient separation between the liberal and the servile arts. Among all the learned men who played a leading part in the scientific revolution, the geometers were those who retained the closest relations between science and art—a relation which, as we have seen, was retained also, in a different way, by Paré and Palissy in their capacity of artist-craftsmen.

Desargues, who was an architect and a student of architectural engineering, offers the historian a most direct link between the new school of mathematics and the visual artistic tradition. A modern inquirer into mathematical history has written of Desargues, "he composed more like an artist than a geometer."[85] By suggesting, as he does, that a sharp antithesis has always existed between geometry and art, the writer, Dr. E. T. Bell, betrays a modern outlook which is historically false. In the Platonic tradition, geometry, through its close concern with all matters of form and repetition, had always been an essential part of art, especially in architecture and music, but also in painting and in poetry. A close connection existed between the transition from Romanesque to Gothic architecture and the revival of the geometrical sides of Platonism, especially in the school of Chartres during the twelfth century.[86] Throughout the later Middle Ages, geometry and geometrical ideas seem to have played a fundamental role in architecture. Dürer's interest in geometry is well known. He was responsible for the first printed work on plane curves, published in 1525.

The Cartesian influence—through its emphasis on clarity, purification, and simplification—upon the rational nature of French "classicism" in the seventeenth century is a commonplace. The new elegance exemplified in French mathematics contributed to the orderly, precise, and subtle languages invented in France for painting, music, poetry, and prose. These four tongues of delight were the instruments of all the great artists of the reign of Louis XIV. Without these instruments, which owed a good deal to geometrical concepts, French "classical" art could not have attained its great perfection, nor could it have influenced the entire art of Europe—the baroque and the rococo—as profoundly as it did. There was, therefore, an important sense in which French seventeenth-century mathematics, in its inspiration and its methods of work, was the ally of art. This alliance provides further evidence that the scientific revolution resulted from the renewal of tradition, as well as from new experiences and from a break with earlier methods of reasoning.

In so far as the new mathematics, in which France played the leading part, served the artist without making him its slave, the progress of mathematical science partly offset the influence inherent in the scientific revolution to narrow the range of intellectual activity to the establishment of palpable conclusions, positively demonstrable. Yet the very certainty which the Cartesians sought and which has served the natural scientists so well ever since was founded on a separation of the mind from the body and, indeed, from all experience, which makes the modern quantitative approach to phenomena almost inhuman and, in itself, hostile to art. Professor Koyré, whose admiration for the Cartesian philosophy is great, has observed justly that "the distinctness of an idea makes it *valid for our mind*. But how can we be certain that the real world conforms itself to the demands of our reason? Could it not happen that the real [is], on the contrary, something obscure and irrational, something which reason cannot penetrate and make clear?"[87]

That very concept of the real as something obscure and inaccessible to statement in precise, palpable terms had predominated in European history before the scientific revolution. The ways of art and the ways of faith, which were not the ways of modern science and which depend on what Pascal called "nimble discernment" (on the power to reach conclusions in the presence of innumerable experiences which cannot be reduced to clearly provable propositions), were ways men had followed for centuries in order to obtain approximate truths. The same dependence had been laid on nimble discernment in rational judgments, in "reason" as this word was understood by Aristotle and his followers and by the scholastic philosophers. The consequence of ignoring this side of the mind, as the more rigid Cartesians were inclined to do, was to narrow the range of human experience. Such an emphasis on mathematical rigor as Descartes advocated was, in the long run, a serious danger to the imagination and to all qualitative judgments. That is of concern even to scientific progress, which has always depended to some extent on fundamental ideas that are intuitive, and which in the twentieth century seems to depend less than in the nineteenth on quantities and precise measurements.

In so far as mathematics, with its emphasis on "clear and distinct ideas," has banished the real world in which we actually live, it has helped, along with the experimental method, to render science one-sided and narrow. Since the sixteenth century, scientific modes of thought have so largely recolored man's outlook on life that men have forgotten the limitations inherent in the modern concept of "reason," as covering only what is positively verifiable. Now only a great poet can reveal the contradiction between the palpable knowledge which governs us and the creatures that we are. "One had to be Newton," wrote Paul Valéry, "to observe that the moon is falling when anyone can see for himself that it is not falling."[88] There is a sense in which the scientific revolution focused the minds of men on an unreal world which is of little concern in their lives, which may have little to do with their nature and destiny. Whitehead has written that the whole system of organizing the pursuit of scientific truth, which dominates modern learning in the universities throughout the world, "is quite unbelievable. This conception of the universe is surely framed in terms of high abstractions, and the paradox only arises because we have mistaken our abstraction for concrete realities."[89]

What has made this unreal world of the modern scientist seem of the utmost concrete importance has been the success of science in supplying those values which were given novel emphasis at the time of the early industrial revolution by two philosophers whose fame has endured, Francis Bacon and Descartes—the success of science in lengthening lives, lightening labor, and multiplying output. Without the scientific revolution, the infant industrialism which was generated in the north of Europe during the same period would have come to little. By virtue of their consequences, therefore, the scientific revolution and the early industrial revolution are two aspects of a single story. Both were essential parts of the genesis of modern industrial civilization.

V. CONCLUSION

If the two revolutions—in scientific procedures and in industrial values—were aspects of a single story, as we suggest, it is not unnatural to assume that one was the cause of the other, or at least that the two were joint products of the same economic conditions. But the comparisons we have made between English and French history warn us against these ready assumptions. The dialectics of history are not so simple or so mechanical. Unlike many of the phenomena of the physical world, historical cause-and-effect relationships, which are the outcome of the thought and activity of living men in societies, are not susceptible to mathematical statement.

It is obvious that the coincidence in time of the early industrial revolution and the scientific revolution was not merely fortuitous. The speed of industrial, commercial, and financial development after about 1580, in the north of Europe, in Holland, and especially in Great Britain, by increasing the need for complicated numerical calculations, perhaps helps to explain why English (and Dutch) mathematicians should have been more concerned with algebra than with geometry, and why they should have stressed the practical mechanical applications of mathematics more than French mathematicians. The novel industrial progress in northern Europe seems to have helped also to provide an intellectual atmosphere in England favorable to experiments and observations. In draining mines, driving hammers, moving bulky commodities (coal in particular), and in devising furnaces which would make it feasible to substitute coal for firewood and charcoal as fuel in such industries as glassmaking and steelmaking, inventive problems, unrelated to beauty and concerned almost exclusively with cheapening labor costs, arose in a more urgent form in Great Britain than elsewhere. By the middle of the seventeenth century, the reciprocal advantages to "natural philosophers" (as scientists then were called) and industrial technicians of a knowledge of each other's work were beginning to be recognized. Robert Boyle referred to the reductions in labor which might be obtained through the naturalist's insight into trades. The scientists played the central role, through the newly formed Royal Society, in encouraging and co-ordinating efforts in every occupation throughout the country to acquire curious data which might help to reveal nature's secrets and laws. In 1667 or thereabouts, the members noted with satisfaction: "All places and Comers are now busy and warm about this Work and we find many noble Rareties to be every Day given in [to the Society] not only by the hands of learned and professed Philosophers; but from the Shops of Mechanics; from the voyages of Merchants; from the Ploughs of Husbandmen; from the Sports, the Fishponds, the Parks, the Gardens of Gentlemen."[90]

When, in the sixteenth century, men with scientific interests, like Agricola, Paracelsus, Paré, or Palissy, derived helpful information from the occupations of their times, they got it directly as part of their own professional work in mines, saltworks, or metallurgical establishments, or in arts and crafts. A clearing-house, such as the Royal Society presented in the 1660's, for data which might have scientific significance, was novel. Through the elaborate correspondence which the Royal Society established with foreigners and newly formed foreign societies, and also through the election of foreigners to associate membership, the clearing-house became international in scope. New technical problems, whose solutions were made more urgent as a result of the early industrial revolution which placed a new pressure on available natural resources, had a bearing on the scientific researches of Newton, Boyle, and other members of the Royal Society during the later seventeenth century.[91] The scientists, in their turn, were glad to have their knowledge used for practical purposes, though they were sometimes reticent out of an anxiety lest science should contribute to destruction. Boyle actually sought to steer the work of one practical inventor away from destructive toward productive ingenuity.[92]

Such a symbiosis between the progress of modern science and industry as was seen to be possible in Great Britain as early as the

1660's does not seem to have had great practical consequences for nearly a hundred years. Beginning in the mid-eighteenth century, men of learning in Continental Europe as well as in Great Britain turned much more frequently to applied science. After about 1785 in Great Britain, and after 1815 on the Continent, their efforts began to have an immense effect upon productivity and upon the multiplication of the species, until the nature of material existence was profoundly altered in many parts of the world.

It would be an error to push this economic determinism farther than the conditions will bear. It has been shown that Newton and Boyle derived their inspiration, their data, and their methods from many sources besides the early industrial revolution. Among these sources, the inspiration provided by the love of truth for its own sake was important.[93] Furthermore, the work of Boyle and Newton began after the period that concerns us in this essay was over.

It would be rash to assume that new practical problems raised by the early English industrial revolution were of importance in bringing about the fundamental changes in scientific procedures during the critical decades between 1570 or 1580 and 1640, when the scientific revolution actually started. The work of Galileo and Kepler was done in parts of Europe which were little affected by the industrial revolution. Gilbert and Harvey were living much closer to it. What consequences had it for their work?

The loadstone, which had been known from time immemorial, is a variety of magnetite, the magnetic oxide of iron, and Gilbert's interest in the subjects of magnetism and electricity may have been increased by the remarkable expansion of the English ironmaking industry in his time. In *De magnete,* he refers frequently to the multiplication of iron mills, and he describes the roundabout process for manufacturing iron.[94] He studied the behavior of all kinds of iron, but what interested him most was the behavior of the ship's compass with its magnetic needle. That had been in use for many generations, and the voyages of discovery, which preceded the early English industrial revolution, had increased its importance.

Harvey's treatise on *The Motion of the Heart and Blood in Animals* contains less evidence of industrial experience than does *De magnete.* It is true that there are at least two references to bellows.

There is also a comparison of the two motions of the ventricles and the auricles with that "in a piece of machinery, in which, though one wheel gives motion to another, yet all the wheels seem to move simultaneously; or in that mechanical contrivance which is adapted to firearms."[95] But bellows were an exceedingly ancient device, and neither the machines nor the guns, whose mechanical actions Harvey compares to consecutive motions of the blood, were inventions of the early industrial revolution.

The more one considers the direct connections between the scientific and the early industrial revolution, the more they seem to be superficial. Our inquiry in this essay has shown that the use for scientific purposes of data and ideas derived from the arts, crafts, and manufactures was no distinctive feature of the new sciences. Galileo was a great observer; yet what distinguished his scientific work from that of earlier scientists was not the practice of making observations but the way he correlated his observations for purposes of his own intellectual devising. He studied the methods of work employed in building and repairing warships at the famous arsenal in Venice. He observed the loading and firing of guns. He derived material from the work of building craftsmen who were constructing churches, palaces, and fortifications. But his procedures differed from those of artists or craftsmen like Palissy or Paré. His discoveries were not, as theirs were, a by-product of experience with crafts which he followed as a professional. He took his material wherever he could find it—from the movements of a swinging lamp while he was at Mass in the cathedral at Pisa, for example—and, in all he took, he was guided by systematic plans of his own devising for answering fundamental problems of the physical sciences. There is no evidence that the theoretical issues which Gilbert and Harvey set about to solve, in a similar spirit, or their modes of procedure were derived from the industrial revolution that was taking place in their times in England. All these men were examining bodies and conditions of the universe which had been there from time immemorial, and their methods owed little or nothing to practical inventors who were their contemporaries, like De Caus and Worcester, who tried to make a steam engine, or like Platt and Rovenzon, who tried to purge coal of its noxious properties and make it more suitable as fuel.

The coming of modern science and the coming of industrialism had a momentous characteristic in common: Both represented a disposition on the part of man to face the problems of existence—which are spiritual and intellectual as well as material—in a new way, in which the emphasis in human happiness is upon quantity and mathematical precision rather than upon quality and transcendence. Yet, at the same time, in making the break in new directions, the scientific genius of the late sixteenth and early seventeenth centuries turned from all practical industrial experience, whether it was the experience of the ancient arts and crafts, that had furnished scientists of the Middle Ages and the Renaissance with material and ideas, or the experience of the growing heavy industries, that began to flourish in the north of Europe. The "new philosophy" created a world of its own, whose outstanding characteristic was its independence of practical experience, new as well as old, for its basic intellectual decisions. At the period when a decisive change occurred in rational procedures, the mind itself, and not the economic institutions of sixteenth- and seventeenth-century Europe, called the new tunes and most of the variations that the greatest scientists were playing on them.

According to an old, often repeated saying, necessity is the mother of invention. The validity of the saying depends largely upon the kind of invention to which it is applied. If we are concerned with the invention of the artist or if we are concerned, as in this essay, with the fundamental invention of the scientist which has been behind almost every important step forward in scientific knowledge and which has provided the basis for the practical inventions of the modern world, the saying is mainly false. We are nearer truth when we say that complete independence, complete intellectual disinterestedness, which is close to what the practical modern citizen regards as laziness, is the mother of invention. Freedom, rather than necessity, was the power behind the scientific revolution.

It is true, of course, that laziness of every kind, including the laziness conducive to constructive freedom, is impossible without leisure and that leisure is dependent on at least a minimum of wealth. It is also true that the rapid growth of wealth made for more leisure in Great Britain, Holland, Denmark, and Sweden toward the end of the sixteenth century and during the early seventeenth. In Great Britain especially, this growth of wealth resulted mainly from the early industrial revolution and the conditions which produced it, among them a large measure of peace in a warring world. By its contribution to wealth, the early industrial revolution played an indirect part in the scientific revolution. How important was the part?

It was in Denmark that Brahe received the financial support necessary to build and equip his observatory. The remarkable progress in Great Britain and northern Europe generally of new industries outside the older crafts apparently facilitated the manufacture of scientific instruments, which were new and costly, such as the microscope and the telescope. These instruments were of help in the great discoveries which revolutionized the biological and the physical sciences. Both were introduced before 1600. The first telescope was made either in Holland or in England; the first microscope in Holland. At the juncture of the sixteenth and seventeenth centuries, these and other scientific instruments were more readily obtainable in England and Holland than in other countries.

What was fundamental to their discovery and subsequent manufacture, however, was a novel desire to use them. That, in turn, depended upon a fresh interest in the actual structure and content of matter and space and upon a desire to undertake quantitative observations and experiments which were of no immediate use, in order to discover the structure and content. Neither the microscope nor the telescope was of much immediate help in a coal mine, in the conversion of coal to coke, or in constructing the closed pots which made it possible to adopt coal as fuel in the manufacture of glass and steel. The revolutionary scientific discoveries of Gilbert, Harvey, Galileo, and Kepler were of no immediate practical use, and the contribution of the new science to the early industrial revolution was negligible.

By its effect in reducing costs of production, industrial progress in northern Europe and, above all, in Great Britain tended to reduce the proportion of the time of men and women that had to be devoted to getting the bare necessities of life, in a period when, in the Protestant countries of the north, the reduction of holidays left the workmen with more time to give to economically productive pursuits. Economic development in Great Britain was providing little opportunity for the kinds of constructive crafts-manship and art which were at the disposal of the French and other Continental peoples in the small workshops of artisans and in the studios of artists, some of which were subsidized by the French crown. The human energy released by economic progress and by changes in religious worship in England was likely to be put, therefore, to novel purposes. What these purposes should be depended on the predilections of society and on the leadership provided by writers, by the government, and by rich men. This human energy might have been drawn mainly into idle and vapid trifling, as in the twentieth century with the spread of motion pic-tures, picture papers, radio advertising, and television. Or it might have been drawn exclusively into magical fancy of the sort exem-plified by the alchemists.

Progress was insufficient to make it possible to fill people's time with such mechanized entertainment as scientific discovery has provided in the twentieth century, while the fancy of the writer in an age of literary genius was not encouraging the Elizabethan in the study of the occult. In fact, the whole band of alchemists, with their costly drugs and equipment, was becoming a subject of ridi-cule. During the years when Harvey was busy with vivisection and with his estimates of the precise quantity of blood flowing from the heart, Ben Jonson's *Alchemist* (with its lampoons at the expense of the magic formulas of the pseudo-scientist) delighted London audiences even more than Shakespeare's comedies.

As time went on, a growing conflict between the English crown and the wealthy merchants of the kingdom developed over polit-ical and economic policies.[96] But when it came to the use of the leisure time of Englishmen and Scots, the influences of the court and of wealthy individuals were often thrown in the same direc-tion, toward encouraging independent speculative work.

On the Continent, except perhaps in Holland and Denmark, there was no country where the learned man who wanted to try new methods of scholarship and research, without any practical purpose, could count as much as in England on sympathetic recog-nition and authoritative support. For several generations the uni-versities and the ecclesiastical foundations, including the churches set up by the Reformers, had been generally hostile to revolutionary intellectual innovations. Queen Elizabeth's patronage of Gilbert was a symptom of a new attitude among the mighty toward the experimenter and his efforts. Isaac Casaubon (1559–1614), the French classical scholar, could not find satisfactory conditions for his work either at Geneva or at Paris, and in 1610 he finally sought asylum at the English court and became a naturalized Englishman. Casaubon's biographer, Mark Pattison, tells us that the court of James I, for all the king's pedantry, was the only court in Europe where the learned professions were in any degree appreciated.[97] It is significant that Kepler, who must have known of James I's visit to the observatory of Brahe in Denmark in 1590, should have thought enough of the king's scientific interests to dedicate to him *De harmonice mundi,* a work published at Augsburg in 1619, in which the great scientist announced his third law of motion. During James I's reign, with Francis Bacon in office as solicitor-general and later as attorney-general, the outlook on experimental inquiry by learned men was more liberal in England than in other parts of Europe. So the English court provided new experimental work with official approval such as could be obtained almost nowhere else.

Nor was this approach to scientific innovations limited to a favored few surrounding the king. On the eve of the Civil War, England was becoming a country full of amateur "inventors," a title given both to searchers after natural information to satisfy idle curiosity without immediate purpose and to projectors seeking to construct new kinds of clocks or new machines for draining mines. In her delightful essay, "Rambling round Evelyn," the late Virginia Woolf gives us a view of the passionate enthusiasm with which these men sought natural knowledge by amateur vivisection and close inspection of tangible objects, alive and dead. Mrs. Woolf writes of Evelyn:

No one can read the story of Evelyn's foreign travels without envying in the first place his simplicity of mind, in the second his activity. To take a simple example of the difference between us—that butterfly will sit motionless on the dahlia while the gardener trundles his barrow past it, but let him flick the wings with the shadow of a rake, and off it flies, up it goes, instantly on the alert. So, we may reflect, a butterfly sees but does not hear; and here no doubt we are much on a par with Evelyn. But as for going into the house to fetch a knife and with that knife dissecting a Red Admiral's head, as Evelyn would have done, no sane person in the twentieth century would entertain such a project for a second.[98]

How much this naïve curiosity, widely diffused, must have encouraged the more learned and systematic inquiries of a Harvey! The circumstances which produced this curiosity, the conditions which determined that a considerable part of the new-found leisure of the English should be spent in idle reflections and pursuits which were encouraging to the new scientific outlook and research—these circumstances are elusive. For the historian the final explanation of the conditions lies not only beyond John Evelyn's knife but beyond the methods derived from modern science. Doubtless the early industrial revolution contributed to the amount of leisure available in England for such pursuits. But what was behind the early industrial revolution? Certainly not the scientific revolution. It needs to be recognized that many discoveries and inventions essential to the industrial revolution—such as great wheels driven by horsepower and water power to drain mines and to drive bellows at blast furnaces—were products of earlier European culture, of the culture of the Middle Ages and the Renaissance.

In any event, our inquiry shows that the early industrial revolution was not essential to provide leisure for speculative flights, which were no less fundamental to the genesis of modern science than was the establishment of the experiment as the final arbiter in matters of knowledge. The most startling progress of the physical and the mathematical sciences in the sixteenth and early seventeenth centuries occurred in parts of Europe which did not participate directly in that revolution. Furthermore, if the early industrial revolution cannot be understood apart from earlier culture, the scientific revolution is altogether inexplicable without earlier culture. While it is correct to see a fundamental break in emphasis from all previous experience as marking the genesis of modern science, it needs to be recognized that the scientific genius of Galileo, Kepler, Desargues, Fermat, and Descartes, even the scientific genius of Harvey and Gilbert, derived inspiration and sustenance still more from the traditions of earlier science, philosophy, and religion than from the new industrial values which were beginning to establish themselves, especially in the north of Europe. In the case of the geometers the most stunning results were obtained partly as a consequence of their effort to lift mathematics away from any contact with mechanics and to restore the dignity of pure thought independent of any practical purpose.

If the mind was to create, as it actually created, a way of looking at the world unique in its emphasis, abstract but antirationalist in that it eventually denied all rationality to the intellect unless the conclusions could pass the test of palpable experience, the mind had to possess immense confidence in its own powers. Men had to believe that the intellect gave them the capacity to reach judgments that were valid for all creation. This confidence was derived from generations of habit in exact abstract thought, which go back at least to Aristotle. It was derived from the belief in the dignity and reality of pure ideas, independent of palpable experience, which goes back especially to Plato. It was derived from the powers of observation demonstrated in visual form by the great art of Europe and of classical antiquity, which continued to play an important role in the scientific advances of the sixteenth and seventeenth centuries, as the discoveries of artist-craftsmen, such as Palissy and Paré, have shown in the realm of the skilled manipulation of materials, and as the discoveries of geometers, like Descartes, Desargues, and Fermat, have shown in the realm of forms and space relationships. The new confidence in the mind was derived perhaps most of all from the Christian faith, as expounded especially by Augustine, Aquinas, and other great scholastic philosophers (and presented in the Judeo-Christian Scriptures) that God is supremely *rational,* that not only is He the Truth, but that man, by virtue of being made in His image, has the intellectual power to participate dimly in the Truth.[99] It was out of their confidence that man's Christian origin had provided him with an instrument independent of all temporal circumstances, an instrument capable of revealing secrets hitherto known only to God, that the great scientists of the early seventeenth century turned to the experimental method, to mathematics, and to the mathematical treatment of observed phenomena. It was not any dependency of the mind upon the early industrial revolution but a striking independence of all ordinary economic experience, and even of the new industrial wealth, which was responsible for the genesis of modern science.

In more recent times, beginning with the late eighteenth century, the spread of the "new philosophy" has tended to weaken each of the traditional ingredients out of which it had emerged. The scientific outlook has now so completely "recoloured our mentality" that it threatens to destroy the culture and the faith without which there would have been no scientific revolution. The appearance during the early industrial revolution of an emphasis that was new on quantity as an economic end in itself had eventually an important influence in bringing the modern world into being. As the new economic values came into ascendancy after the mid-eighteenth century and especially during the nineteenth and early twentieth centuries, science was provided with an unparalleled opportunity to achieve practical results. The modern scientific mind, which had originated during the late sixteenth and early seventeenth centuries in a sense of intellectual freedom from all material circumstances, lost much of the liberty that had been a condition of its birth.

With the phenomenal material progress made during the last century and a half, it has become usual to attribute all the human blessings which this progress has brought, to the scientific and economic values whose ascendancy among an important minority can be traced to the age of Bacon and Descartes. There is a sense in which it is true that these values are responsible for the condition of the world today. But our inquiry shows that the new scientific speculations themselves would have been hardly possible without the prior existence of a rich world of the mind and spirit which emphasized other intellectual values that learning today too often has come to treat as obsolete.

The part of these older values in bringing into being the modern world, with its unique facilities for production and destruction, has not been confined to their role in forming the scientific mind. One thing that helped to make possible the early industrial revolution was the increasingly peaceful conditions which came to prevail during the late sixteenth and early seventeenth centuries in the north of Europe and especially in Great Britain. Rapid industrial progress everywhere depended upon limitations on war and violence, while limitations on war and violence depended, in their turn, upon the renewal and development of the traditional values which the modern world seems disposed to forsake. These values imposed a brake upon the rapid progress of industrialism and the application of modern science to useful objectives. But they also provided conditions necessary to the progress of both modern science and industrialism. Without restraints on the economic growth which Europeans and Americans since the eighteenth century have come to identify with progress, this very progress which the world now worships would have been hardly possible.

During the last fifty years the researches of great scientists (such as Sherrington, Whitehead, Whittaker, Rutherford, and Einstein) have revealed the limitations inherent in the peculiar scientific view of the physical universe and of man, whose origins have concerned us in this essay. These researches suggest that the future of civilization may depend upon the renewal and development of the very values and procedures that modern science and industrialism have pushed into the background. Does not the history of Europe during the late sixteenth and early seventeenth centuries add to the testimony that recent scientific research itself is bringing forward on behalf of a wider, more comprehensive view of man and the universe? The new emphasis in science and industry which began in this period provided material conditions for a great increase in human happiness. But happiness itself depends on hopes and on services that the new emphasis has circumscribed.

NOTES

BRITISH INDUCTIVE LOGIC AND FRENCH IMPRESSIONIST PAINTING

1. Quoted by Alfred H. Barr, Jr., *Picasso: Fifty Years of His Art* (New York, 1946), pp. 247–48.

2. From "Painting and Reality: A Discussion," *Transition,* No. 25 (Fall, 1936), p. 104.

3. Henri Hauser, Jean Maurain, and Pierre Bennaerts, *Du libéralisme à l'impérialisme (1860–1878)* (Paris, 1939), p. 296.

4. E. A. Burtt, *The Metaphysical Foundations of Modern Physical Science* (New York, 1925), pp. 16–17.

5. Cf. Élie Halévy, *The Growth of Philosophic Radicalism,* trans. Mary Morris (London, 1928), p. 502: "The individual became in some sort the atom of the Utilitarian economist and moralist."

6. Leslie Stephen, *The English Utilitarians,* Vol. III: *John Mill* (London, 1900), p. 76.

7. In *Man versus the State,* Herbert Spencer wrote: "The function of Liberalism in the past was that of putting a limit to the powers of kings. The function of true Liberalism in the future will be that of putting a limit to the powers of parliaments."

8. William James, *The Principals of Psychology* (New York, 1890), II, 357.

9. Quoted in Emery E. Neff, *Carlyle and Mill* (New York, 1926), p. 251.

10. "Vindication of the French Revolution of February 1848, in Reply to Lord Brougham and Others," in *Dissertations and Discussions,* Vol. II.

11. Among others were those by G. H. Lewes, Herbert Spencer, and Mill.

12. Quoted in Hauser *et al., op. cit.,* p. 296: "La vieille et bonne route, si longtemps abandonnée, de l'induction et de l'expérience."

13. J. B. Stallo, *The Concepts and Theories of Modern Physics* (New York, 1884), p. 216 n.

14. F. H. Bradley, *The Principles of Logic* (London, 1922), I, 357. The first edition of this work appeared in 1883.

15. Neff, *op. cit.,* p. 340.

16. John Rewald, *The History of Impressionism* (New York, 1946), p. 16. Since I make extensive use of this work, it may be noted that it comprises detailed data on all the major figures of the impressionist movement as well as a comprehensive bibliography.

17. Camille Pissarro, *Letters to His Son Lucien,* ed. John Rewald, trans. Lionel Abel (New York, 1943), p. 50. The letter is dated 1883.

271

18. Helen Merrell Lynd, *England in the Eighteen-eighties* (New York, 1945), p. 100 n.

19. Rewald, *op. cit.,* p. 213. Quoted from the letters. Compare, however, Rewald's view with that of Signac in regard to the influence of Turner as cited by Mr. Rewald in n. 59, p. 254. Signac's view more nearly coincides with that of M. de Fels in *La Vie de Claude Monet:* "Certes, Turner lui aussi était un impressionniste avant l'invention du mot."

20. Cf. Lionello Venturi, *Modern Painters* (New York, 1947), pp. 46–48.

21. The New Art Club, founded in 1886, represented the earliest formal effort by English artists to support impressionism.

22. Rewald, *op. cit.,* pp. 78–79. Also, see Eleanor Patterson Spencer, "The Academic Point of View in the Second Empire," in *Courbet and the Naturalistic Movement,* ed. George Boas (Baltimore, 1938).

23. Nikolaus Pevsner, *Academies of Art* (Cambridge, England, 1940).

24. Rewald, *op. cit.,* pp. 122–24 and 424.

25. It is now generally believed that the scientific investigations in optics had no influence upon the development of the impressionist technique. If anything, this supports the position taken in this paper. For so strong was the evidence of relationship that it was hard to convince some that there had been no direct influence.

26. Cf. Rewald, *op. cit.,* pp. 271–73. Of many accounts, perhaps as explicit as any is that of J. Carson Webster, "The Technique of Impression—a Reappraisal," *College Art Journal,* IV (1944), 3–22.

27. John Stuart Mill, *Examination of Sir William Hamilton's Philosophy* (London, 1878), pp. 225–26.

28. John Stuart Mill, *System of Logic, Ratiocinative and Inductive* (London, 1873), VI, iv, 3.

29. Alexander Bain, *Mental and Moral Science* (London, 1875), p. 199.

30. Guido de Ruggiero, *Modern Philosophy,* trans. A. Howard Hannay and R. G. Collingwood (London, 1921), p. 131.

31. Lionello Venturi, "The Aesthetic of Impressionism," *Journal of Aesthetics,* I (1941), 36. Italics in original. In addition, see his introductory essay to *Les Archives de l'impressionnisme* (Paris, 1939). Presumably this writer would disagree with my general thesis, since in the article referred to he also writes: "Impressionism has been considered a branch of Realism. But it must be pointed out that Impressionism was a reaction against Realism." However, when he writes in *Modern Painters* of "an empiric or prosaic vision," contrasting it with a "poetic interpretation of light," one questions whether the term "empiric" has any precise meaning for him or if it is not a pejorative term only.

32. John Stuart Mill, *System of Logic,* II, iii, 4.

33. *Ibid.,* 8.

34. *Ibid.,* III, v, 2.

35. *Ibid.,* vii, 2.

36. L. Susan Stebbing, *Modern Introduction to Logic* (London, 1930), p. 335.

37. See J. H. Levy, "His Work in Philosophy," in *John Stuart Mill: His Life and Works,* by Herbert Spencer, Henry Fawcett, Frederic Harrison, and others (New York, 1873).

38. Pissarro, *op. cit.,* p. 234.

39. John Stuart Mill, *System of Logic,* III, vii, 1.

40. Quoted by Myron Lucius Ashley in "The Nature of Hypothesis," in *Studies in Logical Theory* (Chicago, 1913), ed. John Dewey, chap. vii. The Preface informs us that "the pages in the discussion of Hypothesis, on Mill and Whewell, are by" the editor. It is wholly with this section of the essay that we are concerned. In the following paragraphs, I follow closely the argument to be found there.

41. *Ibid.,* p. 164.

42. *Ibid.,* p. 165.

43. *Ibid.,* pp. 167–68.

44. *Ibid.,* p. 166. Italics by Mr. Dewey.

45. Rewald, *op. cit.,* p. 303.

46. For a more detailed study see John Rewald, "The Realism of Degas," *Magazine of Art,* XXXIX (1946), 13–17.

47. Rewald, *The History of Impressionism,* p. 176.

48. It is perhaps worth noting that during these same years Hermann von Helmholtz was defending the empirical view of mathematics with greater sophistication than Mill had shown and also with a full knowledge of the development of non-Euclidean geometries (see Edwin G. Boring, *A History of Experimental Psychology* [New York, 1929]), esp. pp. 296–98.

49. R. L. Nettleship (ed.), *Works of Thomas Hill Green* (London, 1911), II, 251.

50. Rewald, *The History of Impressionism,* p. 370.

51. Pissarro, *op. cit.,* p. 132.

52. Meyer Schapiro, "Nature of Abstract Art," *Marxist Quarterly,* I (January–March, 1937), 82–83.

53. Beatrice Webb, *My Apprenticeship* (London, 1926), p. 41.

54. Rewald, *The History of Impressionism,* p. 424.

55. Pissarro, *op. cit.,* p. 163: "I firmly believe that something of our ideas, born as they are of the anarchist philosophy, passes into our works." The argument which follows does not concern any systematically complete philosophy of anarchism—any more than, probably, Pissarro had such in mind.

56. Halévy, *op. cit.,* pp. 500 ff.

57. Hauser, *et al., op. cit.,* p. 297. "Même en Angleterre, en 1878, la veine de l'empirisme semble épuisée."

58. Rewald, *The History of Impressionism,* pp. 411–13.

JOHN WESLEY AND THE AMERICAN REVOLUTION

1. John Telford (ed.), *The Letters of the Rev. John Wesley, A.M.* (8 vols.; London, 1931), VI, 143; *The Works of the Rev. John Wesley* (11th ed.; 14 vols.; London, 1856), XII, 303.

2. Wesley to North, June 15, 1775 (Telford, *op. cit.,* VI, 161).

3. Wesley to Dartmouth, June 14, 1775 (*ibid.,* VI, 158).

4. A. Murphy (ed.), *The Works of Samuel Johnson* (new ed.; 12 vols.; New York, 1811), VIII, 144–89.

5. Wesley, *Works,* XI, 76–86.

6. Johnson to Wesley, February 6, 1776, quoted in George Birbeck Hill, *Boswell's Life of Johnson* (6 vols.; New York, 1904), V, 39 n.

7. Wesley, *Works,* XI, 77.

8. *Ibid.*

9. *Ibid.*

10. Dora Mae Clark, *British Opinion and the American Revolution* (New Haven, 1930), p. 257.

11. Wesley, *Works,* XI, 78–79.

12. *Ibid.,* p. 80.

13. *Ibid.*

14. Johnson, *Works,* VIII, 155–56.

15. Clark, *op. cit.,* pp. 259–60; see also *London Magazine,* February, 1766, p. 78; *ibid., January,* 1771, p. 42; *Letters of Junius* (2 vols.; London, 1876), II, 102–3.

16. *London Magazine,* September, 1775, p. 457.

17. *Ibid.,* p. 457; Clark, *op. cit.,* pp. 262–63; Ross S. J. Hoffman and Paul Levack, *Burke's Politics* (New York, 1949), p. 58.

18. James Macpherson, *The Rights of Great Britain Asserted against the Claims of America* (Aberdeen, 1876), p. 96; William Knox, *The Present State of the Nation* (London, 1768), pp. 80–81; Adam Smith, *Wealth of Nations* ("Everyman's" ed.; London, 1910), II, 118–21; Richard Price, *Observations on the Nature of Civil Liberty* (London, 1776), p. 28; see also the interesting article on Price by Carl B. Cone, "Richard Price and the Constitution," *American Historical Review,* LIII (1948), 727–47; *Gentleman's Magazine,* January, 1775, p. 38; F. D. Cartwright, *Life and Correspondence of Major Cartwright* (2 vols.; London, 1826), I, 58–59; William Adam, *An Examination into the Conduct of the Present Administration* (London, 1778).

19. Wesley, *Works,* XI, 76–77; see also C. T. Winchester, *The Life of John Wesley* (New York, 1906), pp. 230–32.

20. Quoted in C. E. Vulliamy, *John Wesley* (New York, 1932), p. 326.

21. George Otto Trevelyan, *The American Revolution* (new ed.; 4 vols.; New York, 1917), III, 262.

22. *Ibid.,* p. 264; Luke Tyerman, *The Life and Times of the Rev. John*

Wesley, A.M., Founder of the Methodists (3 vols.; New York, 1872), III, 191; Wesley, *Works,* XI, 124.

23. For an able account of the criticism and Wesley's response see Thomas Walter Herbert, *John Wesley as Editor and Author* (Princeton, 1940), pp. 108–10.

24. Wesley, *Works,* XI, 124.

25. *Ibid.,* pp. 13–32.

26. *Ibid.,* pp. 32–43.

27. *Ibid.,* p. 41.

28. *Ibid.,* p. 39.

29. *Ibid.,* p. 40.

30. See Vulliamy, *op. cit.,* pp. 241–43.

31. Wesley, *Works,* XI, 89, 127.

32. *Ibid.,* pp. 123–24.

33. *Ibid.,* p. 130.

34. Quite consistent in his view of mobs, Wesley was later to deplore the Lord Gordon riots, however affecting his sympathy for the young nobleman himself (*ibid.,* IV, 185).

35. *Ibid.,* XI, 84.

36. *Ibid.,* pp. 114–23.

37. *Ibid.,* p. 116.

38. *Ibid.,* p. 114.

39. *Ibid.,* p. 132.

40. Francis J. McConnell, *John Wesley* (New York, 1939), p. 258.

41. *Ibid.* For Wesley's opinions see also Wesley, *Works,* XI, 27; XII, 40, 136; Telford, *op. cit.,* V, 199; Nehemiah Curnock, *The Journal of the Rev. John Wesley, A.M.* ("Standard" ed.; 8 vols.; New York, 1910), V, 458; VI, 23. Once Boswell asked Johnson if he thought Rousseau as bad as Voltaire, to which Johnson replied, "Why, sir, it is difficult to settle the proportion of iniquity between them. He always appeared to me a bad man. That he was mad I never doubted" (Curnock, *op. cit.,* VI, 23 n.).

42. Curnock, *op. cit.,* VI, 100; see also Herbert, *op. cit.,* pp. 104–5. Wesley frankly acknowledged that he was a Tory in believing "God, not the people to be the origin of all civil power" (see Telford, *op. cit.,* VII, 305). For a study of Wesley as a Tory see W. W. Sweet, "John Wesley, Tory," *Methodist Quarterly Review,* LXXI (1922), 255–68.

43. Wesley, *Works,* XI, 123–24.

44. Robert Southey, *The Life of Wesley and the Rise and Progress of Methodism,* ed. Maurice H. Fitzgerald (2 vols.; London, 1925), II, 244.

45. Herbert, *op. cit.,* pp. 107–8; see also *ibid.,* p. 134, n. 21; Southey, *op. cit.,* II, 244–45; J. M. Buckley, *A History of the Methodists in the United States* (New York, 1896), pp. 176–78; W. W. Sweet, *Religion on the American Frontier: The Methodists* (Chicago, 1946), p. 37; Edward Frank Humphrey, *Nationalism and Religion in America, 1774–1789* (Boston, 1924), pp. 123–25; Winchester, *op. cit.,* p. 240.

46. Quoted in Buckley, *op. cit.*, pp. 167–68.

47. *Ibid.*, pp. 174–76.

48. Humphrey, *op. cit.*, p. 168.

49. See *ibid.*, pp. 19–47; Vulliamy, *op. cit.*, p. 338; Alfred Plummer, *The Church of England in the Eighteenth Century* (London, 1910), pp. 180–81; Arthur Lyon Cross, *The Anglican Episcopate and the American Colonies* (New York, 1902), pp. 268–72.

50. *Minutes of the Annual Conferences of the Methodist Church for the Years 1773–1823* (New York, 1840); see also Nathan Bangs, *A History of the Methodist Episcopal Church* (2 vols.; New York, 1838), I, 80, 149; Abel Stevens, *The History of . . . Methodism* (3 vols.; New York, 1859), II, 211.

51. John M. Mecklin, *The Story of American Dissent* (New York, 1934), pp. 278–79.

52. *Ibid.*, p. 279.

53. Wesley, *Works*, XIII, 238.

54. Coke soon ordained Asbury as associate superintendent, and within five years the two men were calling themselves bishops.

THE IRISH REPUBLIC

1. *Journal of Dail Eireann Debates,* May 10, 1949:

"Notices of Motions.

"Dail Eireann,

"SOLEMNLY RE-ASSERTING the indefeasible right of the Irish nation to the unity and integrity of the national territory.

"RE-AFFIRMING the sovereign right of the people of Ireland to choose its own form of Government and, through its democratic institutions, to decide all questions of national policy, free from outside interference,

"REPUDIATING the claim of the British Parliament to enact legislation affecting Ireland's territorial integrity in violation of those rights, and

"PLEDGING the determination of the Irish people to continue the struggle against the unjust and unnatural partition of our country until it is brought to a successful conclusion;

"PLACES ON RECORD its indignant protest against the introduction in the British Parliament of legislation purporting to endorse and continue the existing partition of Ireland, and

"CALLS UPON the British Government and people to end the present occupation of our six north-eastern counties, and thereby enable the unity of Ireland to be restored and the age-long differences between the two nations brought to an end.

"Amendment:

"DENYING the right of British Armed forces to occupy any part of Ireland,

"SOLEMNLY DECLARES THAT the national territory is integrate, that the jurisdiction of the Oireachtas embraces the whole island of Ireland, its islands and the territorial seas and that the laws enacted by the Oireachtas shall henceforth apply to the whole of Ireland; and

"RELYING on the Proclamation of the Irish Republic in Dublin on Easter Monday, 1916, on the Declaration of Independence made at the first meeting of the First Dail Eireann in the Mansion House, Dublin, on January 21st, 1919, on the Constitution of Ireland enacted by the People of Ireland on 1st July, 1937, and on the sovereign rights of the People of Ireland

"WE, THE MAJORITY OF THE ELECTED REPRESENTATIVES OF THE IRISH PEOPLE, PLEDGE ourselves in the name of the Irish People to make this declaration effective, by every means at our command."

2. Constantia E. Maxwell, *Irish History from Contemporary Sources* (London, 1923), Introd., p. 47. For some fifty years the O'Connors and O'Mores had harassed the English residents of the Pale and had exacted black rents with impunity. At one time they had quite daringly captured the vice-deputy and held him until ransom was paid.

3. *State Papers, Ireland, Elizabeth* (hereafter cited as "*S.P.I.E.*"), XXVI, 14 (November 5, 1568). Cecil to Sidney: "In the latter end of this summer I labored so much to her Majesty that she was well content to establish two councils, one for Munster, the other for Connaught. To the first Mr. John Pollard has been appointed—to the other Sir Ed. Fitton. The grievous sickness of Pollard with the gout has delayed the enterprise in regard to Munster."

4. *Calendar Patent and Close Rolls, Chancery Ireland,* ed. J. Morrin (3 vols.; Dublin, 1861–63), I, 533.

5. *S.P.I.E.,* Vol. XVI (January 4, 1570). Mr. Rafe Rokeby to Cecil: "Books made of every man in Connaught. A provost marshal appointed to truss up such as none will brook or undertake for. Some of the greatest malefactors in Connaught executed, others saved by the benefit of clergy. Such as do come in we cause to cut their glibbes, which we do think of as the first token of obedience."

6. *Ibid.,* XXX, 43.

7. William F. T. Butler, *Confiscation in Irish History* (Dublin, 1917).

8. Dorothy Macardle, *The Irish Republic* (London, 1938), chap. xii. From a speech of Patrick Pearse at Glasnevin Cemetery, July, 1915:

"Deliberately here we avow ourselves Irishmen of one allegiance only. We must stand together in brotherly union for the freedom of Ireland. And we know only one definition of freedom. It is Wolfe Tone's definition, it is Mitchell's definition, it is Rossa's definition. We stand at Rossa's grave not in sadness but in exaltation and here we pledge to Ireland our love and to England our hate. . . . They think they have pacified Ireland, they think they have purchased half of us and intimidated the other half . . . but the fools, the fools, they have left us our Fenian dead and while Ireland holds their graves, Ireland unfree shall never be at peace."

9. *Ibid.*

10. *Ibid.*

11. As an executive of the Irish Republican Army, Mr. de Valera concurred in its program of militant resistance to the pro-treaty government of Mr. Cosgrave.

12. Speech of Mr. Brian MacGiolla Phadraig at the Celtic College of Bangor, North Wales (*Irish Times,* August 11, 1949).

13. *New York Times,* June 17, 1951.

14. Mr. William Carleton, *Yale Review,* spring, 1951.

15. Sean McBride, "Ireland and the Atlantic Pact," *Round Table: Quarterly Review of British Commonwealth of Nations,* Vol. XXXIX (June, 1949).

SCOTTISH WITCHCRAFT CASES

1. See, e.g., G. L. Kittredge, *Witchcraft in Old and New England* (Cambridge, Mass., 1929), pp. 279, 371–72.

2. F. Legge, "Witchcraft in Scotland," *Scottish Review,* XVIII (October, 1891), 259–61; George F. Black, *A Calendar of Cases of Witchcraft in Scotland, 1510–1727* (New York, 1938), Introd., pp. 11–12; *The Acts of the Parliaments of Scotland* (12 vols.; Edinburgh, 1814–75), II, 539.

3. William K. Boyd and H. W. Meikle (eds.), *Calendar of State Papers Relating to Scotland and Mary, Queen of Scots* (Edinburgh, 1936), X (*1589–1593*), 365: R. Bowes to Burghley, Edinburgh, July 23, 1590 (hereafter referred to as *"Cal. Scot., 1589–1593"*).

4. R. Pitcairn (ed.), *Ancient Criminal Trials in Scotland* (Edinburgh: Maitland Club, 1829–33), I, Part III (*1584–1596*), 186, 206.

5. Legge, *op. cit.,* 261–62.

6. *Cal. Scot., 1589–1593,* p. 425.

7. *Ibid.,* p. 434.

8. G. B. Harrison (ed.), *Newes from Scotland* (1924), pp. 12, 14, 15, 26; or *Newes from Scotland,* printed in Pitcairn, *op. cit.,* pp. 213, 220 (see n. 9).

9. It was reprinted by the Roxburghe Club in 1816; in 1924 G. B. Harrison edited it, together with James VI's *Daemonologie;* R. Pitcairn published it in his *Ancient Criminal Trials,* I, Part III, 213–23. A copy of the 1591 London edition is in the Bodleian Library, Douce f. 210. The University of Pennsylvania has a film of this, which shows very clearly the realistic detail of the woodcuts.

10. References are to the Maitland Club publication, not to the Bannatyne Club edition.

11. The mark placed by the devil on his subjects when they first entered his service. The part of the body covered by the mark was supposed to be insensible to pain. A common way of detecting witches was by "pricking" them with pins to discover this spot.

12. *Newes* (Harrison ed.), pp. 8–14.

13. *Cal. Scot., 1589–1593,* p. 502; Pitcairn, *op. cit.,* I, Part III, dittay against Barbara Napier's jurors, June 7, 1591.

14. *Newes,* Pitcairn, *op. cit.,* p. 219.

15. Pitcairn, *op. cit.,* pp. 239–40, item No. 50 of Sampson's dittay; p. 245, dittay against Napier's jurors.

16. *Ibid.,* pp. 236–37, item No. 40 of Sampson's dittay; p. 211, items Nos. 6, 7, 8, Fian's dittay.

17. *Ibid.,* p. 245, dittay against Napier's jurors.

18. *Ibid.,* p. 246.

19. *Newes* (Harrison ed.), pp. 18–29; Pitcairn, *op. cit.,* I, Part III, 209–13, Fian's dittay; *Cal. Scot., 1589–1593,* p. 463. David Calderwood, *The History of the Kirk of Scotland* (8 vols.; Edinburgh: Wodrow Society, 1842–49), V, 115–16, in a brief account of these prosecutions in the winter of 1590–91 said: "John Feane, schoolesmaister of Saltprestoun, confessed he was clerk to their assembleis; yitt at his executioun he confessed onlie he had abused the people that way, and had committed adulterie with two and thrittie weomen, but denied witchecraft."

20. *Newes* (Harrison ed.), p. 10.

21. Calderwood, *op. cit.,* V, 115.

22. John Spottiswood, *History of the Church of Scotland* (3 vols.; Edinburgh: Bannatyne Club, 1850), II, 411–12.

23. Pitcairn, *op. cit.,* pp. 231–41. Bowes in his letter to Burghley, February 23, 1591 (*Cal. Scot., 1589–1593,* p. 467), said she confessed 58 out of 102 articles of her dittay.

24. *Cal. Scot., 1589–1593,* pp. 464–67; Pitcairn, *op. cit.,* p. 232, item No. 15, and pp. 234–35, items Nos. 32 and note and 33. According to Pitcairn (*ibid.,* p. 232, item No. 11), if she stopped once in her prayer, the sick person was bewitched; if she stopped twice, the patient would die. Another conjuration by which she healed the sick was a five-line prayer calling on Christ's name, the Mass, the nails that were used in the Crucifixion, and his blood (*ibid.,* p. 237, item No. 44; *Cal. Scot., 1589–1593,* p. 466). George Sinclair's *Satan's Invisible World Discovered* (reprinted Edinburgh, 1871, from the original edition, Edinburgh, 1685), p. 23, quotes two short rhyming "prayers" which Agnes Sampson was said to have taught to people, the "White Pater Noster" and the "Black Pater Noster," quite different from the charms referred to above. The "White Pater Noster" read:

> "White *Pater Noster*
> God was my Foster.
> He fostered me
> Under the Book of Palm Tree.
> Saint *Michael* was my Dame,
> He was born at *Bethelem.*
> He was made of flesh and blood,
> God send me my right food:
> My right food, and dyne two,
> That I may to yon Kirk go.
> To read upon yon sweet Book,

Which the Mighty God of Heaven shoop,
Open, open, Heavens Yaits,
Steik, steik, Hells Yaits.
All Saints be the better,
That hear the White Prayer, Pater Noster."

The "Black Pater Noster" follows:

> "*Four newks in this house for haly Angels,*
> *A post in the midst, that's Christ Jesus,*
> Lucas, Marcus, Matthew, Joannes,
> *God be into this house, and all that belangs us.*"

25. Both her successes and her failures were charged against her in her dittay, e.g., Pitcairn, *op. cit.*, pp. 231–33, items Nos. 1–12 inclusive, 16–25 inclusive.

26. *Ibid.*, p. 232, items Nos. 13, 14.

27. *Ibid.*, p. 237, item No. 41; p. 240, item No. 51.

28. *Ibid.*, p. 237, item No. 42.

29. *Ibid.*, p. 238, items Nos. 45, 46.

30. *Ibid.*, p. 235, item No. 34.

31. *Ibid.*, p. 236, item No. 38.

32. *Ibid.*, p. 238, item No. 48. Apparently she was not convicted on this charge of attending the convention where she was said to have upbraided the devil.

33. *Ibid.*, pp. 230, 241; *Cal. Scot., 1589–1593*, p. 464.

34. *Cal. Scot., 1589–1593*, p. 467.

35. Pitcairn, *op. cit.*, p. 238, item No. 49 of Sampson's dittay. David Seaton was chosen by the king to seek out those witches who had fled into England because of his knowledge of them (*Cal. Scot., 1589–1593*, p. 457). A certain David Setoun in Fowlstruthir sat on Barbara Napier's assize (Pitcairn, *op. cit.*, p. 242).

36. Pitcairn, *op. cit.*, p. 211, items Nos. 6, 7, 8, Fian's dittay; pp. 236–37, item No. 40, Sampson's dittay.

37. See below, p. 110.

38. *Newes* (Harrison ed.), pp. 14–15; Pitcairn, *op. cit.*, pp. 211–12, items Nos. 9, 15, Fian's dittay; pp. 239–40, item No. 50, Sampson's dittay.

39. *Cal. Scot., 1589–1593*, p. 430; cf. Pitcairn, *op. cit.*, p. 245.

40. *Newes* (Harrison ed.), p. 10, lists Agnes Sampson of Haddington and Agnes Tompson of Edinburgh among those incriminated by Geillis Duncan's testimony. Yet in the same pamphlet the two names seem to be used interchangeably (pp. 12–17). The dittay against Barbara Napier's jurors said a Margaret Thomson was intrusted with the poison attempt (Pitcairn, *op. cit.*, p. 245).

41. Spottiswood, *op. cit.*, II, 411–12.

42. *Cal. Scot., 1589–1593*, p. 467.

43. He was the son of John Stewart, prior of Coldingham, an illegitimate son of James V, and was therefore a cousin of James VI. His mother, Lady Jane Hepburn, was a sister of the Earl of Bothwell, Mary Stewart's third husband.

44. See, for example, Annie I. Cameron (ed.), *The Warrender Papers* (Edinburgh: Scottish History Society, 1932), II, 156.

45. David Masson (ed.), *Register of the Privy Council of Scotland* (Edinburgh, 1881), IV, 610 n. (hereafter cited as *"Reg. P.C. Scot."*); *Cal. Scot., 1589–1593,* p. 453.

46. *Cal. Scot., 1589–1593,* p. 504.

47. *Ibid.,* pp. 509, 531.

48. See *The Dictionary of National Biography,* article on Francis Stewart Hepburn, fifth Earl of Bothwell.

49. Jos. Bain (ed.), *The Border Papers* (2 vols.; Edinburgh, 1894–96), I, 486–87; *Cal. Scot., 1589–1593,* pp. 501–2; *Warrender Papers,* II, 161.

50. *Cal. Scot., 1589–1593,* pp. 462–64, Bowes to Burghley, February 23, 1591.

51. *Ibid.,* pp. 463, 501–2. There is a certain confusion of time. Bowes was absent from Scotland in the summer of 1589, when the witches may have been raising storms to interrupt Anne of Denmark's voyage, and in the autumn, when the king sailed for Norway and Denmark. He was certainly in Scotland in 1590, having been ordered north about December, 1589, during the king's absence. It seems clear that the witches' meetings at Newhaven and North Berwick, where the king's destruction by poison or by a wax image was allegedly plotted, occurred in the summer and autumn of 1590, after the king's return, when the ambassador was resident in Scotland.

52. *Cal. Scot., 1589–1593,* p. 504.

53. Bothwell had succeeded his uncle, Mary Stewart's third husband, in such offices as lord high admiral, sheriff of Edinburgh and of the county of Haddington, sheriff of Berwick County and balliary of Lauderdale.

54. There was some story that the death of Archibald Douglas, eighth Earl of Angus, in 1588 had been accomplished by witchcraft. See, for example, Napier's dittay (Pitcairn, *op. cit.,* p. 243), although she was acquitted of this charge. Cf. *ibid.,* p. 240, item No. 51, of Sampson's dittay; *Cal. Scot., 1589–1593,* p. 465.

55. *Border Papers,* I, 487.

56. *Cal. Scot., 1589–1593,* p. 504.

57. *Ibid.,* pp. 505–6. Sir John Carmichael was reckoned one of "the Queen of Inglandes knyghtes." Bothwell blamed him and the Edinburgh minister, Mr. Robert Bruce, as agents of England in causing his troubles.

58. *Ibid.,* pp. 511–13.

59. See *Cal. Scot., 1589–1593,* pp. 506–7, where Bowes admitted that he had not been idle in furthering the exhortations of the ministers, who urged

the king to examine these matters thoroughly, protect the innocent, and punish the guilty (cf. *Warrender Papers*, II, 158–60).

60. Pitcairn, *op. cit.*, pp. 242–43; *Cal. Scot., 1589–1593*, pp. 514–15.

61. Pitcairn, *op. cit.*, pp. 243–44 and note, quoting Home of Godscroft.

62. Calderwood, *op. cit.*, V, 128–29.

63. The king wrote to Maitland: "Trye by the medicinairis aithis gif Barbara Nepair be uith bairne or not. Tak na delaying ansour. Gif ye finde sho be not, to the fyre uith her presesentlie [*sic*], and cause bouell her publicclie" (*Cal. Scot., 1589–1593*, p. 510).

64. *Ibid.*, p. 506.

65. *Ibid.*, pp. 514–15.

66. Calderwood, *op. cit.*, V, 129–30.

67. *Cal. Scot., 1589–1593*, pp. 522–25.

68. Pitcairn, *op. cit.*, pp. 245–47; cf. also *The Memoires of Sir James Melvil of Halhill* (London, 1683), pp. 194–95.

69. Pitcairn, *op. cit.*, p. 245.

70. The *Newes* (Harrison ed.), pp. 15–16, said Agnes Tompson undertook this task. See above, p. 100 and n. 40.

71. Euphemia MacCalzean's dittay (Pitcairn, *op. cit.*, p. 254, item No. 23) mentions this meeting or another like it as held twenty days before Michaelmas, 1590.

72. Pitcairn, *op. cit.*, p. 246.

73. Cf. *ibid.*, p. 239, item No. 50 of Agnes Sampson's dittay; p. 246, dittay against B. Napier's jurors.

74. *Cal. Scot., 1589–1593*, pp. 514–15.

75. Pitcairn, *op. cit.*, pp. 247–57.

76. *Ibid.*, p. 250, item No. 5 of her dittay.

77. *Cal. Scot., 1589–1593*, p. 510.

78. Calderwood, *op. cit.*, V, 128–29.

79. *Cal. Scot., 1589–1593*, p. 530; cf. also Pitcairn, *op. cit.*, p. 256, which lists nine points plus an inclusive one, "convict of commoune Wichcraft and Sorcerie, and vsing of the said Wichcraft aganis sindrie his hienes liegis."

80. Pitcairn, *op. cit.*, pp. 256–57.

81. Calderwood, *op. cit.*, V, 128–29, said she was "wirried and burnt to ashes...."

82. *Cal. Scot., 1589–1593*, p. 531.

83. *A Chronicle of the Kings of Scotland from Fergus the First to James the Sixth, in the Year M.D.C.XI.* (Edinburgh: Maitland Club, 1830), p. 143. Cf. *Cal. Scot., 1589–1593*, p. 537: "This afternone Effam Mackalzon was executed by fyre and dyed very obstynatly without confessing any cryme."

84. *Cal. Scot., 1589–1593*, p. 501. James wrote to Maitland: ". . . garr see that Richie Grahme uant not his ordinaire allouaince quhill I take farther ordoure uith him" (*ibid.*, p. 510).

85. *Ibid.*, pp. 506–7, 531.

86. *Ibid.,* pp. 514–15, 518, 520, 530–31.

87. *Ibid.,* p. 513.

88. *Ibid.,* p. 531.

89. *Ibid.,* pp. 534–35.

90. *Ibid.,* pp. 535–36; cf. also *Warrender Papers,* II, 163.

91. *Warrender Papers,* II, 163 and note; *Cal. Scot., 1589–1593,* pp. 506, 535–37; Annie I. Cameron (ed.), *Calendar of State Papers Relating to Scotland and Mary, Queen of Scots, 1593–1595* (Edinburgh, 1936), XI, 61–62 (hereafter referred to as "*Cal. Scot., 1593–1595*").

92. *Reg. P.C. Scot.,* IV, 643–45; Pitcairn, *op. cit.,* pp. 181–82; Spottiswood, *op cit.,* II, 411–13.

93. Calderwood, *op. cit.,* V, 148: "Upon Tuisday, the last of Februar, Richard Grahame, the great sorcerer, was wirried and burnt at the Croce of Edinburgh. He stood hard to his former confessioun tuiching Bothwell's practise against the king." Cf. *Cal. Scot., 1589–1593,* p. 652, Roger Aston to Bowes, March 2, 1592: "Ricchy Grame was burnt yesterday, 'whoo has taken it uppon his ded.' All he spake of the Earl Bothwell was true." Neither his depositions against Bothwell nor any records of his trial have been found.

94. *Reg. P.C. Scot.,* IV, 730 n.; Calderwood, *op. cit.,* V, 150–56. Cf. his declaration of February, 1593, in *Cal. Scot., 1593–1595,* pp. 61–64.

95. *Cal. Scot., 1593–1595,* pp. 142–43; *Border Papers,* I, 486–89.

96. *Warrender Papers,* II, 161.

97. Pitcairn, *op. cit.,* p. 245.

98. M. A. Murray, "The 'devil' of North Berwick," *Scottish Historical Review,* XV (1917), 310–21, *passim.* Why should Bothwell, if he believed in the efficacy of the ritual with the image, have hedged on delivering it to the witches if he was actually present at the North Berwick meeting in the character of the devil? Why should Bothwell have exposed himself, even disguised, to the sight of so many who might in the future betray him? The claims of Lennox and of Hamilton to the throne were better than Bothwell's, as he well knew. Why go to the trouble to remove James for the sake of another? Miss Murray's argument based on the king's words when Bothwell seized the court in July, 1593, as recorded in Burton's *History of Scotland,* V, 283—"Came they to seek his life? let them take it, they would not get his soul"—seems to me to read too much into a natural expression that anyone might have uttered when he thought he faced death.

99. *Cal. Scot., 1593–1595,* p. 62; *Warrender Papers,* II, 160, 203; *Border Papers,* I, 486–88.

100. *Cal. Scot., 1589–1593,* p. 510. Cf. *Exchequer Rolls,* XXII, 160, cited by Black, *op. cit.,* p. 24, col. 2.

101. *Border Papers,* I, 487–88. Cf. *Cal. Scot., 1593–1595,* p. 141.

102. See *Newes* (*passim*) for references to the torture of Fian, Sampson, and G. Duncan; *Border Papers,* I, 488, for Graham; *Cal. Scot., 1589–1593,* pp. 509–10, for the king's instructions to torture various witches. In one

of his dispatches Bowes spoke of the death of R. Greyson, a wizard, whose death, he said, may have been caused by the torture to which he was subjected (*ibid.*, p. 502).

103. *Border Papers,* I, 487; *Cal. Scot., 1593–1595,* pp. 141, 142–43.

104. *Cal. Scot., 1593–1595,* p. 62, copy of Bothwell's declaration, February 7, 1593. Note that this was before Bothwell seized the court.

105. Pitcairn noted a gap in the Criminal Records from October, 1591 (long after the death of many of the witches), until May, 1596, which may have conveniently suppressed information about Murray's murder and about the Catholic earls, whom the king at times favored (Pitcairn, *op. cit.*, pp. 257–58).

106. John Colville, *The Historie and Life of King James the Sext, 1566–1596* (Edinburgh: Bannatyne Club, 1825), pp. 241–42.

107. For instance, he had stabbed Sir William Stewart, brother of Captain James Stewart, Earl of Arran, in the High Street in Edinburgh in July, 1588, and his followers had then dispatched the ill-starred Sir William in a cellar near by (*Dictionary of National Biography*).

108. *Cal. Scot., 1589–1593,* p. 538.

109. James, Bishop of Winton (ed.), *The Workes of the Most High and Mightie Prince James . . . King of Great Britaine, France and Ireland* (London, 1616), p. 136.

ROLE OF THE HOUSE OF COMMONS IN
BRITISH FOREIGN POLICY

1. Recapitulated by Sir Nevile Henderson to Lord Halifax in 1938 (see *Documents on British Foreign Policy, 1919–1939* [3d ser.; London, 1948], I, 294).

2. This is evident from a telegram to the Minister at Prague from Lord Halifax, dated May 30, 1938, ending with the words: ". . . there is no doubt that Dr. Beneš has been very reluctant to move for the past two years" (*ibid.*, p. 401).

3. *Ibid.*, p. 151.

4. *New York Times,* March 17, 1938, p. 1.

5. Keith Feiling, *The Life of Neville Chamberlain* (London, 1946), p. 296.

6. "The Memoirs of Eduard Beneš," *Nation,* June 19, 1948, p. 681.

7. André François-Poncet, *The Fateful Years* (New York, 1949), p. 222.

8. Winston S. Churchill, *The Second World War* (Boston, 1948), I, 240.

9. At the time of the signing of the Anglo-Italian agreement in April, 1938, the German Ambassador at Rome sent a telegraphic report to the German Foreign Ministry of a conversation in which the British Secretary for War declared himself a confirmed supporter of the new course in British policy, "which not only had a clear conception of existing realities but also drew the logical conclusions from them." The entire conversation is

very damaging if correctly reported by Mackensen (see *Documents on German Foreign Policy, 1918–1945,* Ser. D [Washington, 1949], I, 1095).

10. Churchill, *op. cit.,* p. 242.

11. *Ibid.,* p. 249.

12. *Documents on German Foreign Policy,* Ser. D, I, 29–39.

13. *Ibid.,* p. 40.

14. *Ibid.,* pp. 52–54.

15. *Documents and Materials Relating to the Eve of the Second World War* (Moscow, 1949), I, 25.

16. *Documents on German Foreign Policy,* I, 58.

17. *Ibid.,* pp. 147–48.

18. *Ibid.,* pp. 183–84.

19. On the very day of Lord Halifax' "unceremonious" conversation at Berchtesgaden in November, President Roosevelt had written to Mr. Davies, the Ambassador at Moscow, that there was no longer hope of composing the situation. He would therefore transfer Mr. Davies to Brussels instead of to Berlin, as previously planned. He said that he preferred now to have the Berlin post filled "distinctly formally by a conventional representation," not by a personal friend (Joseph E. Davies, *Mission to Moscow* [New York, 1941], p. 253). The Prime Minister of Great Britain was less wise. He aimed at increasingly close personal relations between himself and the Nazi leaders and, in order to achieve this, perpared to meet their wishes as expressed to Sir Nevile Henderson and Lord Halifax.

20. Churchill, *op. cit.,* p. 255.

21. *Hansard* (5th ser.), 327, col. 618, November 1, 1937.

22. A quaint feature of the official reports is that the costumes worn by the mover and seconder of this particular motion are always stated in parenthesis—in 1937, both wore "court dress."

23. Lord Vansittart, "The Decline of Diplomacy," *Foreign Affairs,* January, 1950, p. 177.

24. *Hansard* (5th ser.), 327, cols. 41–42, October 26, 1937.

25. These statements were as follows:

1934: "They will continue to make the support and extension of the authority of the League of Nations a cardinal point in their policy."

1935: "My Government's foreign policy will as heretofore be based on firm support of the League of Nations."

1936: "The policy of the Government continues to be based on membership in the League of Nations."

1937: No reference to the League.

26. *Hansard,* cols. 363–65, October 28, 1937.

27. *Ibid.,* cols. 425–39, October 29, 1937.

28. *Ibid.,* col. 455, October 29, 1937.

29. *Ibid.,* cols. 579–95, November 1, 1937.

30. See above, pp. 152–53.

31. *Hansard,* cols. 579–95, November 1, 1937.

32. Mussolini made this declaration on October 28, while the debate on the address was in progress, and soon after his return from Germany, where he had agreed to support German policy.

33. *Hansard,* cols. 618–20, November 1, 1937.

34. *New York Times,* August 29, 1937.

35. London *Times,* November 29, 1937, p. 15*b, c.*

36. *New York Times,* November 26, 1937, p. 1.

37. *Ibid.,* November 29, 1937, pp. 1 and 10.

38. *Ibid.,* November 30, 1937, editorial.

39. *Hansard,* 337, col. 852, June 20, 1938.

40. *Ibid.,* col. 954, June 21, 1938. On this occasion Lady Astor, referring to the party, declared, "I would like to say there is not a word of truth in it," a statement which she found it necessary "to explain" to the House soon afterward, for everyone knew it to be, at the very least, misleading.

41. "Ineffective Debates," *Times,* December 21, 1937, p. 15*b.*

42. *Documents on German Foreign Policy,* I, 245–46.

43. *Hansard,* 330, cols. 1811–12, December 21, 1937.

44. *Ibid.,* cols. 1832 ff., December 21, 1937.

45. Holinshed, *Chronicles* (1543), III, 956.

46. *The Ciano Diplomatic Papers, 1937–1938,* ed. Malcolm Muggeridge (London, 1949), pp. 161–62.

47. *Ibid.,* p. 183.

48. *Hansard,* 322, col. 258, February 22, 1938.

49. Above, p. 141.

50. *Hansard,* 333, col. 1407, March 24, 1938.

51. *Ibid.,* 334, col. 39, April 4, 1938.

52. *Ibid.,* col. 144, April 4, 1938.

53. *Ibid.,* 336, cols. 1233–34, May 25, 1938.

54. See above, p. 154.

55. Churchill, *op. cit.,* pp. 209–10.

LONDON MERCANTILE ACTIVITY DURING THE REIGN
OF QUEEN ELIZABETH

1. Farmed out in 1567 and not reported again until 1592, when an official was appointed to check the Farmers' Accounts (cf. F. C. Dietz, *English Public Finance, 1485–1588* [London, 1920], p. 314).

2. It must always be borne in mind that this Port Book does not include the extensive wine trade of London, which reduces the reports on France, Spain, Italy, Malaga, and the Canary Isles.

3. Ephraim Lipson, *The Economic History of England* (London, 1931), I, 494–95.

4. Cf. A. Friis, *Alderman Cockayne's Cloth Project and the Cloth Trade*

1603–25 (London: Humphrey Milford, Oxford University Press, 1927); Lipson, *op. cit.,* chap. x; W. E. Linglebach, "The Merchant Adventurers of Hamburg," *American Historical Review,* IX (1901), 265 ff.; George Schantz, *Englische Handelspolitik gegen Ende des Mittelalters* (2 vols.; Leipzig, 1881).

5. Friis, *op. cit.,* p. 53.

6. *Ibid.,* p. 55.

7. *Ibid.,* p. 54.

8. Cf. *ibid.,* pp. 55–56.

9. *Ibid.,* p. 54.

10. *Ibid.*

11. Bertill Ohlin, *Interregional and International Trade* (Cambridge, 1935), pp. 9–13.

12. Sir William Foster, *England's Quest of Eastern Trade* (London, 1935), chaps. i–iii.

13. Friis, *op. cit.,* pp. 54–57.

14. E. 190 7/8, fols. iv, 2r, 3v, 13r, 14v, 15r, 16r, 16v.

15. W. R. Scott, *The Constitution and Finance of English, Scottish, and Irish Joint Stock Companies* (3 vols.; Cambridge, 1910–12), III, 39, n. 2.

16. Foster, *op. cit.,* chaps. i, ii, and iii.

17. Friis, *op. cit.,* pp. 54, 56–57; Scott, *op. cit.,* II, 57–67.

18. This suggestion is put forward as only one reason for the later difficulties of the company.

19. See E. 190/7/8, fols. 2r and 2v, 14v, 16r. Sir Francis Walsingham married Anna Carleill, daughter of Sir George Barnes (or Barne) in 1562. She died in 1564 (Conyers Read, *Mr. Secretary Walsingham and the Policy of Queen Elizabeth* [3 vols.; Oxford, 1925], I, 26). Sir George Barnes was one of the two councilors of the Russian Company when it was incorporated in 1555. He was the Lord Mayor of London in 1552 (*Analytical Index to the Remembrancia of the City of London, 1579–1664,* p. 181, n. 1). He died in 1557 (John Stowe, *Survey of London* [Kingsford ed.], II, 302, notes for p. 185). The Sir George Barnes referred to here is the son of the first Sir George. The second Sir George began his aldermanic career on October 26, 1574, as alderman for Bridge Without. He became Lord Mayor in 1586 and died in 1592 (*Analytical Index,* p. 18, n. 1).

20. Read, *op. cit.,* III, 371.

21. E. 190/7/8, fols. 2v ff.

22. Read, *op. cit.,* III, 371.

23. Scott, *op. cit.,* III, 52.

24. *Ibid.;* also British Museum, Additional Manuscripts, 12,503, fols. 318–31.

25. *Op. cit.,* III, 50–51.

26. *Ibid.,* III, 46–49.

27. *Ibid.,* I, 19.

28. Friis, *op. cit.,* p. 55; V. M. Shillington and A. B. Wallis Chapman, *The Commercial Relations between England and Portugal* (London), pp. 313–26; C. T. Carr, *Select Charters of Trading Companies A.D. 1530–1707* ("Publications of the Selden Society," Vol. XXVIII [1913]), Introd., pp. xxiii ff.

29. Cf. above, n. 1.

30. Cf. above, p. 189.

31. Foster, *op. cit.,* p. 90.

32. *Ibid.,* pp. 68–70; Read, *op. cit.,* III, 371; Scott, *op. cit.,* III, 38.

33. E. 190/7/8, fols. 71r and 72v.

34. E. 190/7/8, fol. 8v.

35. E. 190/7/8, fol. 46r.

36. E. 190/7/8, fol. 46r.

37. E. 190/7/8, fol. 45r.

38. E. 190/7/8, fol. 45r.

39. E. 190/7/8, fols. 3r and 52r.

40. E. 190/7/8, fol. 45r.

41. E. 190/7/8, fol. 12r.

42. E. 190/7/8, fol. 46r.

THE GENESIS OF INDUSTRIALISM
AND OF MODERN SCIENCE

1. *Science and the Modern World* (1925) ("Mentor Books" [1948]), p. 2.

2. Figures derived from Eli F. Heckscher, *Sveriges ekonomiska Historia frän Gustav Vasa* (Stockholm, 1935–36), I, Part I, 28, 30, Appendix; Part II, pp. 443–44.

3. N. W. Posthumus, *De Geschiedenis van de Leidsche Lakenindustrie* ('s-Gravenhage, 1939), II, 304.

4. J. U. Nef, *The Rise of the British Coal Industry* (London, 1932), I, 21.

5. *The History of the Rebellion and Civil Wars in England* (Oxford, 1843), p. 30.

6. See also J. U. Nef, "Mining and Metallurgy in Medieval Civilization," *Cambridge Economic History,* Vol. II (Cambridge, 1952), chap. vii, secs. i and vi.

7. Nef, "Note on the Progress of Iron Production in England, 1540–1640," *Journal of Political Economy,* XLIV (1936), 401–3.

8. J. E. Neale, *The Elizabethan House of Commons* (London, 1949), chap. i.

9. J. U. Nef, *The Rise of the British Coal Industry,* Introd.

10. Jean Lejeune, *La Formation du capitalisme moderne dans la Principauté de Liége au 16e siècle* (Paris, 1939), p. 133 and *passim.*

11. See also Nef, *War and Human Progress* (Cambridge, Mass., 1950), pp. 280–81.

12. John Ruskin, *La Bible d'Amiens* (Paris, 1947), Preface by Marcel Proust, p. 92 n.

13. See Nef, *War and Human Progress,* chap. ii.

14. C. F. von Weizsäcker, "The Spirit of Natural Science," *Humanitas,* II, No. 1 (1947), 3.

15. Herbert Butterfield, *The Origins of Modern Science, 1300–1800* (London, 1949), pp. 34–35.

16. Charles Sherrington, *The Endeavour of Jean Fernel* (Cambridge, 1946), *passim.*

17. *Four Treatises of Theophrastus von Hohenheim Called Paracelsus,* edited by Henry E. Sigerist (Baltimore, 1941), pp. 46–47, 49, 52, 54, 135, 139, 188–89, 198, and *passim.*

18. Richard Hooker, *Of the Laws of Ecclesiastical Polity* (1592–94), Book I, chap. vii, sec. 1.

19. Whitehead, *Science and the Modern World,* p. 16; see also pp. 14, 42.

20. Sherrington, *op. cit.,* pp. 144–45.

21. Paracelsus, *op. cit.,* p. 220.

22. Butterfield, *op. cit.,* pp. 30, 38–39.

23. Sherrington, *op. cit.,* p. 96.

24. For contrasts between French and English industrial history, see also my "A Comparison of Industrial Growth in France and England from 1540 to 1640," *Journal of Political Economy,* XLIV (1936), 289–317, 505–33, 643–66; "Prices and Industrial Capitalism in France and England, 1540–1640," *Economic History Review,* VII, No. 2 (May, 1937), 155–85; *Industry and Government in France and England, 1540–1640* (Philadelphia, 1940). It was Dr. Read who first interested me in the comparative method as a means of discovering the nature of historical processes. That was a long time ago, in the spring of 1917, when he offered at the University of Chicago a course in the comparative history of political institutions in England, France, and Germany.

25. Sherrington, *op. cit.,* p. 144.

26. Butterfield, *op. cit.,* p. 47.

27. William Osler, "Harvey and His Discovery," *Alabama Student* (1908), p. 330, as quoted in J. F. Fulton, *Physiology* (New York, 1931), p. 13.

28. *The Works of William Harvey,* ed. Robert Willis (London, 1847), p. 29.

29. Cowley, *Works* (London, 1721), II, 524.

30. Butterfield, *op. cit.,* p. 36.

31. Girolamo Fracastoro, *Syphilis, sive morbus Gallicus* (Verona, 1530).

32. *Works of William Harvey,* p. 19.

33. *Ibid.,* p. 6.

34. *Ibid.,* pp. lxxiii–lxxiv.

35. *Ibid.,* pp. lxix–lxx.

36. See Étienne Gilson's notes to his edition of Descartes's *Discours de la méthode* (Paris, 1925), pp. 280–82, and also Gilson, "Descartes, Harvey et la scolastique," *Études de philosophie médiévale* (Strasbourg, 1921), pp. 244–45.

37. T. C. Allbutt, *Science and Medieval Thought* (London, 1901).

38. For these attacks on Harvey's results see *Works of William Harvey,* pp. xlii ff.

39. See Nef, *War and Human Progress,* chaps. xv and xvi.

40. C. Gide and C. Rist, *Histoire des doctrines économiques* (4th ed.; Paris, 1922), pp. 20–21.

41. Descartes, *Discours de la méthode,* Part V; see also Gilson, *Études de philosophie médiévale,* pp. 217–23.

42. *Works of William Harvey,* p. xliv.

43. Butterfield, *op. cit.,* p. 50.

44. See Nef, *War and Human Progress,* pp. 195–96.

45. See also Jacques Maritain, *Art et scolastique* (3d ed.; Paris, 1935), p. 33.

46. Francis R. Packard, *Life and Times of Ambroise Paré* (New York, 1926), pp. 15–16.

47. See T. C. Allbutt, *The Historical Relations of Medicine and Surgery* (London, 1905), pp. 99–100.

48. Packard, *op. cit.,* pp. 27–28.

49. *Ibid.,* pp. 92–93.

50. *Ibid.,* pp. 106 ff.

51. *Ibid.,* p. 25.

52. Cited by B. Hessen, "The Social and Economic Roots of Newton's 'Principia,'" *Science at the Crossroads* (London, 1931), pp. 167–68.

53. See below, p. 251.

54. L. L. Woodruff (ed.), *The Development of the Sciences* (New Haven, 1923), p. 51.

55. *William Gilbert of Colchester,* trans. P. Fleury Mottelay (New York, 1893), p. xviii.

56. *Ibid.,* pp. xlviii–xlix.

57. Packard, *op. cit.,* p. 189.

58. W. C. D. Dampier-Whetham, *A History of Science* (New York, 1929), p. 137.

59–61. The text to which these footnotes pertained has been deleted.

62. Dryden, *Epistles,* II, "To My Honoured Friend Dr. Charleton," in *Miscellaneous Works* (London, 1767), II, 117–18.

63. See Mrs. Mark Pattison, *The Renaissance of Art in France* (London, 1879), II, 256–57, and *passim.*

64. Nef, *Industry and Government,* p. 83.

65. See my *War and Human Progress,* pp. 51–53, 128.

66. *The Development of the Sciences,* ed. L. L. Woodruff, p. 198. Palissy

has even been called the founder of the science of geology (Allbutt, *The Historical Relations of Medicine and Surgery*, p. 64).

67. Butterfield, *op. cit.*, p. 56.

68. *Ibid.*, pp. 53 ff.

69. E. A. Burtt, *The Metaphysical Foundations of Modern Physical Science* (London, 1925), p. 53.

70. Butterfield, *op. cit.*, p. 68.

71. Alexandre Koyré, "Galileo and Plato," *Journal of the History of Ideas,* IV, No. 4 (1943), 17 and *passim*. Exception has been taken to this argument of Koyré's (Hiram Haydn, *The Counter-Renaissance* [New York, 1950], p. 249, n. 319).

72. See Whitehead, *op. cit.*, pp. 31–33.

73. Plutarch, "The Life of Marcellus," *The Lives of the Noble Grecians and Romanes,* trans. Thomas North (Oxford, 1928), III, 75.

74. For the content of this paragraph I am heavily indebted to one of our graduate students at the University of Chicago, Mr. Marshall Kaplan. In connection with a course of mine on the interrelations of intellectual and economic history, he undertook a comparison of French and English mathematics from 1540 to 1640 and obtained what seem to me to be interesting results. I hope to return to this subject in more detail at a later time. Much of Kaplan's material was obtained from Julian Coolidge, *History of Geometrical Methods* (Oxford, 1940).

75. Jacques Besson, *Théâtre des instruments mathématiques et méchaniques* (Lyons, 1579), *passim*.

76. Étienne Gilson, *The Unity of Philosophical Experience* (New York, 1937), pp. 133–34.

77. See Alexandre Koyré, *Descartes after Three Hundred Years* ("University of Buffalo Studies" [1951]), *passim*.

78. *Discours de la méthode,* ed. Étienne Gilson, Part VI, pp. 62–63.

79. Alexandre Koyré, *La Gravitation universelle de Képler à Newton* (a lecture delivered at the University of Paris, April 7, 1951), p. 8.

80. Martha Ornstein, *The Role of the Scientific Societies in the Seventeenth Century* (Chicago, 1928), p. 241.

81. W. R. MacDonald, *The Construction of Logarithms* (Edinburgh, 1889), p. xv.

82. For the information about "Napiers bones," I am indebted to another graduate student in my course, Mr. Robert A. Meier.

83. See my *War and Human Progress,* chap. xvi.

84. A point called to my attention by my colleague, Professor S. Chandrasekhar, for whose help in connection with this essay I am most grateful.

85. E. T. Bell, *The Development of Mathematics* (New York, 1945), p. 158.

86. For this information I am indebted to a lecture of my colleague,

Professor Otto von Simson, given under the auspices of the Committee on Social Thought in January, 1952.

87. Koyré, *Descartes after Three Hundred Years,* p. 26.

88. Cited by Louis de Broglie, *Savants et découvertes* (Paris, 1951), p. 34.

89. *Op. cit.,* p. 56.

90. Thomas Sprat, *History of the Royal Society* (London, 1667), pp. 71–72.

91. See also Hessen, *op. cit.,* pp. 157–74; Nef, *The Rise of the British Coal Industry,* I, 240–56.

92. Nef, *War and Human Progress,* pp. 193–98.

93. G. N. Clark, *Science and Social Welfare in the Age of Newton* (Oxford, 1937), pp. 68–91.

94. *William Gilbert of Colchester,* p. 48.

95. Harvey, *op. cit.* ("Everyman's Library" ed.), pp. 18, 29, 37–38.

96. See Nef, *Industry and Government in France and England.*

97. Mark Pattison, *Isaac Casaubon* (2d ed.; Oxford, 1892), pp. 263–64.

98. Virginia Woolf, *The Common Reader* (New York, 1925), pp. 114–15.

99. On all these matters, see the argument in Whitehead's *Science and the Modern World.*

INDEX

Abbey Theatre, 83
Abyssinia, 138, 155, 170
Acland, Roger, 161
Adam, William, 55
Aevnow, Alexander, 198
Agen, 239
Agreements Reached at the Cairo, Tehran, Yalta, and Potsdam Conferences: Implementation and U.S. Policy, 48
Agricola, Georgius, *De re metallica,* 206, 259
Alexander, Mr., quoted, 178
American Historical Association, v, vii, 43
American Policy on Establishment of Relations with Foreign Countries, 48
American Recognition Policy in Regard to Changes in Latin American Governments by Revolution or Coups d'État, 48
American Revolution, 52–64 and *passim*
    Congress, 53, 59
    Effect on Ireland, 77
    Loyalists, 59
Amsterdam, 189, 198, 203
An Old Fox Tarr'd and Feather'd, 56
Ancient Criminal Trials in Scotland, 98, 107
Ancusen, 189
Anglican, 70
Anglo-Irish Treaty, 65, 86–89, 91–92, 95
Angus, 106
Angus, Earl of, 96
Angus, Lady, 106
Anne of Denmark, 97, 101
    attempt by witches to delay, 96, 99, 102
Anschluss, 141, 145, 174, 176–78
Antwerp, 192
Apollonius, 248
Aquinas, 267
Archangel, 193
Archimedes, 223, 246, 248, 250
Arctic Sea, 189
Aristotle, 8, 220, 224, 234, 236, 242–43, 250–51, 257, 266
Arkwright, 201
Armstrong, Elizabeth, xii
Arnold, Matthew, 27
Arran, Earl of, 96

Art
    defined, 213–14, 218–19
    and industrialism, 210, 218, 220, 235
    and science, 219–20, 234–35, 239–41
    see also Impressionism
Asbury, Francis, 62–63
Asquith, 152
Astor, Lady, 167
Astor, Viscount, 165
Atlantic Pact, 95
Attlee, Clement, 142
Augustine, 267
Austria, 151, 161, 178–79, 202
    German threat to, 151, 153, 160, 174
    nazism in, 147
    see also Anschluss
Austrian and German Problems in the Council of Foreign Ministers, 48

Bacon, Francis, 4, 21, 209, 257, 265, 268
Bain, 7–9
    quoted, 16
Baldwin, (Lord) Stanley, 149, 164, 171, 176, 181, 183
Balfour Declaration, 87, 89
Balkans, 202
Baltic Sea, 191
Barbary, 189–90, 198
    items of trade, 196
Barbary Company, 192, 195, 198
Barber-surgeon, 231–32, 234–35, 241
Barbizon School, 9
Barnes, Sir George, 194, 198
Bassard, Thomas, 194
Baxter, James P., 3rd, xi
Belfast, 67, 71, 82, 86, 93–95
Belgium, 202, 209
Bell, E. T., quoted, 255
Beneš, Dr., 147–48
Bennaerts, Pierre, 4
Bentham, Jeremy, 5, 9
Berchtesgaden, 156, 165, 170, 172, 178, 180
Berlin, 141
Bernard, Claude, 219
Berwick, 107
Besson, Jacques, 249, 251
Bevin, Ernest, 142